*f*P

AMERICAN CHINATOWN

A People's History of
Five Neighborhoods

BONNIE TSUI

Free Press

New York • London • Toronto • Sydney

FREE PRESS
A Division of Simon & Schuster, Inc.
1230 Avenue of the Americas
New York, NY 10020

First Free Press hardcover edition August 2009

FREE PRESS and colophon are trademarks of
Simon & Schuster, Inc.

For information about special discounts for bulk purchases,
please contact Simon & Schuster Special Sales at 1-866-506-1949
or business@simonandschuster.com.

The Simon & Schuster Speakers Bureau can bring authors to your
live event. For more information or to book an event, contact the
Simon & Schuster Speakers Bureau at 1-866-248-3049 or visit our
website at www.simonspeakers.com.

Manufactured in the United States of America

10 9 8 7 6 5 4 3 2 1

Library of Congress Cataloging-in-Publication Data

Tsui, Bonnie.
   American Chinatown / by Bonnie Tsui. — 1st Free Press hardcover ed.
      p. cm.
   "Free Press non-fiction original hardover"—T.p. verso.
   Includes bibliographical references.
      1. Chinatowns—United States. 2. Chinese Americans—Social life and
customs. 3. Chinese Americans—Social conditions. 4. City and town
life—United States. 5. Chinatown (New York, N.Y.)
6. Chinatown (San Francisco, Calif.) 7. Chinatown
(Los Angeles, Calif.) 8. Chinatown (Honolulu, Hawaii) 9. Chinatown
Plaza (Las Vegas, Nev.) 10. United States—History, Local. I. Title.
   E184.C5T834 2009
   973'.04951—dc22   2008055095

ISBN 978-1-4165-5723-4

To my grandparents,
Shau Yip Dong and Suey Lin Dong,
for beginning our family's story in
New York's Chinatown

CONTENTS

INTRODUCTION

Personal Geography

S ome people unpack when they first arrive in a city. Me, I look for Chinatown.

It started, I suppose, with my grandparents. Traveling halfway around the world from Hong Kong, they settled in Manhattan's Chinatown in 1960. Even after moving to another Chinese enclave in Flushing, Queens, they kept going back, like clockwork, to their old neighborhood. Every morning they took the Q26 bus and the No. 7 subway train to the 6 train to Canal Street, where my grandfather worked in a fortune-cookie factory and my grandmother was a seamstress. Every night they brought home fresh vegetables bought from street vendors they'd come to know.

I picture a set of footprints marking a path from Queens down to Lower Manhattan, traceable on a map of the New York City transit system. When I come here today, I'm keenly aware that it's their route I follow.

NEW YORK, 1977. I am born in Flushing. My family's first apartment is a dingy affair with a leaky ceiling, and my brother is careful to pull me away from the drips. It's around this time, at the end of the 1970s, that economically depressed Flushing starts to change, departing from its roots as an Italian and Greek neighborhood to become, eventually, its own Chinatown. I never get a chance to build loyalty for my first Chinatown; before we hit school age, our parents move us to Long Island, where good public schools are a selling point. But it's not where we go to be Chinese—Manhattan's Chinatown is.

My personal history with Chinatowns begins here, where we have wedding banquets, christenings, grocery shopping, daily life with my extended family of aunts, cousins, great-uncles, fake-uncles. Everyone's a relative, even when he's not.

I don't love coming here. At my height, the negatives are magnified: the filth of the streets, old takeout containers littering the gutters, sharply jostling knees. But at the child's eye level of experience, there is fascination, too. We children stick together, sidestepping dark, smelly puddles and eyeing strangers warily, but eagerly poking fingers at tanks of lobsters or plastic kiddie pools of tiny turtles imported from Hong Kong. In the narrow aisled shops, open buckets of candied plums and orange peels beckon while the grocery ladies glare. Even so, when we sidle up to the displays, they bark assent and give us a taste.

The Chinatown of my childhood occupies the same cultural epoch as Roman Polanski's eponymous film noir. I am wholly unaware of what the director has done, of his construct of some inexplicable "Forget it, Jake . . . it's Chinatown" idea lurking beneath the surface that will dominate American cinema for decades. Still, because I'm not entirely of that place—I have, after all, one foot in the almost exclusively white Long Island suburbia of the early 1980s—I recognize the peculiarities, both small and large. Chicken feet at dim sum. A brusqueness of manner to outsiders, sizable extended families living under one roof, butting into each other's business. Competitive noise.

The quirks hint at larger ideas, values, even then. Eating is about appreciating flavors and textures, whatever the vessel, and about the symbols behind them—"phoenix claws" being lucky—and is not to be limited by squeamish ideas of what is clean or dirty. A superiority is bred from thousands of years of culture established somewhere else, and not from mere snobbery or unfriendliness; investment in family protects against outsiders who threaten prejudice and misunderstanding, so that you are never alone, without a community. Finally, if you don't speak up, no one will hear what you have to say. *Dai seng di*—"Make a bigger sound," my mother says, pushing me forward into the world.

When I get my first job after college, I can walk to Chinatown for lunch every day. There is a complicated feeling inside me when I go. I'm here by choice, not dragged along for some family errand or event. What am I here for, now, on my own? I feel unobtrusive, invisible, a little nervous. My tongue is rough; I have to speak Cantonese. The sounds are like an envelope, and I put myself inside it. The street is still dirty, the people still loud, pushy. But I like it. Something here is bigger than me, a history, other people's stories that are somehow my stories, anchoring me in this city. I belong in a way that is deeper than a job or mere geography.

A few years later, I move to the East Village, also a short walk from Chinatown. I make an effort to integrate Chinatown a little more into my regular life. For a year or two, I even visit Mr. Wen, an elderly teacher on Grand Street, a couple of times a week, to learn the workday vocabulary that I never heard in my house growing up. It will help with my travel and my writing, I tell the top editor at the magazine where I work, and he agrees. He pays for my lessons with Mr. Wen.

Family friends sent their kids to Chinese school when I was growing up—weekend classes in Chinatown that emphasized language and crafts and songs. It was the familiar effort to "stay Chinese" in a larger society that doesn't make it easy to be different. Somehow, I had escaped the requirement, and in the lazy way of youth, I was grateful at the time. But it's harder to learn now, even things I want to learn. It's funny to find myself coming here voluntarily, after work, trudging up the subway steps at Grand Street station to Mr. Wen, my adult version of Chinese school.

Mr. Wen is crotchety, funny. He is the chief Cantonese-dialect instructor at a small Chinese-language school called Wossing, but he teaches Mandarin, too. All the kids learn Mandarin now—*potungwa*, the common dialect of all China—but I'm of that in-between generation, just after the last great wave of Cantonese immigrants, a born-in-America daughter who can still speak her parents' language. Mr. Wen and I sit around chatting in a cramped classroom on the third floor of the school's old tenement building. Or rather, I sit and he stands, even though it's just the two of us. He's smart, trained as a professor, but messy-looking. On a hot summer evening, he will sweat visibly through his button-down shirt, strands of thin gray hair glued to his forehead. He's the age of my grandparents, and he's from the same area, Toisan, located in southern China's Guangdong Province. Guangdong was once called Canton, and most of the Chinese immigrants to American Chinatowns throughout the nineteenth and twentieth centuries were Cantonese from Guangdong's Pearl River Delta region—today a major manufacturing center of China that encompasses Hong Kong and Macau. On the other side of the world, they established communities of the same people, and many more followed them, finding safety in numbers. They were the trendsetters of their time.

Mr. Wen is nothing like my *gung-gung*, my mother's father, but I think of the two of them together anyway. Mr. Wen talks a lot more than my grandfather, who is quiet and stoic. Translucent, my father calls him, referring to his pale skin, threaded delicately with thin blue veins. But he could have been talking about the impression my *gung-gung* leaves, which is often faint, hard to discern, an effort to pin down. I never know what my *gung-gung* is thinking.

Perhaps that's why I feel such affection for Mr. Wen, who is the opposite. Oration is his gift. He steamrolls on, trying to get me to write Chinese. Why don't you want to learn characters? he asks me, drawing on the board. It makes it easier to learn new words. I'm too old for that, I say. I just want to talk more, get my mouth in shape. Learn some travel vocabulary so I can ask questions about the Chinese destinations I profile. His method of teaching is unlike that of any other language teacher I've known. It's circuitous, capricious, winging around the world from hotels and airports to cities and professions. Often, his topics have nothing to do with any of the things

I've asked to learn about. He teaches me whatever occurs to him. He teaches me what he thinks I should know.

Eventually, somewhat reluctant to leave New York but in need of a change of pace, I move across the country. I am surprised to find unfamiliarity in its oldest Chinatown, in San Francisco. Its main street feels empty the first time I visit, in the middle of the day. Shops seem to be closed, and I can't find a steamed bun to save my life. A couple of Chinese grandmothers come toward me. As they pass, I realize that they are speaking English, and their accents born-and-bred American, not Chinese.

And I wonder: *What makes a Chinatown?*

SAN FRANCISCO, 2003. Things happen in this Chinatown that I've never seen before. On my way to dinner one evening, I hear the familiar honking whine of a fire engine. I turn, expecting to see prototypical white male firefighters hanging out of the truck. Instead, I see an all-Chinese fire crew, with a stocky young Chinese woman in command, steering the back of the engine as it careens up Kearny Street and disappears around the corner.

The age of this Chinatown, the country's oldest, has earned it a place of respect in the hierarchy of American Chinatowns. I find that the San Francisco Fire Department even teaches fire safety classes in Cantonese to benefit the Chinatown community. On the other hand, Chinese American families have been here for generations, and many of those families now identify more with American than Chinese. The neighborhood is right up there with the Golden Gate Bridge and Alcatraz as the city's most-visited tourist attractions. And it's true that it's very much a tourist's place. To know San Francisco's Chinatown is to recognize that it exists as a kind of first planet to several satellites—the Richmond and Sunset neighborhoods within the city, the revived Oakland Chinatown across San Francisco Bay. Many new Chinese immigrants now settle outside of the original Chinatown, but it remains a gateway for lower-income immigrants. And still Chinese Americans of all generations gravitate back to it, on weekends or holidays, for school or camp or special events. The same questions come up for them as they did for me. What brings them back? What do they hope to find? I begin to give voice to these questions outside my own head.

Non-Chinese people tell me all the time that they love Chinatown. "There's so much to look at," they say, pointing at family-owned kite shops, nineteenth-century Taoist temples, traditional herbalists, sidewalk displays showcasing ceramic rice bowls for sale. My friend Jane tells me that as a child, she was never satisfied until she had shot every pop gun in a certain knickknack store on Stockton Street. Other friends say they can't resist the food, which is so cheap, and so fun to eat. They point to restaurant menus, to swinging slabs of roast pork in the windows, and to *dan tat*, delicate yellow egg-custard tarts, at the corner bakery. There is the promise of the unfamiliar—the exotic and the adventurous—paired with the comfort of being in a place that is, in fact, quite well known by now on the Western cultural radar. Still, they find something meaningful, exciting, intriguing there. "It feels authentic," a woman I work with tells me. "Not like anywhere else."

The more I hear about Chinatown, the more I want to hear from Chinatown. Or, rather, from its people, be they new arrivals or old. They make the neighborhood continue on as it does. As early as the 1920s, sociologists predicted that Chinatowns would eventually disappear in the United States, with the assimilation of immigrants into mainstream America. San Francisco Chinatown has not disappeared. But if many of the immigrants no longer live here, why does it persevere? What gives this community its long-standing, cohesive energy? What is San Francisco Chinatown today? And if this Chinatown is so different from the other I know in New York, what about those other American Chinatowns in between? The bigger questions, I realize, don't make sense until I ask the smaller ones, and find out what Chinatown means to ordinary people.

Why are you here?

■ ■ ■

I BEGIN TO collect these neighborhood stories. And I begin to feel that if the stories were seen alongside one another, they would create a complex and fascinating contemporary portrait of a distinctly Chinese American kind of community. The picture is, of course, a dynamic one: I'm constantly surprised by new waves of Chinese immigration and the unusual locales in which those populations are established, and by the way the old ones shift and assimilate into mainstream America while still holding themselves slightly apart. The scattering has occurred all over the world, establishing Chinatowns in places as far-flung as Vancouver, London, Yokohama, and Caracas, enriching the cultures of all of those cities. I don't mean to suggest that American Chinatowns eclipse these in significance. And for many Chinese, of course, traditional Chinatowns have never figured significantly in their lives. But the immigrant experience has always been vital to the mythology of America, and so the iconic status of Chinatowns in this country commands particular attention. It captures my own attention precisely because it is close to home; in more practical terms, it offers a strict organization for this examination, to rein in what could certainly have been a sprawling book and topic. But the rest of the world, of course, is always there and always felt—it's because of the current global focus on China and its diaspora that I am ever more intrigued by the roots and lively, little-known details of prominent American Chinatowns. In these places, Chinatowns have grown, changed, and thrived, exerting influence beyond their borders.

I BEGIN MY work on this book in San Francisco's Chinatown. It seems right to start here—it's the oldest of the prominent American Chinatowns still in existence, and it's where I live now. In investigating what made San Francisco's Chinatown so distinctive, I get to know my adopted city more intimately. I come to appreciate the Bay Area as the ancestral home of Chinese America. The Chinese called San Francisco *dai faw*: "big port," or "first port." It was through this gateway that tens of thousands of Chinese came during the Gold

Rush—looking for *gum saan*, or "gold mountain"—and railroad boom times, when China suffered from famine, war, and natural disaster and its people were welcomed to the Western frontier as cheap labor. That welcome didn't last long—racism quickly built up to the exclusion acts that rescinded that invitation—but the deep roots of a community were already established. In a republic that was constantly renewing itself with new immigrant pools, xenophobia moved rapid-fire from one group to the next. In this way, American xenophobia was the first force to shape the first port's Chinatown. The 1906 earthquake, which remade Chinatown and the city itself, marked the point at which the community began to take charge of its own image through the shaping of its skyline. It was perhaps the first time an American Chinatown did this so explicitly, but certainly not the last—the building of self-image is a compelling and enduring theme resonating through the Chinatowns included here. It continues in the modern day, with youth leaders who seize the opportunity to "show-and-tell" their own Chinatown stories to San Francisco's tourists, and with today's new immigrants, who struggle to find their voice in the gilded ghetto. They come face-to-face with the paradox that is Chinatown: a vibrant, jam-packed community that speaks their language, but also an insular home that makes it harder to communicate with the larger world outside.

Back in New York's Chinatown, I find I can't escape my family history there. As in San Francisco, I explore the neighborhood with an eye to different generations and their stories, observing the circumstances and geographies that have made the community unique. On streets I had walked a thousand times—the historic main street of Mott, quiet, crooked Doyers, busy East Broadway—I try to slow down and see them anew. This being New York, I track the biggest economies in Chinatown, talking to predominantly female labor organizers for the ubiquitous garment trade, and trace the thread of my grandmother's story as a longtime seamstress in several Chinatown garment factories. To find out about the history of ruling family associations, I seek out the unofficial mayor of Chinatown—the current president of the Chinese Consolidated Benevolent Association, what was for a century the supreme organization of the Chinese in New York—and am startled to learn that, in the early 1970s, he shared Cookie Machine No. 2 with my grandfather in a tiny mom-and-pop fortune-cookie operation in Chatham Square. And when I visit Chinese schools new and old, including a venerable institution on Mott Street, based out of New York's oldest Catholic church, I end up standing at the spot where I was baptized, three decades before. And so I incorporate that personal history in my travels through Chinatown. It becomes inevitable that I embrace the idea of a city within a city—that as big as New York is, and as large as its Chinese population has grown to be, spreading out across the boroughs, the still-small world of Chinatown is where everybody knows somebody, and, chances are, that somebody knows you. Over time, it has found itself inextricably tied to the ups and downs of the city outside. Chinatown became something the city *needed*, in good ways and bad.

In Los Angeles, I find a close-knit Chinatown community that was also uniquely necessary to the larger city—indeed, it was wed to Hollywood at an early age. The movies shaped Chinatown in surprising ways, and not just through their representations of the Chinese on celluloid. Those who saw it happen tell me that Hollywood had more of a hand in the actual creation of the Chinatown of the 1930s than most people know. In this Chinatown, reality and fiction came together to shape not only how America pictured Chinese and "Orientals" in the world, but also to shape the construction of the physical place in which L.A.'s Chinese resided. In the last several decades, the scattering of the Chinese American community to other pockets of L.A.—Monterey Park, Alhambra, and the San Gabriel Valley are just a few—has lessened the day-to-day importance of Chinatown here, but these new enclaves are still connected to the original. As other Chinatowns do, L.A.'s Chinatown persists as a cultural touchstone, indisputably compelling to generation after generation of Chinese Americans. In a way that these other communities do not, Chinatown sends a signal to explore your cultural identity.

What happens when Chinatown ceases to be all Chinese? Can Chinatown be itself and something else, too? A longtime melting pot of cultures, the Kingdom of Hawaii pulled in the Chinese as contract laborers beginning in 1852. For a time, in the 1880s, the Chinese even outnumbered Caucasians in the islands. In 1900, Hawaii officially became a U.S. colony. Throughout the twentieth century, Honolulu's Chinatown became home to successive waves of Asian immigrants, and finally to an arts community. Here, Chinatown feels open. Many aspects of Chinese culture have made their way into Hawaii's everyday. In a social environment that was friendlier than that which was found on the mainland, the Chinese community achieved widespread success and acceptance. It paved the way for Honolulu Chinatown's distinctive renaissance. Listening in on the conversation here, I find insight into what it means to be Chinese and something new at the same time—an acceptance of self-invention that is a lesson for the rest of America.

Finally, Las Vegas. Perhaps most of all, a man-made Chinatown in a man-made place reveals fascinating things to me about America and what sway Chinatown holds over it. On the surface, a Vegas-brand Chinatown seems the ultimate American commodification of ethnic identity. What do I expect? A cheap imitation of the original, a cartoon world empty of substance. But the community that has sprung up around this Chinatown has startling parallels to the traditional one, fulfilling many of the functions of the old neighborhood. The depth of experience to be found here shows that as much as Chinatown is a tried-and-true attraction in this country, darker elements persist, even in shiny, happy Vegas. "In American culture, 'Chinatown' also means negative things," James Chen, the founder of Las Vegas's Chinatown, says. "It means filthy, gritty, dirty, produce on the street, people only speak Chinese, isolated, doesn't care about anybody else, or even worse—gangsters, prostitution, that kind of thing. And to be in a new city, Las Vegas, I knew we had to be better." The story of this founding, and how Chen confronted his image problem, is a telling commentary on the direction that other Chinatowns are headed.

I could say that my nostalgia for the past is what spurs me to seek out Chinatown wherever I go, but I think that's only part of it. I don't go there for the same reasons my grandparents did; I grew up around the fringes of the neighborhood, and the insularity and security of their community never existed for me. They sought out Chinatown for the comfort of a place where people still spoke the same language they did, where they could simply feel at ease. In a still-strange country, it was a sort of homecoming. Hong Kong and China were places I would travel to, not from.

Though it's nice every once in a while to hear Cantonese and eat food that I know well—rice porridge and egg custard when I want to be reminded of my mom, soy-sauce chicken when I think of my grandfather—my fascination with Chinatowns has more to do with being able to see how other Chinese communities integrate into their larger surrounding communities. By looking at the distinctive American Chinatowns of New York, San Francisco, Los Angeles, and Honolulu—fingers of land on the Atlantic and Pacific Oceans, key entry points for multiple generations of Chinese immigrants to the United States—alongside that of Las Vegas, I find unlikely intersections of the new and the familiar.

Chinatowns as we have known them are captivating places to explore. By digging deeper into a group of iconic Chinatowns in important cities across the United States, we get a sharper, more profound sense of immigrant experiences that are specific to place. As we take a look at several different generations in each, we also find out what it is that prevails in culture and tradition across the diaspora. And in examining diverse stories that include those of a newer, unusual Chinese enclave in Las Vegas, we create a moving picture of a population has always flourished in community form. Of course, these are not the only stories, nor are they meant to be wholly representative of every Chinatown. Rather, they are simply points of view—compelling ones that show us new ways of seeing the Chinese in America today.

Notes on Usage

To avoid confusion, I've used the Western convention of writing a person's given name followed by the family name (in my case, Ling Fung Tsui—Tsui being the family name—instead of Tsui Ling Fung, as in the traditional Chinese form). Most Chinese I interviewed, even very recent immigrants, gave their names to me in this way. As Cantonese is a colloquial language, there is tremendous variety in its romanization; for simplicity, I've transcribed any Cantonese phrases or words phonetically. Mandarin has been rendered in pinyin. Finally, a handful of names have been changed, at the request of interview subjects who would like to protect their identity.

① chinatown senior housing

② spofford alley (rosa's old house)

③ sam wo (good noodles)

④ portsmouth square chinatown's "living room"

⑤ i-hotel

transamerica pyramid

financial district

⑥ AAA youth tours (led by alleyway kids)

⑦ sing chong building

⑧ sing fat building

⑬ gordon j. lau elementary

⑫ chinese historical society of america (founded 1962)

⑪ chinese newcomers service center (english classes)

union square shopping district

⑩ joy lok family resource center (for mrs. chan)

⑨ chinatown gate (a gift from taiwan in 1969)

COLUMBUS AVE

broadway
pacific
jackson
washington
clay st.
sacramento
california
pine st.
bush st.
sutter st.

POWELL
STOCKTON
GRANT
KEARNY
MONTGOMERY

CHINATOWN
san francisco

Grant Avenue, San Francisco. *Bonnie Tsui*

ONE

AMERICAN PAGODAS

Behind the tourist architecture.

On my first visit to the City by the Bay's famous Chinatown, I was reminded of Disney World.

Here were multilevel pagoda tops, sharply curving eaves, and Orientalized cornices decorating everything from the bank to the school to the McDonald's. Brightly colored lanterns and flags hung liberally, and trolley cars running down one of its streets added to what seemed to me a "Straight from Old China!" amusement-park air. The big dragon welcome gate at Grant Avenue, the main drag, actually did come from the Far East—a gift from Taiwan—but in 1969, not 1869. No imperial-period importation, but a contemporary of the civil rights era and Woodstock. It was just before the United States under Nixon famously extended the olive branch to Communist China in the 1970s, acknowledging their political position that there was only one China, and that Taiwan was part of that state. But most of Chinatown, comprised of immigrants with memories of escaping the Communist takeover of China to come to the United States in the first place, remained loyal to the Nationalist government that had fled to, and remained in, Taiwan.

It was in that era that my father himself first came to San Francisco's Chinatown, from Hong Kong, in 1968. The trip was his first to America—indeed, his first experience with an American Chinatown—and when I ask him what he remembers about that time, he says it was the neighborhood's distinctively "old" look that struck him most.

He wondered how Chinatown, in a supposedly modern America, could seem even older than the oldest parts of Hong Kong's historic Kowloon district. Shouldn't an American Chinatown be ultra-urban, with the tall buildings and gleaming, metropolitan feel of his home city's commercial center? Instead, it was ornamented with the kind of Chinese flourishes that hadn't been used in China for decades. Plus, it looked run-down, crowded, and dirty. What was it, he wondered, that kept the Chinese neighborhood from looking like all the rest of San Francisco?

The same small, high-density buildings, jumble of sidewalk stalls, and Sinophilic streetscapes that my father saw as a new immigrant in 1968 are what we have come to know as characteristic of San Francisco's iconic Chinatown. But dig into its history and you'll find that the "authentic Chinese" look is a fabricated one, its self-stylization actually begun only a century ago, when the 1906 earthquake leveled the original Chinatown and presented an opportunity for city developers to force the relocation of the Chinese American community and claim the valuable real estate that the neighborhood occupied. "Let Us Have No More Chinatowns in Our Cities," read the *Oakland Enquirer* on April 23, 1906, five days after the quake hit. It wasn't until this point that the Chinatown familiar to us came to take shape; the Oriental city of "veritable fairy palaces" was a conscious, East-meets-West attempt by Chinese merchants to change the community's image from that of a vice-filled slum and ensure its continuing survival as, in part, an attractive tourist draw.

The reading of the physical attributes of this Chinatown, the nation's oldest, can tell us surprising things about its story. In the same year of my father's arrival, Chinatown residents were rebelling against the neighborhood establishment for promoting tourism while neglecting social reforms that would benefit the community. The exoticization that saved the neighborhood in the past became fuel for protest; in black-and-white photos of a 1968 Chinatown demonstration, young radicals rejected the old guard with signs that lampooned a dated way of thinking: "KEEP GRANT AVE NARROW, DIRTY, AND QUAINT FOR TOURISTS!" "Looking for an exotic place to live? Come join our community *rats *overcrowding *poverty *roaches" "PRESERVE CHINATOWN'S UNIQUENESS—HIGHEST TB RATES, NO UNIONS, THE MOST SUICIDES, LOWEST WAGES!"

When I began to look into the story behind the neighborhood's deliberate tourist architecture, and the social currents that led to its subsequent renewal, everyone I asked about it—in this Chinatown and outside of it—pointed to Philip P. Choy.

PHIL CHOY IS an old-timer. Born in Chinatown in 1926 and raised there, he is an architect and historian who, along with fellow Chinese American studies pioneer Him Mark Lai, taught the first college-level Chinese-American history course in the country, in 1969. The reading of the Chinatown skyline to determine what it could reveal about the people's history within the district was also a perspective of his innovation. Many academics operate at some remove from their subjects, but Choy's connection is intensely personal.

Throughout his lifetime, he has been a conscious observer of the sweeping changes that have happened in the neighborhood where he grew up. When we met, Choy was, at eighty-one, a calm, well-spoken man with a head of white hair and a mustache to match. Years of teaching have given him a strong, measured way of talking, and he knows his opinions. He is candid with his stories and experiences in Chinatown and as a Chinese American encountering racism over an all-too-recent span of the twentieth century. Together with Lai, his novel accomplishment is to have documented Chinatown and Chinese American history when there was no such discipline. "I'm just plain Phil," he told me when I visited him. "But I can tell you all about Chinatown and its evolution."

Choy is an architect by training—he designed and built the modern, light-filled house he lives in today, with his wife, Sarah, about five blocks northwest of Chinatown—but he says his interest has always been in the history of the Chinese in America. It was when civil rights arrived in Chinatown in the sixties that Choy began to take on his most important role, as an interpreter of history. By that time, though he was working in an architecture firm—mostly designing restaurants and homes—and living outside of Chinatown, he had become actively involved with the neighborhood's Chinese Historical Society, which was founded in 1963.

The physical condition of Chinatown created a context for rebellion to flourish with the community's youth. Due to more relaxed immigration laws in the 1960s, a flood of new immigrants had begun to populate the area, and a gap had opened up between the conservative old guard and a younger generation who agitated for higher wages, cleaner streets, better schools equipped to educate non-English–speaking kids, and more and better housing for the poor. "They criticized the Chinatown establishment for not confronting the real issues of Chinatown—for maintaining the status quo, maintaining its isolation, and maintaining the decades of 'well-behaved good Chinese' who never rocked the boat," Choy said. "The conservative elements who ran the community for so long looked upon these young people as rabble-rousers who were bringing disgrace to Chinatown."

Like the rest of the nation, Chinatown was burning for change. And it was 1968—the year of Chinatown protest, when my father observed a blighted, dilapidated neighborhood—that students at San Francisco State College, now San Francisco State University, drew national attention by staging the Third World Student Strike in support of establishing an ethnic studies program there.

A vacuum of knowledge about the ethnic community became painfully apparent. When San Francisco State came calling in the wake of the student strike, to ask if anyone at the historical society would want to teach a class, Choy and Mark Lai realized that they knew things no one else knew about. "For me, it was a moment of enlightenment," Choy said. "We could help give the students information and a good dose of history, because up until that point, nobody really knew much about the background of the Chinese in America."

They held classes back to back—the original class syllabus is still heavily referenced today by teachers in the school's Asian American Studies Department—but nonetheless there was over-enrollment. "That was the period when Chinese American students were angry, but they didn't know what they were angry about," Choy said. "They didn't know why they were second-class citizens. They didn't know why their parents were so passive—there was a lot of resentment." In other words, they needed someone to put their lives in the context of something larger than themselves.

Choy's own life gave him useful perspectives that he could pass on to his students. As a boy growing up in Chinatown in the 1930s, he felt a cloud of insecurity over the area, a feeling of "illegality" that he got from listening to his parents talk. "We had a very common saying in Chinese, *m-ho duk joi di faan gwei*—'don't offend the white people.' When you were getting into trouble, or when you were not behaving, you were always being admonished not to offend the white people. My father being an illegal immigrant, there was always the possibility of investigations, and they were always afraid." The 1906 earthquake had destroyed a huge chunk of the city's birth and immigration records; like hundreds—perhaps thousands—of other "paper sons," Choy's father had come into the United States by purchasing false American birth documents. After the quake, Chinese already in the United States could claim citizenship, and they could also claim children born in China as American citizens. These identities, real or false, could be sold to others for a profit. The numbers were impossible to trace, but a 1957 *New Yorker* article reported that if all claims of burned birth certificates were true, "every Chinese woman living in San Francisco before 1906 had had eight hundred sons."

Choy himself had only moved out of Chinatown in the mid-1950s, after laws were changed to allow Chinese to buy property outside of Chinatown. He could explain the fears and inaction of a certain Chinatown generation to his students. He could describe the insularity and self-protection of his parents' generation, a conservative sector of the community that was still afraid to socialize with whites. And he could also go beyond the immediate past and take the long view, contextualizing the life of Chinese America within the larger history of America. That, he says, has always been his goal.

A major perspective of Choy's on Chinatown has been through its buildings. One of his earliest memories involves borrowing Charles Caldwell Dobie's *San Francisco's Chinatown* from the library; published in 1936, it was one of the first general history books written about Chinatown. Choy admired the pencil illustrations in the volume, and carried the book from street corner to street corner, comparing each drawing to the actual subject. Afterward, he tried his own hand at sketching the houses and schools and stores that populated his daily life.

From the library in his architect's study, he pulled down a copy of Dobie's *Chinatown* and showed me its well-preserved pages. "If you know the buildings, you know the history," he said, flipping past drawings of the Chinese school he attended as a youth. "We're always considered foreigners, generation after generation. But look at the evidence. There is a story to be told, and it is that the community of Chinatown has been here since the founding of San Francisco itself."

IN THE BUILDINGS of Chinatown, Choy sees the social climate in which the modern community took shape. With his background in architecture, Choy brought together under scrutiny the two major characteristics that have established San Francisco Chinatown so firmly in the American imagination: its long history, and the hybrid Sino-American architecture unique to it. The Chinese had been coming to San Francisco in large numbers since 1848, when word of the California Gold Rush reached Guangdong—a region that was being ravaged by civil war, drought, and famine. They called California *gum saan*: "gold mountain." In the following decades, Chinese immigrants, mostly Cantonese male peasants from the countryside, settled in the United States by the thousands to build the railroad and to work as farmers. By 1870, there were about 63,000 Chinese in America, more than three-quarters of them in California. Many had formed powerful family and business associations to protect their interests and help newcomers settle into the country. Despite these facts, Choy has written, visitors to Chinatown today continue to see Chinatown as an "unassimilated foreign community" where traditional culture and architecture dominate and are "mere transplants" from China. In their haste to view Chinatown as an exotic oasis, Choy says, most fail to understand the true history of the community that is bound up in its buildings.

I only have to think back to my most recent visit to Chinatown—cameras clicking on every block, slow-walking tourists showing a pervasive fascination with the colorful, festive atmosphere—to see his point. Hundreds of thousands of visitors come to Chinatown every year seeking authenticity and cultural flavor. As Choy has written, these exotics take on a different meaning upon the discovery that the appearance of Chinatown today is due in large part to Chinese merchants who, after the 1906 earthquake, paid white architects to come up with an Oriental look that would be appealing and acceptable to a general public that had come to view the Chinese with racist eyes.

In his telling of Chinatown, Choy first points to the fact that Chinatown before the quake had a largely Western appearance. Consult pre-1906 drawings, photos, and literature, he says, and brick houses and Italianate Victorian facades and balconies dominate. When I researched old images of San Francisco Chinatown, I found street scenes of wood-shingled residences with awnings, cobbled streets, and horse-drawn carriages, discernibly Chinese only in decorative signs and details. After white residents moved out of Chinatown in favor of newer, more affluent neighborhoods in San Francisco, the Chinese occupied their vacated buildings. Architecturally, Chinatown of the latter nineteenth century was a typical American frontier settlement, only with Chinese characters.

But even before the earthquake, Choy says, many of the Chinese wanted to change their image. By 1854, California laws had been put in place in to ensure that violence against Chinese immigrants—which was already on the uptick—could not be prosecuted in court. In 1882, the Chinese Exclusion Act was passed—the first U.S. law ever to ban immigration based on race or nationality—and it would not be repealed until 1943, when China became an ally to the United States in World War II. That period became known as the exclusion era. Though the law exempted merchants, travelers, students, and those born in the United States, most Chinese left in America were essentially in limbo: they couldn't vote, they couldn't reunite with their families, and their rights were not protected. Legal residents could not become citizens. Racism was rampant. At the time of the quake, the immoral Chinatown presented by anti-Chinese forces—the one filled with gambling, prostitution, opium dens, and cheap labor competition—needed to be replaced by a better face, and fast, since the San Francisco Board of Supervisors had increasingly threatened the community with forcible removal. The opening of the earth, at five twelve A.M. on April 18, 1906, became the moment for reinvention. Soon afterward, the specifics of Chinatown's new construction were determined by Chinese merchants Look Tin Eli and Tong Bong, who hired the architect-engineer team of T. Patterson Ross and A. W. Burgren to build the Sing Fat Co. building and the Sing Chong Co. Chinese bazaar.

"From an architectural point of view, the buildings are medio-cre," Choy says. "What was the first thing they thought of in Chi-nese architecture? The pagoda. So immediately that becomes the model for the building. They turned up roofs, made the curlicues, and so on. Basically they were taking a lot of standard architec-tural ornaments and creating a new vernacular, neither Chinese nor American, neither East nor West. It's just a figment of the imagina-tion of a white architect. But what's important is that it tells us a story of what happened, why these buildings came about, and it was because we were promoting our ethnicity to please the white man at the time. It was self-preservation."

One weekday afternoon, I walked to the intersection of Grant Avenue and California Street. It's a corner where people in S.U.V.s cruise by and hang out the window to snap photos of the landmark Sing Fat and Sing Chong buildings, those two edifices that exemplify the reinvention of Chinatown at the turn of the twentieth century. The pagoda-stacked Sing Chong first housed a dry goods shop; the ground floor has since been home to a McDonald's and is now the Chinatown Food Court. Next door, the Asian Image Boutique sells art. Across the street, the Sing Fat is a plain brown brick building with green stone detailing and a plopped-on pagoda cap painted in red, green, and yellow. Its retail windows trumpet "Fine Jewelry Everything 70% Off!" On this main tourist drag, traffic is predomi-nantly non-Chinese: groups of sightseers wait for the cable car to come pick them up, and other visitors sit on the steps of Old St. Mary's Church with maps to plot their next moves. One hundred years later, the architecture of Look Tin Eli and Ross & Burgren—literally Chinese American, in that it was invented in the laboratory of this American Chinatown—has been an unqualified success at attracting outside visitors.

"It was purposely done by the insider, to promote our ethnicity," Choy says. "Architecture is not just a happening, or stereotyping. The people of that generation were trying to prove their ethnicity, and change their image as the good versus the slum. They were promoting and earning the goodwill of the outside community with this nice-looking Oriental village. Today we promote our ethnicity in Chinatown with a certain purpose as well." Tourism dollars have transformed Grant Avenue, once the main functioning thoroughfare of Chinatown, into a soulless, yet lucrative, retail drag selling all things Asian-themed: T-shirts, silk pajamas, tea sets. By many measures, Choy says, "We're still doing the same thing."

The initial post-quake building frenzy in Chinatown succeeded in pacifying the white authorities. On May 26, 1910, the *Washington Post* ran an ad declaring that the "gilded domes of her pagodas add striking features to the beauty of the new city." Choy's colleague at San Francisco State, Marlon Hom, has called the stylizing of Chinatown an "ingenious move, selling a fake China to white folks who didn't know any better." But it was all for self-preservation; in the years following, Chinatown turned inward. In a 1997 PBS documentary on Chinatown, filmmaker Felicia Lowe dramatized the human fact of the ghetto: "Throughout history, Chinatown provided for itself what the outside world would not: by the 1930s an entire parallel community had grown in the dozen square blocks of Chinatown, with its own schools, hospital, night clubs, and marching bands. There was even a Chinese Telephone Exchange, called the China Five." In the thirties and forties, benevolent and family associations continued to add more chinoiserie, and renowned architect Julia Morgan built the Clay Street YWCA with inspiration from Chinese forms. Building remained static in "Cathay by the Bay" through the fifties, but the influx of a new population in the sixties—after the 1965 Immigration and Nationality Act lifted country quotas and once again allowed vast Chinese immigration of the scale seen before exclusion—forced a crowding issue. Modernization and increasing rents took apart and shifted the streetscape again, this time with neon signs and big glass storefronts.

When I asked Choy why he thought it was important to know

that the Chinatown skyline was created not by accident but by design, he was silent for a long minute. Finally, he admitted that he continues to see a lot of work about Chinatown by non-Chinese, writing that "doesn't have much to do with Chinatown itself." Most concentrated on the symbolism of design features, he says, not the buildings themselves or the history thereof. The creation of modern Chinatown was done by Chinese who had already built long lives there and been there since the beginning, he says, and it is valuable to know the truth about why it was done in the first place—as a response to racism. The feeling he had growing up was that the Chinese stay in the United States was not a welcome one; that hostile cultural environment gave rise to the "sojourner" mentality, the expectation that many Chinese had of ultimately returning to China. In his lifetime, he is grateful to see that his children and grandchildren don't have the problems he faced. As China continues to ascend on the world stage—especially on the heels of its extraordinary 2008 Beijing Olympics coming-out party—the younger generations are more likely to feel pride than shame in their heritage. But knowing what happened, he says, is a reminder of why his own generation was spurred to activism.

"Even today, people don't really understand the history—they quote dates and events," Choy said. And it is hard to understand the history of the Chinese in America without recognizing the depth of anti-Chinese virulence they faced from the beginning. They were lynched for accepting so-called "starvation wages" during the Gold Rush; their settlements were burned. The intensity of that racism was what inspired California to pioneer the kinds of laws that eventually led to the U.S. ban on Chinese immigration in 1882. Chinatown, then, was at the same time a forced ghetto and a safe haven. Knowing this reveals something of why Chinatown is the way it is today. By drawing on his own experience, Choy offers an exploration of Chinatown's history as the history of the city itself, warts and all—its migrations, social geography, urban development, and longtime anti-Chinese climate. Marking the significance of the connection between Chinatown history and American history, he says, is something he has tried his whole life to do.

UP UNTIL DOBIE'S *Chinatown*, Choy says, little was written about or by the Chinese in America. There were not many Chinese writers at the time, since most Chinese were busy finding the limited blue-collar work available to them. Since the ethnic awakening of the 1960s, however, there are countless histories, plays, and novels by Chinese Americans concerning their experiences. Choy's childhood friend and coteacher Him Mark Lai went on to build an unrivaled personal archive of papers relating to Chinese-American history; his soon-to-be-digitized collection is particularly noted for Chinese-language media published in America. The modern wave can certainly be attributed in part to Lai and Phil Choy's academic efforts to shape the discipline of Chinese-American studies as it exists today.

Choy has been retired from formal architectural practice for about ten years, but he continues to write and curate exhibitions for the Chinese Historical Society. A permanent gallery in the museum there is named for him. On a large worktable in his study at home, Choy was finishing a book on the history of the Chinese in Sacramento. One of the photos in the manuscript was of his grandfather's meat-market shop, where Choy himself once worked. "I'm an accomplished butcher, you know," he said with a smile. "I can break up a beef into all its parts."

Throughout his sunlit home, the walls and tables showcase an impressive array of art, including several works by Joan Miró, illustrations by a favorite contemporary American artist (when taking me on a tour of his collection, Choy assured me that he doesn't just collect things that are Chinese), and jade miniatures. There are also nineteenth-century engravings of political cartoons depicting the Chinese in America. His 1994 book, *The Coming Man*, written with Marlon Hom and Lorraine Dong, is a detailed survey of this collection and the era's visual consideration of Chinese immigrants. Upstairs, a family gallery features old portrait sittings of his parents, and more recent photos of his three children and five grandchildren. He has come far from Chinatown, but he has not forgotten it.

Choy's work in Chinatown still preoccupies him. In 1986, a proposal he worked on for landmark preservation of Chinatown as a historic district was rejected by the city. "But I was actually a little bit relieved," Choy said. "Many preservationists are of a mind to arrest an historic district in terms of the buildings—they think of it as a museum, therefore you can't change or touch anything. Well, Chinatown is still living. It's still growing, and progressing, and it has a lot of needs. So you can't all of a sudden stop it and make it stand still." The tension between the city's concept of historical preservation and his own, he said, is "something I have grappled with for a long time."

IN MODERN-DAY CHINATOWN, the skyline continues to figure significantly into the survival of the neighborhood. Zoning has restricted high-rise development, and according to local historian Judy Yung, over thirty community organizations that rose out of the youth activism of the 1970s and 1980s now address the economic and social needs of Chinatown.

It was after another big earthquake, in 1989, when Norman Fong—a prominent community leader and a director of the non-profit Chinatown Community Development Center, or CCDC—was asked by a popular Hong Kong magazine if he thought Chinatown was going to disappear. What, in light of thriving neighborhoods like Oakland Chinatown and "satellite Chinatowns" like the Richmond and the Sunset, made this Chinatown any different? "What makes it different is the history," Fong said decisively when he related this story to me. "This is heartland Asian America. People feel a connection with this community, and in fact, it increases their identification as Chinese American. As long as people care, Chinatown is going to be around."

Recently, Fong came up with the idea to affix bronze plates in the shape of monkey pawprints around Chinatown's newly improved alleyways, as a way to track family legacies in the neighborhood. Different families, including Fong's own, have bought plates to honor their heritage and roots here. The paw prints are a physical expression of pride—in many ways a reclamation of the physical space of Chinatown, from tourists, for residents.

Norman Fong says that he shares Phil Choy's passion for the history of their neighborhood. But he also emphasizes that they both think it is the low-income immigrants who actually live here that deserve the highest priority. To accommodate these residents, the skyline needs to shift again.

"Economically, some of the family associations, they really want to turn it into a tourist place," Fong said, citing the continuing battle between Chinatown interests. "More restaurants, more offices—they think we don't need this poor housing here, we should get rid of it all, and do all high-rises. But even though the housing is so crappy, even though the people are real poor, we have a jam-packed community that adds vitality and life here."

"What is the uniqueness of Chinatown?" Tan Chow, a Chinatown community organizer, asked me. "It's the street life." A skyscraper that casts a big shadow on Chinatown's main square has serious consequences for a community that spends most of its time there, he says. Getting developers to defer to how people in the community actually live is not easy. But advocates like Chow can draw from the tradition that Phil Choy has set down. Choy agrees that it's the immigrants who keep this place alive. As he is accustomed to doing, he looks both behind and ahead to illustrate his case.

"As far as the life of Chinatown is concerned, a continuing influx of people will sustain a Chinatown," he says. "Your first generation sustains the culture and the habits. Your second generation becomes more affluent, they move out. Once people stop living there, the fate of Chinatown is to disappear. That was what was happening in the fifties, because of the embargo on trade with China, and also people like myself moving out, after all, because we didn't want to raise our children there." It is because of the post-1965 wave of immigration that Chinatown is still vital, but Choy says the conditions are not a choice for those who live there. "It is still basically a slum area beyond the façade of some of the festivities and so on. It's kind of ironic—the new immigrants are the ones who are sustaining Chinatown, and we want to improve life for them, but if there isn't a continuing influx of the less affluent, then the Chinatown itself becomes merely ornamental." But, I asked him, what do you make of the fact that Chinatown still holds deep importance for Chinese Americans, whatever generation they may be?

"My perspective is that my generation has spent our whole lives trying to get the hell out of there, so I have a different kind of attachment to Chinatown than many of the young kids today," Choy says. It's through our conversations that I understand more fully the reasons each generation has for being here. Chinatown today fulfills two essential needs: as a spiritual and historical touchstone for older generations, and as a physical home for new immigrants.

"I've been involved in the community and its welfare, but certainly not to preserve it as a ghetto—in fact, everything we do is in the hope that the poor will be able to get out of this area," Choy says. "The way I want to preserve it is by making a statement that we've been here, using it as evidence, using it as important piece of history." He taps his hand on the table for emphasis. "It's not a contradiction."

Tim Ho and Rosa Wong-Chie, Portsmouth Square. *Bonnie Tsui*

TWO

ALLEYWAY KIDS

*How youth is reinvigorating
the neighborhood.*

As I approached Chinatown's Portsmouth Square one afternoon, the ground seemed to vibrate. School groups marched through, like trains passing through a station. Kids screamed from the two playgrounds, bouncing between the sandpit on the square's lower level and the bigger play area on the upper floor; true to this Chinatown's characteristic architecture, even the green-and-purple play structures have pagoda-shaped swish tops. Mothers and babysitters sat together; local office workers ate their lunches in the sun, kicking away pigeons as they chewed. Elderly men clustered around park benches and played brisk games of cards and mahjong while others quietly observed the action from a few feet away, hands folded behind backs with a casual grace. Some seniors made slow loops around the square, greeting familiars: "Have you eaten yet?" To each visit, they brought their Chinese newspapers and gossip. Everywhere, I saw people clutching red plastic bags containing the day's shopping.

From a flagpole in the square, twenty-three-year-old Rosa Wong-Chie glanced at the upper-level playground. It is one of her self-proclaimed favorite places, a diversion that for years occupied the greater part of her childhood summers. She turned and squinted into the sunlight, smiling at me as I joined a group of visitors assembled in front of her. "Welcome to Chinatown's 'living room,'" she told us.

31

When I first met her, Rosa Wong-Chie was the newly minted coordinator for Chinatown Alleyway Tours, a program in which high school and college kids who grew up in Chinatown launch walking tours around the neighborhood. The general premise of the outings, she told me, is to take guests off the dim sum path and explore the history and modern-day life of this San Francisco community, through five of its key alleys. Though she now manages the youth initiatives, Rosa began, just like everybody else, as a high school volunteer.

A small, slight girl with glasses and hair often pulled back in a ponytail, Rosa has a serious look and a commanding voice (though, in the way of young people, her sentences occasionally end with the upward tilt of a question mark). She speaks quickly and tells neighborhood stories from memory. It might not be her own memory—she was, after all, born in 1984—but she draws from a collective memory of Chinatown in a way that is both earnest and encyclopedic. That afternoon, as she walked down a set of stairs to the street level, she kept up a running commentary of some of the key neighborhood stories she has internalized over the years: Portsmouth Square is not only the center of Chinatown, but served as the first town square in Yerba Buena, the settlement that would become San Francisco; 60 percent of Chinatown's housing is composed of crowded single-room-occupancy apartments, or SROs, "which partly accounts for why everyone is outside in Portsmouth, using the public space"; the struggle for low-income, affordable housing for Chinatown's seniors and families continues even today, though the 104 apartments in the newly rebuilt I-Hotel—from which elderly residents were infamously evicted in 1977—are finally, triumphantly, open for business; the alleyway program helps youth leaders work on public speaking abilities as well as their skills in history and research within the community.

Beyond this, she added, young guides see the tours as a chance to clear up misconceptions about the place where they grew up. From Chinatown's living room, we followed Rosa, her youth-program colleague, Tim Ho, and seventeen-year-old guide Jason Tong on a two-hour survey of its "front yards" and "backyards"—the narrow lanes that have long served as shortcuts for neighborhood residents who want to avoid crowds on main thoroughfares like Stockton Street or Grant Avenue.

"These alleyways are quick routes for both cars and people," Rosa explained, as two delivery vans rolled by behind her and a mother and child squeezed hurriedly through the remaining space. She pointed out Spofford Alley, the one that contains the cramped SRO apartment in which she grew up. Jason jokingly called it Rosa's Alley.

"Actually," she said, "I call it my 'playground.'"

IN MANY CHINATOWNS across the United States, youth exodus is the norm. The things that many visitors find unpleasant about Chinatown—its crowded feel, dirty streets—are the same factors that spur residents to leave once they can afford to. Despite its splashy outward facade as a popular tourist destination, San Francisco's Chinatown is a place where, internally, most residents skirt the poverty line. This dichotomy makes it what the historian Judy Yung has called a "gilded ghetto."

Here, the cycle of immigrants is still a revolving door—a constant flow of families moving out and newer immigrant families moving in to take advantage of cheap rents and neighborhood services. Conditions have gotten dramatically better in the last two decades. But some in the community worry that young people who grow up here fail to return and contribute meaningfully to its continuing improvement. That return, they say, is key to the neighborhood's survival.

"A lot of kids who move out, they will come back to Chinatown because of the cheap food—that's what they always tell me," Rosa says with a laugh. "They hang out here, either because it's close to their house, or because their friends live here, or their school is around here, or because they go to Chinese school. Maybe their parents work here. So there are a lot of reasons why they're in Chinatown. But those that have more knowledge and a deeper connection—they're the ones who really incorporate Chinatown into their lives after they grow up."

Norman Fong says that very few people have stayed in the neighborhood to do empowerment work. As a boy in the 1960s, Fong ran around with a Chinatown gang. "Everybody needed to be part of a gang then—there was a lot of racism going on that the cops could care less about." He says he has always valued young people. "I valued myself as a youth, even when society really didn't value youth. I've always felt that youth power was not really respected or understood, especially in the Asian community, where reverence for seniors is very important." A short, stocky fireball of a man with shaggy hair, he still seems to be a big kid himself, despite his age (at the time we met, he was fifty-five). He has become, if not a father figure, then a sort of big-brother figure to kids in the community. A minister in the San Francisco Presbytery for more than twenty-five years, Fong also serves as a parish associate for the Presbyterian Church of Chinatown. Many people in Chinatown address him as "Rev."

He founded CCDC's Adopt-An-Alleyway, or AAA (read as "triple-A"), youth project in 1991, to jump-start the thirty-year-old organization's youth-based initiatives; previously, he had been in charge of the youth program at Cameron House, a Chinatown community organization that was originally founded in 1874 as a Christian mission home for Chinese women and girls (to satisfy the demands of a mostly male Chinatown population during the exclusion era, thousands of Chinese women and girls were smuggled into San Francisco). AAA began with a group of eight high school kids and Fong, who asked them what they wanted to change in the neighborhood.

"I said, 'This is your turf,'" Fong told me. "'This is your home, too, no matter where you live now. Chinatown is the birthplace of Asian America. Tell me what you don't like about it, and what should be better.' And they kind of focused on the alleyways. They said, 'Alleyways stink really bad. The city doesn't take care of them.'"

When Fong called San Francisco's Department of Public Works, he was appalled to find that the city still had not integrated Chinatown's alleyways into its plans for maintenance and sanitation. "This was the nineties," Fong said, shaking his head at the memory. "And here we were, still getting screwed." Push the garbage to Sacramento Street, they told him, or push it to Washington or another one of the main streets, and then we'll pick it up. Since cars drove through them all the time, the alleys were not really private lanes (in which case the responsibility for clean-up would have fallen on the landlords). But the DPW foisted responsibility on the landlords anyway, who, similarly negligent, pointed fingers right back.

The eight students began doing alleyway patrols every Friday after school, adopting a several-block area and dividing it into four regions. They walked the blocks, learned the history, and recorded what they saw. Finally, Fong says, they "got smart": they invited a local newspaper reporter to walk around with them as they graded the alleyways.

"The next thing we knew, Chinese TV was coming along with us, and all this press happened," Fong says. "Youth get graded by society—they have the right to grade back. That was the principle behind it." The youth group started recruiting Chinese clubs in high schools around the city to come and do alleyway and graffiti clean-ups in Chinatown, and the social network continued to grow. In 1995, Fong worked with Jasmine Kaw—a student at the University of California at Berkeley who did her thesis on Chinatown's alleyways—to draw up a Chinatown "master plan": an analysis of all the alleyways that led the city to adopt them for maintenance.

"We got it," Fong says. "We won. It was a victory. So, for the youth, I tell them this—and I might exaggerate just a little bit— 'AAA is the story of the greatest youth movement in Chinatown!' Basically, San Francisco screwed the Chinese community as they have for many years, and they helped to turn it around. They earned a piece of it for themselves." The alleyway tours followed later, in 2000, with each student personalizing a tour with his or her own experiences and favorite stories from the neighborhood (many of which originated with Fong, who used to lead his own excursions through Chinatown).

"I love Norman," Rosa told me, adding that she thinks that he is "a really cool guy." Fong's street cred comes from growing up in Chinatown—he is a third-generation Chinese American whose father came through Angel Island Immigration Station, where many Chinese were infamously detained and deported—and his effectiveness clearly stems from a tireless championing of the neighborhood. He is still considered a Chinatown boy. He rarely sleeps (his college-age son, Micah, says that his father has more energy than he does).

When I asked Rosa why she thinks Norman puts such a premium on keeping the youth engaged in the community, she said it is because he wants to keep Chinatown alive—and in good shape—for many years to come.

"I think part of it is definitely because the youth is the future. He always starts out with a story: 'What better way to keep Chinatown clean than to have students' involvement to shame the merchants and shame the government about it?' That's how he started the program. He really believes that youth should have a voice, in everything, and it shouldn't just be about adults. That's one of his big, big priorities."

INSIDE SAM WO, a narrow, three-level Chinese restaurant on the corner of Grant Avenue and Washington Street that became legendary in the 1980s after *San Francisco Chronicle* columnist Herb Caen wrote about its histrionically rude waiter, Edsel Wong, the subject of math came up over a noodle lunch I had with Rosa and Tim Ho.

"My sister is two years older than me," Tim said. He, like Rosa, was born in 1984.

"So, she was born in 1986?" I asked. Silence. Then laughter. Tim pointed to his gray T-shirt, which read, in red block letters, "I SUCK AT MATH."

"It's our stand to disprove the idea that all Asian Americans are good at math, 'cause the stereotype is that we're all geniuses at it," Tim explained, running a hand through his spiky black hair. "We should get you a T-shirt, too." I was, I admit, strangely flattered.

A decade ago, Tim didn't have a particular affinity for Chinatown, despite the fact that it was where he spent all of his time, playing basketball and hanging out with his friends. His family lived in an SRO for a few years, before moving to the outskirts of the neighborhood. But they continued to come back every day. "If you only know Chinese, where else are you going to go?" Tim asked, playing with his chopsticks. "My day care was at Commodore Stockton"— the main Chinatown elementary school, now named Gordon J. Lau, after a local civil rights and community leader—"and I hung out at Chinese Playground every day. My whole life was here, except for high school." At fourteen, he was neither proud of being Chinese nor ashamed, but it was something that made him feel different from many of his classmates. There was, he says, a sense of dislocation. "You don't see many Asians on television. And when you do, you don't see them as normal human beings; you see them flying, kicking, and punching. How does an Asian American kid grow up normal without seeing a person similar to himself or herself as a normal human being? And when immigrant parents have different ideals and morals that clash with the American lifestyle, kids feel like they don't fit in even more."

These feelings have a compelling echo across the generations. "Growing up in this community, you only saw certain things that you were proud of and not proud of," Norman Fong told me. He remembers an era of black power and civil rights organization, and, for a long time, a lack of identity and self-respect in his own community. "Your parents you're not that proud of, because they're immigrants or they're not wealthy, so you end up rebelling a lot of different ways."

One of the main reasons Tim says that he and Rosa continue to be active in Chinatown, even after graduating from high school and even after their families moved out of the neighborhood, is that they learned about themselves by working in the community. Tim attended a small alternative high school called Wallenberg, in the Richmond district, an Asian American neighborhood north of Golden Gate Park that is sometimes described as a satellite second Chinatown, albeit a wealthier one. But he credits his education through the youth program in the history and community of Chinatown for giving his life experience there a real, meaningful context. "The Chinese kids at Wallenberg, from that neighborhood, they have a lot more money than me and Rosa, so they never had the need to go to Chinatown, for child care or anything. Their parents owned stores on Clement or somewhere else in the Richmond. They didn't feel the same type of associations for Chinatown that I do, not just for the area but for the people."

A deeper sense of connection—the sense, Tim says, that "there's just so much history that could all be forgotten"—is crucial to getting beyond the physical push and pull of Chinatown. He says his peers at Wallenberg didn't see the point of Chinatown—they felt that it was "just a dirty place, too crowded, with a lot of pushing and shoving from grannies and grandpas. It didn't mean anything beyond that to them. For them, it wasn't a real place."

Tim and Rosa's work in Chinatown has not been without its high points. "Tim was an extra in a Spike Lee movie once," Rosa told me, proudly. How did the director manage to find him? I asked. "It was easy—he asked us to do a tour for him," Tim said, laughing. "And when he mentioned that he needed some young people as extras, I told him I might be able to help him out."

The waitress brought bowls of steaming noodles and wonton soup, and plates of fried vegetable rolls and curried chicken with rice.

The widely told story of Edsel Wong, which made Sam Wo famous citywide, is simply a tourist's tale now, one before Rosa and Tim's time; to them, Sam Wo is a good place for cheap noodles, a restaurant that's open late and has quiet tables on the third floor. They make their own memories here. In between slurps, Rosa compared the kids Tim described to some of the tourists she sees coming into Chinatown, who think that the neighborhood is just for their benefit. "I remember having a tour group, and telling them that Chinatown is a mixed community—that the bottom is the commercial, the top is the residential, and I pointed out the places where people would go to go into their buildings, and they're like, 'Oh, wow, I didn't even know that this is how people live.' So people without a sense of connection probably think that Chinatown is just a tourist attraction, too."

Rosa says that the history of Chinatown makes her proud. "Okay, well, some parts of the history make me proud and some parts make me just so mad about society," she said. She laughed at her own intensity. "Like the reason why Chinatown existed in the first place is racism—people weren't allowed to leave. It was a ghetto, so the community had to survive on its own. The history taught me to be proud of my own community. I think that if people don't have a sense of pride, then they don't care about the community. I think that's maybe why some of the students that Tim was talking about, and maybe some of my high school peers, don't understand. Some people, even the students living in Chinatown, if they don't get the history themselves, they probably feel the same way—even if they live here, and hang out here, they just see the bad conditions, nothing else. The crowdedness, all the negative stuff and none of the positive. It overshadows the good stuff. That's the reason why my parents moved to Visitacion Valley"—a growing Chinese American neighborhood in the southern part of San Francisco. "My sister and I were in high school, and I was about to go to college. They thought that Chinatown was too crowded for us. But they come back all the time, to go to the bank, for groceries, because it's cheaper, because everyone can speak Chinese with them. It still matters."

Rosa Wong-Chie's experiences living in SROs as a child have shaped her interest in housing issues in particular. "Rosa was a senior at Galileo High School when I first met her," Jane Kim, CCDC's former youth coordinator, told me. The alleyway tours began under Kim's tenure. "She wasn't the most outspoken young person—we had a lot of guides who were funny, and many who were outgoing. But Rosa has an ability to convey genuineness that people really connect to. And because she grew up in one of the alleyways, it gave her an added level of authenticity on the tour. One of the major issues in Chinatown is housing, and she really wanted to concentrate on that, because she grew up in an SRO. It was something that most of her classmates didn't even know about."

Though she no longer gives regular tours, Rosa still cuts through Spofford Alley. We walked there from her office, and along the way, she pointed out childhood landmarks like her old Chinese school, now closed, and a favorite bakery. I asked her what it was like to live in such a crowded environment. One of her strongest early memories is of an SRO apartment on Grant Avenue, in a building that had hundreds of units—a maze of hallways in which she would play tag or hide-and-seek with the other kids. She shared a bunk bed with her sister, in the same room as her parents, who shared another bunk bed.

"My grandmother was in there, too," she said. "And my aunt and uncle had another room, with my cousin. It was really, really crowded; there was no space at all. I remember one time I was sitting on the floor, because there were no chairs, and I had a cup of water next to me. And my dad warned me not to knock it over, but I accidentally did. And then he started yelling at me, and I started crying." She paused, thinking. "That's how I remember feeling about that room."

She and her parents and younger sister eventually moved out of the Grant Avenue unit when the family found its own SRO in Spofford Alley, one with slightly more space. As a young girl, she despised having to take a shower, since her unit had no bathroom, only a toilet.

"We had to share a shower with the other people on the floor. Which I *hated*. I hated showering, because I had to run to the bathroom and then come back to the room." She shuddered. "I actually ended up showering a lot at my cousin's place, because they had their own shower and bathroom, and I could get privacy."

At 34 Spofford Alley, we stared at the heavy metal door on the pink building for a moment before Rosa walked up and gave it a shove. It opened easily, and she looked at me and laughed. "Still no lock," she said, holding the door open so I could pass through. We stood in the cramped entryway, and she looked around at the broken mailboxes. According to recent legislation in the city, all buildings in Chinatown must have working mailboxes; it had been seven years since Rosa lived here. "No," she said. "It's not changed at all."

Our voices echoed in the stairwell. A middle-aged woman came down the stairs and squeezed past us, and as the door closed again, Rosa pointed out its makeshift wood panel. Once, someone kicked through the bottom half, she said, and building management had boarded up the hole. It was still broken.

As we clomped up the narrow stairs, Rosa noticed new lighting, and a banister. There was also what appeared to be an earthquake retrofit, evidenced by patches of exposed beam and broken plaster. She explained to me that SRO residents are now classified as homeless by the city, so that they can receive the same benefits, including food and public transportation assistance. The average SRO costs $350 to $600 per month, for an eight-foot-by-eight-foot room. Two flights up, we quietly opened the throughway door to her old floor. "That's the bathroom," Rosa said, her voice low, pointing to the dark end of the hallway opposite from the street window.

A wire running down the length of the hallway along the wall drooped under the weight of hangers laden with drying laundry: bras and underwear, T-shirts, pants. The jury-rigged drying apparatus extended through the window to the fire escape, where more plastic hangers rattled in the light breeze. Stacks of shoes sat outside each of the four units; at the dark end of the hall, a child's tricycle looked forlorn, as did a pair of tiny pink Hello Kitty sneakers, surfacing in a sea of adult-sized slippers.

Rosa pointed out the one-room studio where she had lived. To show how me big it was, she used her arms to measure the width of the room from the outside, against the stairwell wall. "Basically, our bunk bed was from here to about here, leaving a little space for us to walk," she said, describing the plan of the room, as if she could see through walls. The entire width of the SRO apartment was equivalent to the span of her outstretched arms, plus another arm's length: somewhere shy of seven-and-a-half feet.

"We eventually moved across the hall to this unit, which was a lot better, because it had a bathroom," she said, pointing to another wall and sketching the layout of a living room, bedroom, and kitchen with her hands. "And the living room and then the bedroom, and the kitchen is on the side. The kitchen is like the size of this hallway, this wide. And I'm amazed, because my mom put our desk in there." She laughed at the memory. "So we were studying inside the bathroom and the kitchen. The bathroom is partitioned off, with a bathtub to the side, and then there's a door for the toilet. So you could use the bathtub area, but someone else could use the toilet."

An elderly couple emerged from the unit at the front of the building, and they eyed us as they opened the door to the stairs. Another man wandered into the hallway. "Are you looking for a place to live?" he asked, in Cantonese.

"Oh—no, we're not," Rosa said, ducking her head. We headed for the stairwell and returned to the world outside.

Later, I ask Rosa if she would ever want to live in Chinatown again. She says maybe. Her life is based around Chinatown, and it would be convenient. "But now that I can afford to live somewhere else, then probably not," she told me thoughtfully. "Because I understand why people need to live here more than me."

THE LIFE OF a Chinatown kid in San Francisco reflects life in much of inner-city America. Crumbling, overcrowded apartment buildings, widespread poverty, and parents who often work late hours—it's a recipe for listlessness. But Chinatown also benefits uniquely from a thriving street life and a neighborhood that is today vastly cleaner and safer than it has been in the past.

Like CCDC and Cameron House, many other neighborhood programs try to keep a sense of community alive for young people—otherwise there is no need for them to return or be involved. And youth is a crucial unifying force for change in this neighborhood. "Chinatown is too divided—we have one-hundred-and-fifty-five different family associations and four different merchant groups," Fong says. "Everyone has their own interests, so sometimes it's hard to get that united front. Youth cross over that, because everyone loves youth. Getting the kids who grow up here involved is really powerful."

And at AAA meetings, the kids get to be in charge. On the second Friday of each month, a core cabinet of about fifteen students meets to decide what projects the group wants to focus on for the next four weeks. At a recent meeting, the teenagers settled on an agenda of graffiti clean-ups, a Sunday meeting to educate SRO residents in health and safety issues, and a tenant-services event, which Tim Ho helped to launch in 2002 to "sort of bridge the generation gap." Since many elderly residents in Chinatown are somewhat disconnected from the world, Tim says, the students try to give a "different energy" to their day.

"The last time we played bingo, the seniors were very rowdy,"

Rosa told me. "They got really excited about the prizes. We bought them at the ninety-nine-cent store, but they loved it. Tupperware, grocery bags. Vegetable drainers. Shower caddies. Good stuff." She invited me to the next event.

It took place on a Wednesday afternoon, and when I arrived, the community room at 777 Broadway was jumping. The activity was origami. Five long tables were filled with about thirty seniors, and twenty students helped give demonstrations on folding various paper creations: cranes, frogs, hearts, flowers, collapsible boxes. Carmen, a self-assured, sweet-voiced sophomore who seemed older than sixteen, made announcements about the afternoon's activities in Cantonese, while Darwin, a shy boy in a blue shirt, made the same announcements in English. A dull roar of audience chatter nearly drowned him out. His baseball-capped grandfather, a resident in the building, ambled in to say hello.

Mrs. Lau, white-haired and in a purple paisley blouse and matching purple fleece, sat across from Sarah, a thin girl with bangs, zebra-striped nails, and a fur-trimmed hood. Sarah was new to the program, and had not said much that was not directed at her friends Wendy or Angelina. "Sarah is my daughter's name!" Mrs. Lau said in Cantonese, beaming. In her hands, she twirled a pink paper lily. Sarah smiled timidly, and helped Mrs. Lau fold her own flower as Carmen led the table of seniors in a demonstration.

The seniors were rapt, adoring. It is not a stretch to say that this monthly visit is one of the days they hold most precious—even as their cell phones ring and they chat about day trips to nearby casinos. I watched ninety-year-old Mrs. Tse fold an intricate pink paper heart. "Look how pretty my heart is," she said. I held it up to her chest, and she let out a snort of laughter. Her neighbor, Mrs. Luw, an eighty-year-old ethnic Chinese who came to the United States from Vietnam in 1979, invited me over for dinner, informing me that she was making vegetables and fish that night in her third-floor apartment.

"We love it when the young people come see us," she said in

Cantonese, pushing up her glasses to look at me. "They come every month, you know. We don't have a lot of places to go, so it's nice that they come and talk to us for a little bit."

Two hours later, when I asked Carmen how her flower demo turned out, she gave me a thumbs-up and bounced on her toes. "We finally got it to work, and then I did a speed version at another table," she said, grinning and rolling her eyes dramatically. She said she felt bad when all the other tables were "*littered* with origami, and we didn't finish even *one* yet."

At the end of the day, the Chinatown kids belong here. This is their community, and they have begun, little by little, to take ownership of it. Jeffrey, a quick-witted boy fluent in Mandarin and English and jokey in both, practiced his nascent Cantonese with friends. Rosa asked a couple of new students for their e-mail addresses, and encouraged them to attend the annual camping retreat so they could get to know the other kids better. "It's a lot of fun, you should go!" She knows, she said, from past experience.

A pod of teenagers clustered together over several handheld video games—Nintendo DS Lites, which were a "cooler version of Game Boy," a boy named Brian explained. They all hooked up wirelessly. As I collected my things, Brian and two girls named Queena and Donna recruited Rosa to join their three-player tournament. "Okay, okay, one game," she said. She waved at me to go on without her, the transition from newbie Chinatown community leader back to regular Chinatown kid easily made. Shrieks followed me out the door.

Later, Rosa tells me that being in charge of the youth program is still new to her. But the community is not. "I don't know what I'll be doing later on, but I think it will always come back to Chinatown," she says, pointing to the neighborhood as her anchor. "Kind of like Norman. He's always here."

A field trip from Chinatown. *Bonnie Tsui*

THREE

CHAIN MIGRATION

*Family ties pull a new generation through
Chinatown Gate, but not without difficulty.*

Part of what appeals to Americans about Chinatown is the promise of the exotic within a few blocks of home. Cross Kearny Street at Washington, and you leave the Transamerica Building and downtown's office buildings behind for the hubbub of Portsmouth Square. Cut over Bush Street at Grant Avenue, and Union Square's ubiquitous coffee shops give way to Chinatown's ubiquitous souvenir shops. Pass through Chinatown Gate, and there's a world apart to taste—you can listen to a foreign language, try to barter for a trinket on the street, or visit a historic temple, without ever leaving the country. You come to expect this, looking for "something different" in its narrow lanes and fish markets. The streets and alleys entertain for a few hours, and you pass through those few blocks. If you're a resident of the city, maybe you buy some cheap produce on your way out. Then you get on with the everyday.

But consider an everyday contained within that same square-block area. The marvelous becomes simply mundane, and a preference for the foreign quickly gives way to that for the functional. This Chinatown has infinitely more depth than it does for you as a visitor—beneath the cell phone store is the preschool, above the restaurant is a relative's apartment. People might call your name on the street, ask about your aunt's health, tell you that the cherries at the corner grocery are ripe and ready for eating. (Though I visit fairly often, the shopkeepers don't offer me the same courtesy; instead, they frown and tell me that I can't choose my own fruit.) At the same time, the neighborhood has its finite limits, its existence and yours loosely circumscribed by the Chinese-language signs petering out along the edges of the district.

It is in this Chinatown that twenty-eight-year-old Mrs. Chan resides. Four years ago, she moved with her husband to the United States from Toisan. Every Monday and Thursday morning at eleven thirty, she walked the three blocks from her apartment to attend a family playgroup class on Clay Street. One Monday, I met her there to talk about life in Chinatown as a new immigrant.

A full-lipped woman with a ready smile and a deep, resonant voice, Mrs. Chan was shy of speaking with me at first, but soon warmed when I asked about her children. Everyone knew her by her two boys, Edward—a red-cheeked seven-month-old whom she carried in a plaid sling—and David, a bright, talkative three-year-old with a crazy laugh who shared his mother's grin and almost always wore a favorite pair of army fatigue pants. The first time I met him, he was hiding under a table, giggling madly. That day, I helped him make a blue paper butterfly with pipe-cleaner antennae.

Before moving into their own apartment in Chinatown, Mrs. Chan and her husband lived with his relatives in Visitacion Valley. Life is much more convenient in Chinatown; she can get around easily by foot or bus, and she can shop for groceries day by day instead of having to plan by the week. Everyone speaks Cantonese or Toisanese. She has friends here whom she knew previously in Toisan—one of whom, Mrs. Huang, she ran into on the street in Chinatown not long after moving here—and if she wants to take her children to the park or the library or the doctor, all are located within the neighborhood. And all come personally recommended, verbally stamped with approval by a friend or family member.

But there are downsides. She hates her cramped one-bedroom

apartment, which she likens to a "dog pen." In Toisan, she said, she could have her own house. Even though San Francisco is bigger than Toisan, there isn't enough room to live properly in its housing. Chinatown's streets are dirty, and she thinks the shopkeepers contribute to the ever-growing piles of garbage. "No self-control," she said, with a rueful smile, mimicking someone carelessly tossing a piece of trash onto the sidewalk. She knows her ABCs, but she doesn't speak English. This, by far, is the hardest thing about her new American life.

Family is the reason she moved to America. Her husband's mother has lived in Chinatown for eleven years; eager to bring her son and daughter-in-law to the United States, she filed the paperwork to sponsor their passage. Mrs. Chan's own parents, sister, and brother live in Toisan, and she is the only one of them here. She misses them desperately.

Her days in Chinatown have fallen into a routine. Her husband leaves at seven in the morning for his job as a dim sum chef at a Chinese restaurant in Daly City, just south of San Francisco, while she almost always stays behind, taking care of their two young sons. She shops, and cleans, and goes to the park with Mrs. Huang. Sometimes she wishes they could move back to Toisan, but she is resigned to Chinatown for now. In a few short years, it has already become a comfort zone. "The kids were born here, they like it here," she said. "They're used to it. So we stay."

Most new immigrants are employed in restaurant or construction work. "The biggest obstacle is language," Homer Teng, a family support counselor at the Joy Lok Family Resource Center, where Mrs. Chan's playgroup is held, told me. Of the working-age Chinese residents in San Francisco who do not speak English well, two-thirds earn less than $20,000 a year. Teng explained that many new immigrants in Chinatown are employed in restaurant, garment, or construction services, working ten hours a day, six days a week. Even in China, he says, they were mostly blue-collar workers with limited schooling. "Most of the permanent residents who come through this center do so because they are sponsored by family who are already here," Teng said. "Many have inflated expectations of how their life can be like, where they can live, the jobs they can get. Chinatown is a safety zone—it's their own little country here. But their long-term future relies on their ability to become more self-sufficient."

After a century and a half of Chinese immigration to California, Chinatown remains a gateway for new immigrants and a continuing safe haven for old ones, who can live their entire lives within sixteen square blocks. While educated overseas Chinese choose Silicon Valley and bypass Chinatown, poorer immigrants need it. They rarely have to speak English, because the improvement of Chinatown means that all the services are here, offered in their own language. The truth is that a person who has lived in Chinatown for thirty years doesn't necessarily speak better English than a new arrival. And a new arrival may never have the time to learn. For a working-class new immigrant today, passage through Chinatown Gate is a complicated entry to a gilded ghetto. It has its advantages. It can also keep you down.

"OUTSIDERS ARE ALWAYS amazed that people in Chinatown are poor," Norman Fong says. "It doesn't fit the mainstream idea of what poverty is. The face of poverty is not Asian. But a lot of families squeeze into tiny apartments, SROs, and public housing—sardine living. It isn't what those rooms were originally meant to hold, but it's what they can afford." One afternoon, we walked through several SRO and public-housing buildings in the neighborhood. I saw elderly residents living in tiny rooms ten feet by ten feet, each jammed by a bunk-bed frame and every nook stuffed with clothing and pictures and other belongings, all of it illuminated by the wan glow of a clip-on bed lamp. As we stood outside Ping Yuen, a large public-housing project in the northern part of Chinatown, traffic pushed past us on the busy sidewalk, and Fong told me that he is often asked why he remains so entrenched in Chinatown life, since he no longer has to live here.

"If you think about Chinatown as a gateway or transition point, where everyone wants to get a nice house and move out—the logical immigrant perspective—then it can turn into a slum and people don't care about it," he said, sighing. "I think we blew it in the past, when we didn't respect our own community. We've turned it around. But in a way it's even worse now than in the fifties and sixties, because there are more families." He paused to say hello to a man and his son ambling by. "When I look at new immigrants here, I see my parents."

In the last forty years, the major population change in Chinatowns across the United States has mirrored the shift from bachelor-heavy to family-focused immigration, what sociologists call chain migration. This huge demographic change happened with the 1965 Immigration Act, which placed an emphasis on reuniting families and in ending immigration discrimination. Before the change, long-time Chinatowns like New York's and San Francisco's were declining or in stasis, since Chinese immigration was so restricted. After Chinese Communists led by Mao Zedong took over mainland China in 1949—and forced Nationalist leader Chiang Kai-shek and his government to retreat to Taiwan—refugees trickled into the United States, but it wasn't easy to get papers. The year 1965 was a benchmark: the immigration law rejuvenated American Chinatowns with an influx of people seeking to reunite with their families; the post-1965 boom also saw a new class of students and educated professionals from different parts of China, Hong Kong, and Taiwan, as well as ethnic Chinese from Southeast Asia seeking asylum after the Vietnam War. Chinatown survives because of this open door. Between 1960 and 1970, the United States received about 100,000 Chinese immigrants; between 1990 and 2000, there were well over 500,000 arrivals. Chain migration is now at the center of current debate over immigration policy in America; critics argue that skills-based immigration should be given higher priority. The pattern in San Francisco's Chinatown is still strong in immigration from Guangdong Province, especially from Toisan; whole communities may come over on the sponsorship of family members already residing here.

As a result, it is completely possible for a new immigrant to run into old friends on the streets of Chinatown, as Mrs. Chan did. "One day, I was just walking on Clay," she said. "And I saw Mrs. Huang!"—her old friend from Toisan. "She was taking her older daughter to Chinese school. It made me really happy to find her again here." In the absence of her next of kin, Chinatown signifies an extended family.

Her twice-weekly Chinatown playgroup, where I first got to know her, is also part of this extension. Hidden belowground at the corner of Stockton Street—sandwiched between a dried-herb store and a massage parlor that doubles as a hair salon—Joy Lok is a family resource center frequented by new immigrant families to Chinatown. It is where low-income parents with young children look for help with subsidized day care and preschool. Despite its basement location, Joy Lok is a brightly lit, modern space. The walls are painted in pale blues and yellows, and the offices double as playgroup areas, scattered with colorful three-dimensional puzzles and toddler-sized tables and chairs.

To ease the process, a major priority of the center is to expose young immigrant parents to other environments outside of Chinatown. Language barriers ensure that most leave the neighborhood only rarely. "They might know one or two areas outside, like 'This one school is good because I know such-and-such sends his kid there,'" Monica Ng, a resource specialist at the center, told me. "It's very insular, and they're afraid to go outside."

During the course of several mornings spent at Joy Lok, it became clear to me that these women were going to school with their children. Because they can't yet work—if they take jobs, they won't be eligible for subsidized day care, and what they would make in wages would not be enough to cover unsubsidized care—they are essentially held in social and economic limbo. They have limited options for employment—again, primarily due to the language barrier. Playgroups like Joy Lok's are a crucial gateway to an American-style education of their own—a way to learn the alphabet and elementary songs in English and Cantonese, and how to play and interact with their two- and three-year-old kids in a way that will prepare them for life in this country.

Mrs. Chan says that if she's lucky enough to get day care for both of her children, she plans to learn English so that she can find some work. "That would be better, for me, to have a job," she said. Her face grew animated at the prospect.

Soon after meeting Mrs. Chan, I dropped in on an English-as-a-second-language (ESL) class at the Chinese Newcomers Service Center, three blocks south of Joy Lok, just before the Stockton Street tunnel. The class was a new three-day session taught by Yi Zhong, an alert-eyed young woman from Beijing. Though she was dressed casually, in a gray sweater and baggy jeans, she moved and talked with a smart, efficient competence. When she wrote on the board, her green jade bracelet slid quickly up and down her wrist. Like Mrs. Chan, Yi has been in the United States for four years. But unlike Mrs. Chan, who comes from a working-class area in southern China—before she came to the United States, she worked in a restaurant—Yi is part of the educated class in China's capital; she speaks Mandarin and attended San Francisco State, receiving a master's degree in English. She teaches at the center on a volunteer basis.

Geographic and economic separations among immigrants were evident even in the composition of the ESL class. A little over half of the students in the class were middle-aged men and women who chatted in Toisanese. These eight sat at a table on one side of the room. Six others, mostly younger women, sat on the opposite side. They spoke to each other in Mandarin. Eventually, all eyes turned to Yi. As the class progressed, some students murmured to themselves as they copied down basic English phrases into little notebooks or onto scraps of paper.

"Good morning!"

"What's your name?"

"How long have you been here?"

The students were stirred to respond. One of the Toisanese women burst out, "Eight months!" Another woman in a brown coat answered more softly, in Mandarin, "One year, eight months."

Yi asked the woman in the brown coat how her English was.

"Not so good."

"Why is that?"

"Because I don't go out," she answered, giggling and exchanging looks with a friend who sat next to her.

Yi laughed along with them, then wrote, "We are in an English-speaking environment" on the board. "That's why the Chinese like San Francisco," she said, in English. "Even if you don't know English, you can survive in this city—especially if you are living in Chinatown." She explained that while all of us were Chinese, the learning culture was different in America; she encouraged everyone to ask questions and to speak up if they didn't understand what she was talking about. A heavy silence followed.

The class continued for another hour. Yi talked about language topics as diverse as the job interview ("tell them you are learning English"), reality television ("watching a TV show like *American Idol* is a good way to improve your English"), and how to order at McDonald's ("I want a number one"). As she encouraged the students to "practice" ordering, I couldn't help thinking that frequent fast-food orders at McDonald's probably weren't beneficial to their long-term well-being. I looked over at a young mother who had come to the class with her child and sat next to me, so clearly thirsty for a little companionship and conversation. "How long have you been in the U.S.?" she had asked me in Cantonese, her voice hopeful. For better or worse, this was her American education, under way.

IN CERTAIN RESPECTS, Mrs. Chan is already a typical American. She shops for diapers at Costco—on her husband's day off, they go to visit relatives or to the mall in Daly City, just south of San Francisco—and dresses her children in Old Navy. She carries a shiny pink cell phone with a Winnie the Pooh accessory in her back pocket. Though she doesn't speak a lot of English, her conversations are peppered with bursts of "hi" and "okay" and "thank you." The other day, a man asked her where to find a popular children's CD. "He spoke slowly, and I knew what he was saying," she said, in Cantonese. "But I couldn't think of how to say it." She laughed and waved her hands helplessly. "I didn't have the words."

As much as new immigrants like Mrs. Chan are exposed to the American mainstream, there is a gulf here between American-born Chinese, or ABCs, and those "fresh-off-boat," or FOBs. That gap is only beginning to be examined by those in the community, Sabina Chen, director of San Francisco's Chinese Culture Center, told me. The center recently hosted a groundbreaking panel in Chinatown between American-born Chinese and Chinese-born immigrants of similar ages.

In the sprawling "extended family" that is the Bay Area Chinese community, she said, issues of immigration status, language, class, and acculturation cause huge generational divides. "Yet we all call ourselves Chinese," she said. Though there were lots of questions and few answers, she said that plenty of people—from the Chinatown Chinese to the Silicon Valley Chinese, from first generation to second generation—wanted in on the conversation.

"Right off the bat, the first-generation immigrants tossed out

ABC as semi-derogatory, and the second-generations tossed out FOB as semi-derogatory," Chen told me. On the question of how to raise kids in America, language and culture are at the forefront. "For first-generation folks, it is important for their kids to speak English perfectly, and there is a desire and recognition for them to speak Chinese as well, for practicality's sake, because China is a rising power. For the American-born, we mull over what kind of education we want our children to have—do we put them in immersion school or bilingual school?—recognizing that we want them to connect to the culture somehow. There's a lot of talk about families and the generations that came before us. It's more nostalgic."

When I asked Chen where ABC and FOB groups intersect, if they do at all, she said that it was a good, but difficult, question. "There are ABCs who serve the new immigrant population in Chinatown, but there's not a lot of interaction outside of that. New immigrants are either family-sponsored or sponsored by work, which is at the core of the whole immigration debate now, and there's a stigma that goes with both," she said. Work-sponsored immigrants tend to be wealthier, and have less of a connection to previous Chinese generations in America. "The current Silicon Valley generation that is work-sponsored and speaks Mandarin, they don't really have contact with Chinatown the way that the family-sponsored immigrant generation does. The family-based generation has deep roots. It is a question for a lot of Chinatown groups, how to stay relevant to the Chinese community at large outside of Chinatown."

The question of Chinatown's relevance raises an interesting paradox. The Chinese have had significant success in this country and can be considered to be assimilating quite effectively in a lot of ways—and yet Chinatowns still persist. It remains the first stop for a particular class of immigrants, but in addition to that, some insight to the paradox might be found where the ABCs and the FOBs do find common ground. Part of what makes up the new American identity is ethnic identity—the American ideal is no longer confined to a white Anglo-centric model. Chinese Americans of all stripes bring their children to Chinese schools, shop in Chinese supermarkets, read Chinese newspapers, and remain in touch with relatives back in China. For many, Chinatown represents most immediately the heritage of the Chinese American immigrant experience.

For outsiders and tourists—and they include multiple generations of Chinese Americans—there is an authenticity of experience to be sought in Chinatown. For Mrs. Chan and new immigrants like her, the outsiders are part of a community that continually expands and contracts, like a living, breathing thing.

ON A FRIDAY morning in Chinatown, a crowd of forty children, parents, and grandparents gathered outside of Joy Lok. A big yellow school bus was coming to take them just north across the Golden Gate Bridge to a children's play museum in Sausalito's Fort Mason. For many of them, it was their first trip across the famous rust-hued bridge. On the ride over, the children squirmed and the adults pointed; the excitement level mounted. "When they're outside, they just try to see everything," Karen Ho, one of the playgroup leaders, told me. "It's all new to them."

Given that Chinatown is just as popular with visitors as the Golden Gate Bridge is, the irony was not lost on me. During one of our last conversations, I asked Mrs. Chan what she thought about the tourists who come to her doorstep every day. She told me that she is intrigued by what drives them to her neighborhood. "Chinatown to me is nothing special, nothing different," she said. "It's where I live. But every time I leave home, I see all these people who seem to think it's really exciting. Why is it so exciting? I don't know why they think it's so special. Sometimes I wonder what brings them here."

When I asked her what she liked best about living in Chinatown, she thought only for a moment before answering. "The food here is pretty good," she said. "It's definitely better here than where I come from." Chinatown and the Golden Gate Bridge are both places where tourists congregate. But in a Chinatown market or restaurant, it can also be where tourists and residents come together, and this meeting is a poignant repeat event. For newcomers who are isolated here, it's a rare chance to share in the outside world. And in this place, it's an interaction that's as old as San Francisco itself.

I ♥ CHINATOWN new york

↑ uptown

① chinese staff
(where feng ying jiang works)

lower east side →

ccba ☆ ⑩
(once supreme org. of chinese in n.y.)

KENMARE

DELANCEY

② grand st. subway station

BROOME

centre st.

baxter st.

mulberry

mott st.

elizabeth

the bowery

chrystie

GRAND

⊤ transfiguration church ⑨
(where i was baptized, 1978)

CANAL

② ③

⑩

③ grand st. park 🌳

BAYARD

⑧

⑨

CANAL ST.

city hall ←

🌳 columbus park ⑧

WORTH

DIVISION

E.B'WAY

HENRY

MADISON

⑦

⑥

MANHATTAN BRIDGE

④

□ chatham square ⑦

CHERRY ST. ⑤

FDR DRIVE

▲ my grandparents' first chinatown apartment, 1960
⑥

⚓ south street seaport

BROOKLYN BRIDGE

to brooklyn ↓

↟ p.s. 2 meyer london ④
(xue mei + elaine's school)

↟ p.s. 184 shuang wen ⑤
(john tan's school)

Garment workers protest sweatshop labor, New York. *Mario Tama/Getty Images*

FOUR

CITY WITHIN A CITY

*The industry of Chinatown
changes New York.*

When I lived in Manhattan, the ceaseless industry of the city never failed to impress me. And in no other neighborhood, perhaps, is the business of New York more obvious and in-your-face than in Chinatown, where everything from bunches of Chinese broccoli and griddle cakes to knockoff designer wallets and souvenir T-shirts bearing the "I ♥ NY" logo are sold street-side. Chinese Americans have long been entrepreneurs, and New York's Chinatown has by necessity been a place for their business, and for their survival. By 1920, 40 percent of all the Chinese in America lived in San Francisco and New York, pushed from smaller towns to these urban Chinatowns by racism. They took the jobs the white world allowed them to take, in laundries, groceries, and restaurants. And the community established its own internal network of associations, most based on family ties and place of origin, through which new arrivals could find jobs and housing, and even set up bank accounts and businesses. When I went back to the neighborhood, it was with this backstory in mind, to examine more closely what historically have been Chinatown's biggest economies. Given Chinatown's reputation for being a society apart, it was surprising to discover how closely its industry has been tied to the fortunes and labor struggles of the larger city outside.

Take clothing, for instance. For generations, New York made more clothes than any other city in the country. Across the twentieth century, fashion has been the biggest manufacturing industry in Manhattan, with immigrant labor serving as its backbone. In sewing shops tucked away in neighborhoods all around the island, waves of German, Italian, Jewish, Puerto Rican, Chinese, and other immigrants wove the fabric of a city.

These days, Manhattan persists as America's fashion capital. Though much of the clothing production continues to be moved off-island, fashion is still the biggest source of manufacturing, most of it concentrated in the midtown Garment District and—surprise— Chinatown. Top labels like Nicole Miller, Marc Jacobs, and Oscar de la Renta continue to have their clothes made in Manhattan. The rise and fall of the Chinatown garment industry tells us a lot about how connected the neighborhood is to the forces at work in the city. Chinatown, it turns out, is not as isolated as people think. It was forty years ago that Chinatown became instrumental in keeping the American garment industry afloat. And my mother's mother, Shau Yip Dong, was one of the legions of Chinatown ladies whose labor helped the industry to survive. It makes sense, then, that I should start with her story.

AS MY GRANDMOTHER tells it, her life in Chinatown began in 1960, when she moved with my *gung-gung* and three of their five children into a shabby three-room apartment in a brownstone tenement at 86 Madison Street. Along with another family on the floor, they shared a bathroom in the hallway that was so dirty that people were afraid to use it. There was no refrigerator, so my *paw-paw*—the name in Cantonese for maternal grandmother—put the daily groceries for dinner out on the fire escape. The rent was $80 a month. Here on the east side of the neighborhood, their lives were largely conducted under the span of the Manhattan Bridge, looming overhead and leading across the East River to Brooklyn.

Like other immigrants filtering into New York at the time, my grandparents had fled the Communist takeover of mainland China in 1949. After making their way from the rural rice paddies of Toisan to Guangzhou, the capital of Guangdong Province, my grandparents managed to get to Hong Kong, where they stayed for seven years, biding their time until they could gain passage to America. Hong Kong had yet to become a booming commercial center, and there were no jobs for the mostly rural population of Chinese refugees—some 3 million of them—who landed there between 1950 and 1960. My family survived on money sent to them from my *gung-gung*'s father, who was already working at a laundry in New York. Years before, my great-grandfather had himself become a "paper son," buying someone else's documents in order to come to America. Eventually, after immigration laws were relaxed, he was able to secure papers to bring my grandparents and some of their children—the immigration lawyer thought that five might be too many, so he drew up documents for only three—to New York. Because my mother was the oldest, and my aunt Rosena the second oldest, they stayed behind in Hong Kong, in the care of relatives, uncertain when they would see their parents and siblings again.

My *paw-paw* told me that when she arrived, she was eager to find work. The sense that she had relied on other people for far too long gnawed at her. Almost immediately, she started a job at a Chinatown garment factory alongside her mother-in-law, my great-grandmother, first snipping threads and then moving on to piecework as a seamstress.

Like other garment shops occupying Manhattan's limited real estate, the factory she worked at on Division Street wasn't very big—just forty people sewing in a room. It was one of several Chinatown shops that had begun to take on sewing work from the midtown Garment District as the older unionized workforce of Italian and Jewish immigrants retired. A serious labor shortage was making itself felt, and since American textile manufacturers were starting to get pushed out by overseas competition, cutting costs was also a priority. The center of the textile universe began to shift, from the center of Manhattan down to Chinatown, where cheaper space could be found, and cheaper labor, too, in newer immigrants willing to work for less. In the factory where my *paw-paw* worked, all of the seamstresses were women; almost everyone was from Guangdong, and almost everyone spoke Cantonese or Toisanese. A handful of men distributed bundles of fabric and pressed the finished garments. My grandmother, a gregarious, talkative woman, quickly made friends with the women who sat at the sewing machines next to her.

Their earnings depended on how much they could sew—someone who was just starting out wouldn't even make a hundred dollars a week. But most women earned weekly wages of $140 to $250. The work fluctuated with the fashion seasons, sending the ladies home early on some weeks and working them around the clock on others to fill an order on time. During the busy season, the boss closed the doors to the factory and the women worked quietly into the night, without speaking, so as not to attract the authorities. My *paw-paw* says that overtime pay was not an option in a Chinese-owned shop. "The boss asked who wanted to work extra hours, and those who wanted to work stayed," she explained, matter-of-factly. "Of course we wanted to work. If you have no money, you don't eat."

Her workplace was a whirl of colors and patterns bundled into piles of unfinished sleeves and collars and pant legs, brought to her to be stitched together, only to be sold somewhere else. As the factories became more efficient, an assembly line system was gradually adopted, and the work was divided up into departments. My *paw-paw* worked in zippers, buttons, waistbands. "It was layers of business—the fabric was cut upstate, and we did all the sewing in

Chinatown," she recalled. "They never told us where the clothes went after that."

The factory was located four blocks from home. Though the family lived in poverty—my *paw-paw* told me, with a good-humored laugh, of the time my five-year-old uncle noted the leaky bulges and cracks corrugating the ceiling of their Chinatown apartment and asked her plaintively, "*This* is America?"—the three children could go to public school, and eventually even to college, for free. By contrast, an education in Hong Kong was impossible without money.

Their lives fell into a tightly circumscribed pattern. In the mornings, my *paw-paw* brought my two aunts and my uncle to P.S. 2—Meyer London, the neighborhood elementary school—before continuing on to work. In the afternoons, when the bell rang at dismissal, she was there to meet them for the walk back home. "The boss was a good man," she says. "He let us have breaks to do what we needed to do." As my grandmother related these details to me, I was struck by the commonality across Chinatowns and between the generations therein. Forty years later and a continent away, Mrs. Chan's life echoed Mrs. Dong's. Whether in New York or San Francisco, at the inception of the neighborhood or in the present day, the convenience of Chinatown, with its chockablock community and everything within walking distance, makes it easier to get by.

FITTINGLY, my earliest memories of my grandmother involve her sewing machine. On Sunday visits to my grandparents' house in Flushing, Queens, I sometimes wandered into her bedroom and watched her finish off a skirt hem or the elastic on a pair of trousers; her fingers moved quickly with the fabric, the light from the lamp glinting off her glasses. My grandmother made the wedding dress my mother wore to get married to my father in 1972; it was a satiny fairy-tale confection that my mother kept stored in the back of my closet throughout my girlhood. Even after I outgrew any possibility of fitting into it—I am half a foot taller than my mother, and was so in sixth grade—I loved that intricately stitched gown, so beautifully and skillfully made. I believe my grandmother when she tells me today that she was one of the fastest in her factory.

When I asked her recently if working in the garment factory was difficult, the intensity of her reply surprised me. "For such a long time, we had nothing," she said. "In the factory, everyone sitting around me was my friend, and everyone was happy to have a job. In Hong Kong, we had no job, no money, nothing to do. We came here, and we couldn't believe that we had the freedom to earn our own living. We didn't think of it as uncomfortable or hard—we just felt lucky to be able to do it." To her, it was simple. Almost fifty years later, the hardship of postwar life in Guangzhou and Hong Kong still colors her view of America. Her uncomplaining, keep-quiet philosophy characterizes her generation of Chinatown immigrants—a generation that Phil Choy, the San Francisco historian, described as conservative and insular, unwilling to rock the boat.

My grandmother's arrival in Chinatown just predated the post-1965 immigration wave. When quotas were lifted, my mother and my aunt were able to leave Hong Kong and join their parents and the rest of their siblings in New York. But post-1965 immigration didn't just change the face of America to a more Asian one—in Manhattan, its coincidence with the labor shortage in the local garment industry funneled the new arrivals into Chinatown's garment shops, filling the gap with a much-needed influx of workers.

Between the end of the sixties and the beginning of the eighties, the number of jobs in the Garment District plummeted by 40 percent. But over the same period of time, the number of workers in Chinatown employed by the garment industry ballooned, from 8,000 to 20,000. According to Xiaolan Bao, a historian who spent ten years interviewing female garment workers in New York, by the early 1980s the Chinatown garment industry was contributing significantly to the city's economy, to the tune of $125 million each year.

In other words, Chinatown wasn't just something that the Chinese needed—Chinatown was something that the city itself depended on. Though the individual factories weren't very big, the collective number in Chinatown made a difference. Sewing shops had popped up all over the neighborhood, changing everything about it—Chinese bosses employed thousands of Chinese women on behalf of mainstream manufacturers, expanding the boundaries of Chinatown into the lofts and old industrial spaces of the Lower East Side and Little Italy, while local Chinese restaurants and groceries opened to feed the swelling population and provide for its needs. In true New York fashion, the Chinatown economy was booming.

MY GRANDMOTHER didn't know or care much where the fashions she made ended up. There were complicated, higher-quality clothing orders that demanded more time and attention, and she did her job dutifully. But even though she never complained, she was savvy enough to know that there was a disparity.

"Of course they didn't tell you where the clothes went," she said, her eyebrows lifting. "Because then you'd say, 'Why do you sell it for so much money and pay us so little?'"

By the 1980s, the garment and restaurant trades were the two biggest employers for working-class Chinese in New York. In effect, Chinatown had become one big factory. After years of immense growth and unchecked hours, it was inevitable that labor abuses and a worker consciousness would emerge. Any kind of family-style solidarity that might have been fostered between bosses and workers had dissipated, and competition for work drove down wages. In 1979, a handful of restaurant and garment workers founded what was then a radical new organization, called the Chinese Staff and Workers' Association. Over the last thirty years, Chinese Staff has helped workers across different trades and ethnic backgrounds organize and bring legal action to improve their working conditions. One of its most successful efforts was the recent organization of the city's restaurant workers—where tip-stealing by restaurant owners was once rampant, it is now rare due to a pivotal Chinatown restaurant case in 2007 that declared it illegal and awarded $700,000 in back pay and tips to employees. But change has been slower to come in the garment industry.

One afternoon, I went to visit Wing Lam, a Chinese Staff cofounder well known in the community, in the organization's crowded, one-room Chinatown office, near where the Manhattan Bridge off-ramp dumps out onto busy Canal Street. Lam worked as a presser in a garment factory in the 1970s. Across a table piled high with legal files and protest flyers, Lam told me that by 1980, a rift had opened up between the Chinatown management elite and the working class. "After 1965, it took about ten or fifteen years for the Chinese themselves to become the real bosses," he said. "They treated their own workers, the Chinese workers, without respect. Sweatshop conditions. No breaks, no control over their time. The workers finally realized that something had to change. The Chinese were becoming racist against themselves." Three years after Chinese Staff was founded, 20,000 Chinatown garment workers went on a massive strike in New York, forcing all the Chinese-owned garment shops in the city to sign an agreement with the needle trade union.

My *paw-paw* ended up working in Chinatown's garment factories for more than thirty years. In 1992, she retired and moved to Long Island to help raise my cousin, Justin, who had just been born. The union pays her a retirement pension of $104 a month. She is grateful for what Chinatown provided for her when she arrived—a place to live, a place to work, with a community that spoke her language. It was a place to go when she had no choice of where to go. My grandparents still go back periodically to shop or attend a special event, and they follow the news on the Chinese radio, but their daily ties there are falling away. Every time they read the Chinese newspaper, they see that this or that person from the neighborhood has passed on, or moved on. The boss's wife still phones my grandmother from Chicago, where she went to live with her son's family some years ago. When she calls, she always asks the same question: "What's the news from Chinatown?" Though my *paw-paw* sees the changes, it's from afar. She tells me that the question is one she no longer knows how to answer.

THE GARMENT STORY, however, continues. The same year that my grandmother retired and moved to Long Island, forty-six-year-old Feng Ying Jiang arrived in Chinatown. She came from Fuzhou, the capital of Fujian Province, located just east of Guangdong and across the strait from Taiwan. The day after she got to New York, she went straight to work at a Chinese-owned garment factory in midtown.

Jiang was at the front end of yet another wave of Chinese immigrants to New York's Chinatown, this time from Fujian Province. In the last decade and a half, just a block away from my grandmother's first Chinatown apartment, the Fujianese have rapidly transformed the neighborhood's eastern frontier, creating a Chinatown along East Broadway that is largely self-contained and independent of the traditional Cantonese-dominant population clustered around Mott Street. Language barriers separate the two populations, and many of the newer immigrants have further difficulty because they are undocumented, at times owing tens of thousands of dollars to the "snakeheads" who have smuggled them into America. In 1994, a tramp steamer named *Golden Venture* ran aground in the middle of the night in Queens, bearing nearly three hundred illegal immigrants smuggled mostly from Fujian. Ten passengers drowned in the attempt to swim to shore. The notorious incident came to symbolize the swelling human traffic from the province, and the changes the new immigrants have exerted on Chinatown itself.

Some of the most significant changes have been felt in the garment industry, says Jei Fong, a young organizer at Chinese Staff who is kept busy with labor cases involving garment workers. She explained to me that the root of the division between the Cantonese and the Fujianese is simple: most Cantonese are longtime documented immigrants, while most Fujianese are recent undocumented immigrants. In the garment factories, where many look for jobs, it matters.

Fong began working with Chinese Staff as a volunteer, and has been on staff since 2005. "Immigration law says that these people are criminals," Fong told me. "As a boss, you're not supposed to hire undocumented workers. The twist is that instead of preventing undocumented hires, the law has actually encouraged bosses to *prefer* hiring undocumented workers. They say, 'I'm not supposed to hire you, so you better do what I say.'" The squeeze comes from the top, with each level looking to cut costs: mainstream fashion manufacturers hire Chinese factory contractors, offering a fixed price per garment; the factory contractors in turn hire undocumented workers, paying them less and avoiding the legal responsibilities of overtime and benefits, all in order to make a razor-thin profit themselves. Many garment workers tell Fong that they can no longer get jobs if they tell the bosses they are documented. The impact on the community, she told me, is that it "really screws the documented workers— these older immigrants who have their whole families here and have to take care of them, pay taxes, this whole other set of expectations." Most new immigrants she works with come over by themselves, with a limited plan to make money and stay here for a few years—it's the sojourner mentality all over again. This economically driven prejudice, Fong says, extends to social prejudice, and creates rifts in the Chinese community between the two populations.

I met Feng Ying Jiang on one of my visits to Chinese Staff's office.

She is a pretty woman, that day dressed neatly in trim slacks and a flowered button-down shirt, her jet-black hair carefully styled with curled bangs. Before Jiang moved to the United States in 1992, she worked in a tailor's shop in Fuzhou, helping customers with clothing alterations. Jei Fong, who speaks Mandarin, helped me translate Jiang's story.

Right from the beginning, the factory was all Jiang knew of America. "That was it: work, work, work, to make money," she told me. Like my grandmother, she was happy at first to work as many hours as possible—typically at least twelve hours a day, even on weekends—just to survive. The midtown garment shop where she worked was owned by a Chinese contractor for DKNY, fashion designer Donna Karan's high-end clothing label. Jiang says that everyone knew the boss owned other factories in midtown and Chinatown under different names, and simply moved the shops around whenever there was trouble. (On the day I first talked to Jiang, there was a garment sweatshop operating out of the building right next door to Chinese Staff; in a few months, it would be gone.) The women were paid $8 for every piece they finished, which, at the end of the day, amounted to less than minimum wage. But Jiang knew from early on that the fancy trousers, lacy undergarments, and flowing evening gowns she made were luxury goods. She remembers one dress in particular that required so many yards of fabric that she could barely hold it up even while standing; she knew how to make it, but she had no idea how to put it on.

Her husband had been in New York for six years, working in a restaurant, and he had sponsored her and her son to come and join him. The couple's daughter was twenty-one when Jiang immigrated, and no longer qualified as a minor; she stayed behind in Fuzhou while her parents tried to navigate the application process to bring her over. But as it was, Jiang barely had time to see her husband, or her teenage son. Every day she was cloistered in the factory, sewing. When the Department of Labor came to perform surprise investigations, the boss got on the loudspeaker and shouted in Mandarin: "The DOL is here! They're going to investigate! If they ask you if you are paid overtime, you say yes! If they ask you how many hours you work, you say eight hours a day! All you undocumented workers, you need to go hide or go out the back way!" The raids were as regular as fire drills in other workplaces, and the workers grew practiced at the art of escape. A few of Jiang's coworkers were Cantonese, but most were Fujianese. Out of forty workers, about ten were undocumented. During a raid, if they couldn't get out to the street in time, they hid in piles of unfinished clothing and fabrics. When Jiang described the process to me, she put her hands over her head in mock surrender, giving a small chuckle as she did so at the absurdity of what the women were subjected to.

"When you're there, whatever the boss says, you do," she said. "Because if you don't, you're afraid you might not have a job."

Jiang fiddled with my tape recorder before speaking again. "Such expensive clothing, and none of the workers were getting paid what they were owed," she said, her voice soft. "I was one of the workers who worked there longest, five or six years at that point, and even though it was a union shop, during that whole time no one ever got paid overtime."

Workers began to grumble to each other, and in 1999, she and four other workers came to Chinese Staff for help. Through a representative, they approached the boss in May of 2000 with a complaint of overtime and back pay wage violations. The factory closed its doors shortly after they spoke up, and suddenly everyone was out of a job. The next month, Jiang was among five workers who filed a landmark class-action lawsuit against DKNY and all its contractors for failing to pay minimum wage and for withholding millions of dollars of overtime pay for seventy-plus-hour workweeks. Eighteen other workers eventually joined the suit, with most workers owed tens of thousands of dollars each. It was the first class-action suit to accuse a major designer, Donna Karan International, and not just

the factories it employed, of sweatshop conditions and labor violations at those factories.

In 2003, Donna Karan International settled with the workers
out of court. The terms of the settlement are confidential, but the
New York Post reported that the amount was over half a million
dollars. Jiang's employer defaulted in the lawsuit and never paid her
own court-ordered judgment. Jiang reports that the boss sold her
factory off to her son and is currently the owner of a jewelry store
and tea shop in Flushing.

After the DKNY factory shut down, Jiang found part-time work
at other factories in Chinatown before coming to work at Chinese
Staff. "After we stood up and complained, all the midtown factories
that work for DKNY started to pay overtime, and everybody now
works forty-hour weeks," she told me. She's proud of what she has
done, but she knows that the problems she faced in the garment factory are systemic. Under New York labor law, workers in trades that
involve subcontractors—the garment and construction industries,
for example—continue to have problems holding manufacturers and
building developers accountable for working conditions. Now on the
board of Chinese Staff as head of the garment workers' committee,
Jiang is learning about labor organization, helping to form coalitions
with other groups, including Korean nail-salon workers and Latino
construction workers, to change the New York labor law.

It's fair to say that my grandmother's generation of garment workers was isolated in Chinatown, by language, by law, by economics.
But Jiang represents the next generation of garment workers here,
helping to build a labor movement that goes beyond Chinatown to
alter the social fabric of the city itself. In voluntarily tying itself to
other communities throughout New York, Chinatown has changed.
The old Chinatown—the insular, closed society with little contact
outside its borders—is no longer the reality.

■ ■ ■

CHINATOWNS ARE MICROCOSMS of their respective cities. In Manhattan, Chinatown is at once a reminder of the city's nineteenth-century textile glory days and of the continuing role immigrants play in the economic and social life of New York. Today, the challenges to the garment industry speak more generally of challenges to Chinatown and the city. In the four years after September 11, 2001, more than half of the garment factories in Chinatown were closed due to transportation snafus and lack of work, or pushed out to Brooklyn. More have followed. The fabric economy is in decline, and Chinatown has felt this loss acutely. Garment factories still exist, since New York fashion designers still need to be able to make quick-turnaround items, but the business is no longer robust. The change to the neighborhood has also been physical. Since the flight of the garment industry from Chinatown, high-rise condos and hotel developments have begun to buy their way in. As in San Francisco's Chinatown, the New York neighborhood's biggest battle now is over gentrification and the displacement of its working class.

These days, Chinatown has really become three Chinatowns: Manhattan's Chinatown plus the satellite Chinatowns of Flushing, Queens, and Sunset Park, Brooklyn, where many new immigrants are settling. The New York metropolitan area is now home to over half a million Chinese—the largest Chinese population in the United States. The densest concentration is still in Manhattan's Chinatown, but in the last fifteen years, settlement patterns have skewed toward the newer Chinatowns; the biggest increases in average annual Chinese immigration from the 1980s to the 1990s were felt in the Flushing and Sunset Park neighborhoods. With the growth of these new enclaves and the disintegration of what has been its most valuable economy, Manhattan's Chinatown is fighting for its life.

Karin Chien, a Chinatown resident and a curator at the Museum of Chinese in America, has described Manhattan's Chinatown as "the hardest-working neighborhood in a city of workaholics." Over the years, Chinatown immigrants have contributed mightily to the surrounding city's productivity, but the enclave remains a place of survival. As in San Francisco, the veneer of tourism and commerce conceals the fact that the vast majority of Chinese residents are still poor. Every day, they show grit simply by getting by: as garment workers and grocers, busboys and bus drivers. They have eked out a living trying to fill the needs of the bigger city. But with the displacement of working residents due to rising rents, there is an alarming sense of insecurity in a neighborhood that has long been theirs.

When I last spoke to her, Feng Ying Jiang was awaiting the arrival of her daughter—who now has a husband and two children of her own—from Fujian. After sixteen years and repeated sponsorship attempts, the family would finally be reunited. Jiang was excited for her daughter to come to America, but she worried about being able to find an affordable apartment in Chinatown to house the new arrivals. She herself lives in a two-room apartment on Chrystie Street with her son, her daughter-in-law, and her two grandchildren. At more than $600 a month, the rent strains the family's finances. She is less concerned about her daughter finding a job. "She has two choices—she can work in a restaurant or in a garment factory," Jiang said, her tone pragmatic. "There are still many jobs waiting for her." So many decades after my own grandmother's arrival in America, it stunned me to learn that so little had changed in the everyday lives of average working-class Chinese in New York's Chinatown. But Jiang has a longer view. She endures for the same reasons my grandparents did. "My hope is that my children and their children will have a better education, and a better life here," she says. Even though she could live in comfort if she returned to her home city of Fuzhou right now, that's why she stays. And so she waits for the Fourth of July—on that day, her daughter lands in New York to begin her new American life.

Students practice lion dancing, New York. *Bonnie Tsui*

FIVE

THE NEW CHINESE SCHOOL

Learning to read, write, and live a heritage.

I was first introduced to sixteen-year-old John Tan through his YouTube page. Over a period of nine months, he had made three movies and posted them to the video-sharing website. If there is such a thing as a video diary of the chaotic, mercurial brain of a streetwise teenager growing up in New York's Chinatown—"welcome to the life of a somewhat insane asian out to rule the world!"—this was it. The videos show him at school, at home, hanging out with his friends at night, scaling city walls, peeing into alleyways. He called his collective musings "The John Tan Show."

John was born in the Lower East Side and raised in Chinatown. From the get-go, he's had his opinions. New York—NOIR YORK CITY—is a concrete jungle. Eminem is part of his soundtrack. He values his crew of guy friends. He recently got into the traditional Chinese discipline of lion dancing. Though his summer job involves working with younger kids at a church in Chinatown, he doesn't personally believe in religion. He battles contradictions daily. His original vision of high school was different from what he has actually experienced in his freshman year at Brooklyn Tech, a competitive school in the Fort Greene section of Brooklyn. He likes being in a more diverse environment. But he also misses the relative ease of his old school in Chinatown.

The summer before, John was part of the first graduating class of a new kind of Chinese school at the edge of Chinatown. P.S.

184, also known as Shuang Wen Academy, is a bilingual English-Mandarin elementary and middle school. "Shuang Wen" means "double language" in Mandarin. In Chinatown, Chinese schools have been around a long time—early twentieth-century Chinese immigrants wanted a way to preserve the culture and language of their homeland for their American-born children. The traditional Chinese schools were monolingual. "TO OPEN CHINESE SCHOOLS: China Would Prevent Her Children from Forgetting Parent Language," read a 1908 *New York Times* headline announcing the establishment of Chinese schools in various U.S. cities. Because of this, generations of Chinese American kids reluctantly supplemented their attendance of regular public school with afternoon or weekend Chinese-language classes at the local Chinese school. The popular New York Chinese School was founded in Chinatown in 1909, and most of the Chinese Consolidated Benevolent Association's historic building on Mott Street is now given over to it. With roughly 3,000 students taking classes there, it bills itself as the largest Chinese school in North America. Teachings in music, dance, and art are also part of the program, to keep kids versed in their cultural heritage. A couple of blocks away, Church of the Transfiguration, the oldest Catholic church building in New York and the largest Chinese Catholic church in America today, has run its own Chinese school for more than fifty years.

Lately, Chinatown's Chinese schools have seen a renaissance. Most programs now favor Mandarin—the official common dialect of China—over the traditional Cantonese that has been dominant in American Chinatowns throughout the twentieth century. In recent years, the popular shift to Mandarin has reflected the changing priorities of Chinese parents in America, many of whom are themselves a generation or two removed from China as a birthplace: it is less a fear of forgetting and more a striving for future success that is driving up enrollment in these schools. Growing attendance by non-Chinese children—on one visit to an intermediate Mandarin class held after school in Chinatown, I met a diverse group of eleven- to fifteen-year-olds, less than half of whom were Chinese—also reflects wider America's belief in China's global importance.

Opened in 1998, Shuang Wen is a hybrid, one of the first American public schools to offer a dual-language program. By all accounts, it has been a successful experiment. In a time when China is a rising power—within a decade, China is expected to surpass the United States as the world's largest economy—and Mandarin is beginning to challenge English as the lingua franca for the twenty-first-century world, to many parents Shuang Wen has become the most popular alternative public school in the city, with some of the highest scores in reading and math and, perhaps most importantly, a cultural edge on the future.

WHAT IT'S LIKE to go to the school as a kid, of course, is a decidedly different story. Countless Chinese Americans of all ages have shared with me their view of traditional Chinese school as "torture," or that they were happy to "dodge the bullet" of having to attend at all. Wouldn't a newfangled public school with a built-in Chinese school evoke a similar response? "Shuang Wen definitely wasn't like all the 'other schools," John Tan told me. The day is long. School doesn't let out until five thirty in the evening, which is what makes it possible for afternoon classes to be dedicated entirely to Mandarin-language instruction. It can be socially challenging for students who don't conform to the study culture, and it can be short on diversity. John's YouTube postings detail some of his time at Shuang Wen. Most of the kids in his class were Chinese. That in itself didn't bother him, but he felt the school created an overprotective environment that had kids ill-prepared for the reality of racism on the street.

John began school at Shuang Wen, but left after the fifth grade for another junior high in Brooklyn, a couple of miles from where he now lives in Bensonhurst. "It was really sheltered at Shuang Wen," he said, struggling to explain his disenchantment with the school. "My mom knew I didn't really like it there, so we tried something else." At his new junior high in Brooklyn, he saw more racial diversity and witnessed his first school fights. He fell in with a group of troublemakers, and after a year and a half, his mother forced him to go back to Shuang Wen. But he'd already seen that the world outside Chinatown was pretty different.

He described the time around his return as a "period when teenagers get depressed and all that crap"—a time when he was feeling particularly rebellious. It coincided with a tumultuous period in Shuang Wen's history as well, when the Department of Education moved the school from one Chinatown building, where it had been sharing space with another elementary school, to its current location on Cherry Street, a few blocks away. The new school building was occupied by P.S. 137, a largely black and Latino elementary school. Shuang Wen and P.S. 137 also shared space for a year, but then the city decided that it was P.S. 137 that would be booted out to share space with yet another school down the block. Many P.S. 137 parents considered the move a hostile takeover.

"They put us in to take over a school in the Lower East Side that wasn't doing so well," John recalled. "The parents there were kind of mad, and the kids I guess picked up on that. So the kids at that school picked on us because they thought we were taking over their turf. I remember fighting some black kid because he was beating up kids in my class. There was a lot of strife. The thing that made it worse was that the school was so damn protective that they weren't teaching us how to deal with it. Kids were getting kicked out. It was pretty stressful the last couple of years."

One of John's YouTube postings came shortly after his graduation from Shuang Wen. It is a nostalgic look back at his years at the school, with the requisite photos of kids mugging for the camera on class trips and a moony soundtrack by the band Coldplay.

Given what he told me about his disenchantment with Shuang Wen, I was surprised by the wistful tone. He told me that he made it in a moment of reflection, when he realized that he missed the simplicity of life there.

"At Shuang Wen, I was sort of angry—I didn't really like going there that much—so when it was over, I had a chance to think about it and miss it a little bit," he explained. I asked him if he could tell me what he liked best about Shuang Wen, and he paused to think about it. Though the "social stuff" was difficult, he was a bright kid, and school was easy for him academically. "I could F-off all I wanted to and it wouldn't matter," he said, a little longingly. "I got hundreds on everything no matter what I did. High school is harder." He added that learning Mandarin was a positive thing, and he gives props to his old school for it. He still takes Chinese at Brooklyn Tech, and he says that it's probably his easiest subject. "That's because of Shuang Wen."

A good education for their kids is a huge reason that Chinese immigrant parents come to America. A school like Shuang Wen would seem to be the perfect embodiment of values: high academic scores, free (and mandatory) afternoon classes in Chinese, and, for parents who work long hours, an extended, supervised school day that allows them to worry less about keeping their kids out of trouble. By virtue of the school's location in Chinatown, kids of new immigrants make up a large percentage of the student body. Neighborhood residents are given preference. But in this age of pricey SAT prep and high school résumé-padding, non-Chinese and American-born Chinese parents from outside the district have also jockeyed to get their children lotteried into the program. When students graduate, they will likely head to top-performing city high schools like Brooklyn Tech or Stuyvesant, located on the opposite side of Manhattan from Chinatown, overlooking the Hudson. Stuyvesant, one mother told me, was "the dream" for Chinese parents in Chinatown—a meal ticket out of the neighborhood. At five thirty on a warm spring evening, I joined the crowd of parents amassing to pick up their children in front of Shuang Wen, which occupies a squat green-and-white building surrounded by housing projects on the eastern edge of Chinatown. Some parents waited in cars parked along the street, but most came on foot. The younger children spilled out the doors by the basketball courts, almost all of them making a beeline for the battered ice cream truck parked conveniently at the curb.

On the far side of the school building, where the older kids exited and ambled off in their own small posses, I met up with a tall, thin boy wearing a black fleece jacket and backpack. His name was Lin Lin, and he was a fourteen-year-old member of the school's second eighth-grade graduating class. We'd spoken by phone earlier that day; Shuang Wen's principal, Ling Ling Chou, had arranged for us to talk. In person, we continued our conversation about his experiences at the school, and in Chinatown. As we stood on the corner chatting, a few of his buddies slowly passed by and giggled, eyeing me.

Lin's parents moved to Chinatown from Fuzhou when he was three years old. His father is a chef in Brooklyn, and his mother works as a seamstress in Chinatown—both parents working in those twin pillars of industry supporting the blue-collar Chinese in New York. Several years ago, the family moved across the East River to Brooklyn, but Lin says that since he has gone to Shuang Wen since kindergarten and spends all his time in Chinatown, Chinatown is still more his home than Brooklyn is. In his free time, he meets up with his friends to play basketball. They pick their way through various courts around the neighborhood. He spent the previous weekend shooting hoops at Columbus Park, a main hangout for locals.

He said that most of his friends are Chinese, too, so they "get" where he's coming from. "When I'm with my friends, I feel more American," he told me, flashing a mouthful of braces. "But when I'm at home, I feel more Chinese." After spending so many years learning Mandarin, he speaks it pretty well by now. "Everybody's saying

China's the next big power, so it's the most important language to learn. But Mandarin speakers don't understand Fujianese—it's different. I speak Fujianese to my parents. My dad speaks a little bit of English, but we usually have a translator for school meetings." Outside of school, Lin's parents ask him to translate whenever they need to speak English.

Ling Ling Chou, Shuang Wen's principal, says that Lin is representative of many of her students who are recent immigrants from Fujian. When I first talked to her, Chou was preparing to accompany the second annual graduating class trip to China over spring break. Lin told me he wouldn't be joining the expedition. He'd been back to China once already with his family. This time around, he decided to forgo China for Chinatown; he'd rather spend the week hanging out with his friends and playing basketball than go be a tourist. Though he was born in China, Chinatown is where he belongs. He thinks that tourists who come to Chinatown have a lot of stereotypes—for example, how the Chinese are "not open" and "always conservative." But he knows that's not what the community is all about. "They have a lot to learn about us," he said with a wry smile, heading off to join his friends.

MANY KIDS I met told me that going to school in Chinatown—whether it's Shuang Wen or a more traditional public school—makes Chinatown important to their self-identity, in ways that are both positive and negative. On an F train bound for East Broadway station, I watched a group of fifth graders horsing around in my subway car. Three girls perched on the edge of the hard orange plastic seats, daring a pudgy boy to hop on one foot as the train spit and sputtered its way through the tunnel.

One of the girls jumped to her feet. "This is our stop," she announced, jostling to get off the train. "Chinatown!" Her mother gently herded the kids toward the door. When I asked where they were coming from, she told me that the class had just made a trip to see a Broadway play. Their exuberance at getting to go to a new place was palpable, but so was their enthusiasm to return home. After they surfaced to the street and reconvened on the sidewalk, the kids pointed their noses a block and a half away to P.S. 2, Meyer London Elementary School, the same neighborhood school my own relatives attended.

That afternoon I met Mary Ang, the head school aide who supervises school dismissal every day at two thirty. She has been working at P.S. 2 for twenty years, watching generations of neighborhood kids come and go—and, at times, come back again. A high-pitched chorus of "bye, Mary" floated along the sidewalk, and as we watched the crowd disperse, she told me that kids who graduate from P.S. 2 often return to do community service as high school students, helping with office work and translating for parent conferences. Ang herself understands complicated home situations firsthand; she grew up not understanding the dialect her mother spoke. "As bizarre as it sounds, I had to talk to my father to talk to my mother," she told me.

Later that week, Ang introduced me to Elaine Kyi and Xue Mei Wang, two high school juniors who are former P.S. 2 students. We dragged a few chairs into the hallway outside the main office, and as we talked about their ambitions, Chinatown, and what Chinese language and culture means to them, I found that the two girls formed a sort of tag-team comedy duo, the yin to each other's yang. Their energy was infectious. Elaine was the dry straight-talker-with-attitude to Xue Mei's bubbly and garrulous optimist. Elaine spoke Cantonese and Burmese, while Xue Mei spoke Mandarin and Fujianese. Elaine's parents were fairly well-educated, but neither of Xue Mei's parents finished middle school, and her mother couldn't read or write any language. Though Elaine often finished Xue Mei's sentences, it was almost always to pull the existing thought or idea in a completely different direction, like so much saltwater taffy.

One thing they do agree on, though, is that Chinatown is their hood, their center—they identify with it, with the specific intensity that New Yorkers have for their corner of the city. Xue Mei told me that she was born in Fuzhou, but she has lived in Chinatown, across the street from the Chatham Square Library, since she was two years old. "Basically, I've been here all my life, ever since I came here from China—even at the same address!" she said, laughing. She pushed up the glasses on her round face. Her close family lives in New York, but she has gone back to China during some summers to visit other relatives. During those trips, she has seen the effects of the Chinese economic boom in Fuzhou. "It's changing into a pretty big city," she said, nodding. "There are a lot more cars now."

By contrast, Elaine's family is more scattered by the Chinese diaspora—"everywhere, in Burma, and Hong Kong and Macau." She has been to all of these places. At the time, she was living with her aunt in Brooklyn. But during all of her family's peripatetic wanderings, the constant for her has been going to school in Chinatown.

Chinatown is reliable for them, and the reason they chose to fulfill their high school community service requirement at P.S. 2. "We know people here," Xue Mei explained. "We have connections. And we want to help out here. Rather than go to another school, why not just come back to the one we know?"

When I asked them what was best and worst about going to school in Chinatown, they answered immediately and in unison: "Asians." They looked at each other and cracked up, and Xue Mei tried to explain the contradiction. For them, elementary and middle school was 90 percent Asian. "You think that's the way it's supposed to be," she said. It was a familiar pool of students from the neighborhood up until ninth grade, when everyone applied to go to different high schools around New York City. By chance, both Xue Mei and Elaine ended up at a school just a few blocks away from Chinatown, near City Hall. But the new mix of kids came as a shock to them.

"Once you get to high school, you're like, 'Whoa!' Everything is so different," Xue Mei said, her eyes widening. "You see every kind of people you can imagine. It's kind of good in a way, because you get to know all types of people and their culture. But at the same time, it's harder to get close with them. You feel less comfortable. So that's the bad part. Our school is still almost fifty percent Asian, but compared to elementary and middle school, it's really different."

Adjusting to the social environment has helped them to look ahead. Both girls told me that they were most comfortable in Chinatown, since they've been here all their lives. But they were also ready for something else. Xue Mei had tried to convince her parents to move somewhere more suburban, but they would not. "They're like, first, they don't drive, they don't have a car, and then they don't know how to travel alone, and it's too inconvenient, because they don't have as much things as they do in Chinatown," she said. But she herself doesn't want to be trapped in the same boring place. "The biggest reason is that they're used to it, and the language. You basically can't do anything without the language. You can't travel, you can't speak, you can't communicate."

Elaine jumped in. "That's why when Chinese parents tell us, 'Go to Chinese school,' we're like, 'Why?'" she said emphatically. Her parents tried to send her to Chinese school, but she refused. "I say, 'Why do we need to learn Chinese? Why don't you go to English school?' They're like, 'Oh, we don't have to do that.'"

The girls were proud to speak the languages of their community. But they were all too aware of the ironic role that language has here. Chinatown is the place where American-born Chinese come to learn Chinese. It's even a place that American parents who have adopted Chinese children use as a resource—one example of how the narrative of Chinatown is an evolving one, helping to create a new concept of what is Chinese American. But it's also where an old story is told, a place where new immigrants who speak Chinese but no English make their home, often because there's nowhere else to go.

The New Chinese School • 87

A SCHOOL LIKE Shuang Wen may have prepared kids like Lin Lin and John Tan for certain things in life, but there is an undeniable cultural education in Chinatown itself. What Chinatown has to teach its youth can be found outside of school, they said: on the playground, in the basketball court, out on the street, with its never-ceasing social interaction.

"My mom let me walk around by myself in Chinatown from when I was in second grade, so she obviously felt I was safe even though I was small," John told me. John's parents speak Cantonese almost exclusively; his mother works in Chinatown, helping his aunt sell jewelry in a shop there. He says that's why he hung out in Chinatown so much as a little boy. He would roam around the neighborhood, stopping at this store for a pastry or at that corner for a soda and finding favorite hangout spots, like Grand Street Park, a block away from M.S. 131, Dr. Sun Yat-sen Middle School, named for the famous Nationalist leader and father of modern China. In this way, he got to know the landscape. One Chinese New Year, his mother took him to see the annual lion dance festivities, just the two of them. The explosive energy and athleticism of the lion dance grabbed his attention. The cymbals clanged and the drums kept time. The hungry lion was fed a head of lettuce, which represented money. After taking the lettuce into its mouth, the lion tore apart the leaves, exuberantly throwing them to the right and to the left, spreading prosperity to others. All along the narrow streets, the crowd cheered.

Lion dancing goes back at least a thousand years in China, as a ceremonial performance meant to exorcise evil spirits and to summon luck and prosperity. Each lion utilizes two performers, one acting as the head and one as the tail. At Chinese New Year celebrations, weddings, or business openings in the United States, elegantly leaping lions typically perform in the popular Southern Lion Dance style; the kinetic, physically demanding practice involves a lot of jumping and balancing, and relies on a foundation of martial arts. Specific dances represent specific stories in Chinese mythology, and are usually told using a pair of lions who play off one another. Even now, the lion is a vivid Chinese cultural symbol, at times acting as a powerful guardian and at other times as a playful, mischievous character. It, too, has conflicting identities.

Years after his first exposure to the discipline in Chinatown, John was introduced by a friend to Southern Praying Mantis Kung Fu, a martial-arts and lion-dance school headed by Norman Chin, a *sifu*, or master, who teaches the Southern Lion Dance style and leads one of the premier lion dance troupes in New York's Chinatown. Chin holds classes in multiple locations around the New York metro area. But his free youth class is taught at Dr. Sun Yat-sen School, next to John's favorite hangout. John invited me to come and watch one of his practices. "If you really want to find out about Chinatown, you should come to one of our practices and talk to my *sifu*," he told me, a touch of pride in his voice. "He's pretty well known."

So one Thursday afternoon after school, I went to meet the master before practice. We sat at a pastry shop a few blocks from the school, and over milk tea and coffee Norman Chin told me about his own experiences as a kid in Chinatown.

When Chin was brought up in Chinatown in the 1940s and 1950s, lion dancing was taught primarily through family and benevolent associations. "Chinatown was still very small then— surrounding areas like Canal Street and the Bowery were basically Italian and Jewish immigrants," he said. Chin's accent reminded me of my uncle's: pure New York mixed with a tinge of Cantonese. "So everything was still done through the family associations. They were the ones to hire a master who knew kung fu to teach the lion dance." Traditionally, the people practicing it were martial artists, to ensure that the stances were correct and that they learned about the mythology of the lion and the significance of the discipline. To learn the lion dance was to follow a strict set of rules. As a young boy, Chin lived in a building that was owned by the Chin family association; every year, in the months leading up to Chinese New Year, the association's troupe would begin to practice. He began to learn the lion dance from a young age, but didn't take it seriously until he was about ten or twelve years old.

"Lion dancing then wasn't commercial yet," he told me, sipping his coffee. "Nowadays, someone will buy a lion head and all of a sudden they're a lion troupe. They don't go through the discipline of martial arts. To them, a lion dance is, they put the head on, they jump around—it becomes like Ronald McDonald. You wear a costume and you're a clown. Maybe there's nothing wrong with that. But I'm a very strict traditionalist, and I believe that one should at least have some background to know what it means. Because otherwise it's just noise—you lose the essence and the true meaning of what it is."

Part of being a strict traditionalist was recruiting kids from the neighborhood and making sure they went to school. In the 1970s, New York's Chinatown had acquired a gangland reputation for drugs and violence. "Our school was very strict, and we kept the kids in check, but a lot of the other clubs were looser with rules and discipline," Chin told me. "The kids would cut out of school, using the club as a hangout, smoking, drinking, things like that. So New York for a while had the reputation of gangster or punk kids hanging out, using kung fu as a gang-related macho thing. Those were the guys who didn't learn anything but to be the big brother—the *dai gaw*, or gangster head. They didn't really care."

Outside the community, people only saw the negative side—like when people got shot or killed in a fight. But Chin says gangs and drugs weren't just an issue in Chinatown—it was all over the city. "It was a sign of the times. So you can't just point at Chinatown."

Nevertheless, it was tough to be a teen in Chinatown. If you were a good student or interested in school, you were in danger of getting a beat-down. "The gangs try to make you join them, they either beat you up or drag you in," Chin said, shaking his head.

Chin tries to make the lion-dance group more of a community for his young students, while also honoring and respecting the traditions. Sometimes, he says, peer pressure can be positive. Many kids come to his studio through word of mouth; lately, more students have been following their friends in. I asked him about John, who had joined the group about a year before, and he grinned and asked me if John had told me about "eating the head and the tail."

"Anybody who's a new recruit—you don't get hazed, but during the Chinese New Year banquet after the parade, all newbies have to take a bite of the chicken head and the chicken tail. All the kids have to do it. You know why? Because in Cantonese, *yu gaw nei zho yeh, yiu tou yow mei*. It means, when you start something, you have to finish it. If you're not going to put your heart to it, don't do it."

SEVENTEEN BOYS AND girls were waiting for us in the school cafeteria. When they saw Chin, they scrambled to get dressed and arrange the room for practice. Chin put on his strict *sifu* face and began barking orders: "Clean up this room! Why aren't you guys dressed yet? No eating or drinking during practice!" I spotted John, with his spiky hair and glasses, and waved a hand in greeting. He gave me a wave in return, then hustled off with the other kids to change.

A school cafeteria can in fact be transformed into a kung fu studio. Once the students lined up to do their warm-up exercises, their black practice clothes lent them a uniform smartness, and their giggly faces grew serious. They were still nervous, but it was obvious they felt excitement and pride at being able to perform for someone outside of the group. And when they assumed their posts as drummers and cymbalists, lion heads and tails, and the big-headed Buddha, who teases and "tames" the lion, I was enthralled. They practiced the "eating" dance—crumpled paper stood in for the lettuce-money—and a double-stacking routine, in which two performers holding the lion heads jumped up on the shoulders of two others. Strong for his age and size, John was tasked with the role of supporting one lion-head performer's weight. His chin jutted out and his brow furrowed in concentration. The lion head rattled, ferocious and proud.

Later, I sat down with John on a bench to chat, as the other kids continued to practice drum sequences and dance steps. "It's my roots, I guess," John said, referring to why he joined the troupe and continued to spend so much time in Chinatown. "Me being Chinese. And being in Chinatown let me experience my culture in a really easy way. My friends who go to Chinatown and are from here, they definitely have pride in it and represent it, and it represents them. But there are also a lot of my friends who don't care about Chinatown." He paused. "How do I know they don't care? They make fun of me." Here, he put on a doofy voice: "'Praying Mantis, Chinatown all day, every day.'" He laughed. "I guess everyone does their own stuff. What I do seems uncool, what they do seems lame to me. Everyone does their own thing."

Some Chinese Americans never feel a compulsion to visit Chinatown. But Chinatown has an undeniable pull for certain Chinese, no matter what the generation. There was a time when Chin himself left Chinatown, in his late twenties. "Everybody said, 'Oh, I don't want to stay in Chinatown.' But ultimately, you know, we came back. You kind of leave Chinatown physically, but mentally, you still have a connection." He says he has seen many Chinese American friends get a new awareness of their "Chineseness" in college— they become interested in Chinatown as a place to look for their identity, and as a source of language and culture. As some parents informed me, education can be a ticket out of the neighborhood, but I don't think it's as simple as that. There's something important to be gotten here, too.

For a younger generation, Chinatown is a meaningful bridge to the past. Being able to participate in the vibrant street life here is a crucial part of its significance to John. Being able to speak Cantonese and Mandarin is a point of pride—he can help someone on the street, and he can ask for help himself. "I think my life would be a lot different if I couldn't speak Chinese," he told me. It allows him to be close to his mom. And knowing Chinese is important to him in the same way that lion dancing is. "Like I might not be the greatest expert of the Chinese language, just like I'm not the greatest lion dancer," he said. "But since it's in my culture—of what my people have done in the past and are still doing—I want to experience a little bit of it and retain it in myself, so although I'm an American, I don't forget that I'm also of Chinese blood."

I asked John what he thought other people came to Chinatown to find. What he said wasn't yet fully formed, but it was both insightful and funny, and it wasn't just book learning that informed his answer. "People come for the food and the history—it's a cultural thing," he said. "That's what I like about Chinatown. The restaurants are authentic, not American Chinese. Any day in my entire life I'd rather have a Chinese meal than an American meal." If it were possible, he would like to be buried in the neighborhood. His last meal would definitely be in Chinatown. Regarding the dish itself, he was less decisive. "Probably *tsa sew faan*," he said, referring to roast pork with rice. "Something simple, or traditional. Maybe bird's nest soup." Another pause. "Or shark's fin soup—something expensive."

The physical location of Chinatown, he says, helps contribute to its importance. "I guess in a way Chinatown and the Lower East Side are the entrance for a lot of immigrants into America. When you get off the Manhattan Bridge, or the Brooklyn Bridge, you have to go through Chinatown. It's a gateway. If you want to leave, it's the same thing." What was his opinion, if any, of the other key Chinatowns in Flushing and Sunset Park?

"Well, I've been to Flushing, which is considered a Chinatown by some people, but I don't really think anything compares to Manhattan Chinatown," he said dismissively. "Because it's The One."

Fortune cookies and Chinese takeout. *Bonnie Tsui*

SIX

FORTUNE COOKIES

*What the path of the folded wafers tells us
about the movement of communities.*

On a 98-degree day in New York, I took the 7 train to 33rd Street in Long Island City, Queens, to meet Derrick Wong. I didn't go to the end of the line that morning—that would be Main Street, Flushing—but if I had, I would have landed in the middle of New York's biggest Chinatown, home to the city's largest Chinese population, and the place I was born.

It was a day in which power grids went down and subway trains stalled after their third rails warped from the near-record heat. The heavy, humid air was oppressive even at nine thirty in the morning, and the garbage pails left on the street were quickly growing ripe. Wong, a compact thirty-nine-year-old with an easy laugh and thinning hair, picked me up in a silver Acura at the corner of 36th Street and Queens Boulevard, a heavily trafficked area with an industrial pedigree, adjacent to the subway line. From there, I could see the old Swingline stapler factory, recently repurposed to house the Museum of Modern Art's library and archives.

Though he carries the decidedly mundane title of VP of sales and marketing, Wong is a de facto fortune-cookie scion at the helm of the largest fortune cookie manufacturer in the world, family-owned and -run Wonton Food Inc. We were on our way to visit the heat and heart of the cookie oven itself—the company's twenty-four-hour factory and warehouse, dedicated entirely to churning out 4 million cookies a day, six days a week, fifty-two weeks a year, and shipping them out to more than 400 distributors worldwide.

Fortune cookies are arguably the most important restaurant staple not on the menu in Chinatowns across America. Enter any Chinese restaurant and you will spot them: in a bowl near the door, atop a check tray at the waitress station, cracked open and littering a table full of diners finishing their meal. In 2008, the fortune cookie turned ninety—that is, if you believe that Cantonese immigrant David Jung started distributing message-filled cookies outside his Los Angeles noodle company in 1918. Or it hits its hundredth birthday in 2009, if you subscribe to the theory that Makoto Hagiwara, a caretaker of San Francisco's Japanese Tea Garden, created the cookies in 1909. A trail of documents at the U.S. Patent Office pertaining to the fortune cookie supports the idea, at least, that it was invented in San Francisco early in the twentieth century. Still another branch of cookie mythology traces it to Chinese immigrant laborers in the nineteenth century, who created makeshift moon cakes to celebrate the lunar festival. More recent academic scholarship shows the fortune cookie in Japan, where one Japanese graduate student traced early mentions of *tsujiura senbei*—"fortune crackers"—to an 1878 book of stories. Whichever story you buy, one truth persists—the Chinese fortune cookie isn't really Chinese. In fact, when Wonton Food opened the first fortune cookie factory in China in 1994, it promptly closed. "It didn't work," Wong told me. "Fortune cookies are too American."

More specifically, they've become Chinese American. In post–World War II America, they have emerged as the dominant icon of Chinatown and the Chinese restaurant business. And in New York, the growth and movement of the fortune cookie business over the last four decades—from innumerable mom-and-pop shops that sold cookies locally to one monolithic factory in Queens that feeds the world—reflect the economic and geographic movement of

Chinese American populations from Manhattan's Chinatown into the surrounding boroughs and beyond. The cookies themselves are still most beloved across the United States, but Wonton Food also ships to such far-flung destinations as Panama, Morocco, Portugal, Greece, and Belgium. Like many other American cultural icons—from Mickey Mouse to Coca-Cola—they've gone global.

WONTON FOOD's primary business is noodles, but fortune cookies, the company's most well-known product, are sold under the brand name Golden Bowl. Over a third of Wonton Food's business is fortune cookies. The 40,000-square-foot factory in Queens takes up one entire square block, and on the approach to the main building, a delicious, vanilla-tinged aroma wafts out to greet visitors. It is the scent one might imagine as the olfactory accompaniment to Tchaikovsky's dancing sugar-plum visions. Though the fragrance was already familiar to me, I couldn't help but comment on its warmth and sweetness.

"Sugar," Wong said simply, as we dodged several trucks pulling into the loading bay. He meant, of course, that sugar is the leading ingredient in fortune cookies, the other main components being flour and water. The standard recipe is no secret. Dozens of culinary websites and cookbooks offer instructions that play on some variation of the sugar-flour-water ratio; some might include egg whites, oil, or butter to help bind the cookies (Wonton Food uses lecithin and soybean oil). I made the cookies myself in my tiny New York apartment one New Year's Eve, with nothing more than what I had in my kitchen already. That simplicity defies the aura of mystery that has been created around the entire concept of fortune cookies, a fact that has not been lost on Wong. Indeed, the fortune cookie is something of an edible anomaly—what interests most eaters is not the cookie itself, but the cryptic message inside.

Factory protocol dictates that all visitors to Wonton Food's fortune-cookie factory sign into a logbook and don white caps before entering the facility. This is hardly a tourist destination—the vast majority of those who come are bulk-buy customers wanting to know how the products they purchase are made. We began our tour of the facility in the battering area, where stacks of cardboard boxes labeled INTERMEDIATE CAKE FLOUR line the walls. The fluorescent lighting, white tile, snaking tubes, and metallic table surfaces seemed like something out a mad scientist's laboratory, an impression reinforced by the presence of an oversized vat of viscous, bright-orange liquid.

"It's so . . . orange," I said, straining to be heard above the buzzing of the giant mixer.

"It *is* orange—that's the color of fortune cookies," Wong said matter-of-factly, gesturing at the vat of finished batter. Wonton Food's best-selling cookie is citrus, which requires the addition of citrus flavoring and Yellow No. 5 and No. 6 (hence the orange coloring). The second most popular version is vanilla, but cookies can be flavored with anything from chocolate to amaretto. Levels of flavoring are adjusted to make different grades of cookies.

Over time, different regions of the United States have developed particular tastes for what might be called the basic fortune cookie. The East Coast prefers the citrus varietal, while the Midwest always requests vanilla. The West Coast market gets a mix of both. Every once in a while, Wonton Food will experiment with an oddball flavor—cinnamon, for instance, as when Wong tried a joint venture for a South American audience. And as with most of the company's trial deviations away from basic cookie flavor or shape, the response was poor. "People like what they know," Wong says. "They don't like change, especially when it comes to fortune cookies."

IN 1983, WONTON Food bought a small mom-and-pop fortune cookie plant in Manhattan's Chinatown. (The man who sold them the plant was Eric Ng, the recent president of New York's Chinese Consolidated Benevolent Association.) It was how Ching Sun Wong—Derrick Wong's uncle—went into the fortune cookie business. Now well into his seventies, the elder Wong is semi-retired, but he remains the chairman and owner of Wonton Food. The company has been the dominant force in the American—and international—fortune cookie business for more than a decade. There are no other big fortune cookie manufacturers on the East Coast; Golden Dragon in Chicago and Peking Noodle in Los Angeles may come closer to Wonton Food in production capacity than the traditional mom-and-pop shops do, but Wong brushes off the suggestion that the two operations might be his competitors. Approximately forty other fortune cookie factories in the United States also aid in supplying the country's 40,000 Chinese restaurants.

Wong is intimately familiar with every aspect of cookie production. He was born in Guangzhou, and moved to Manhattan's Chinatown when he was fourteen years old. He joined the company in 1991 after he graduated from Brooklyn Polytech, where he was trained as a civil engineer. "Back then, the economy was not so good," he says. "There were no jobs when I graduated. Then my father asked me to come back and join the company. Once I joined it and settled down, that was it. I did almost every job, production job, all the baking, the warehouse, drive the truck, salesman—everything." His training in civil engineering, he says, has been put to use "not at all."

Wong's father, a mechanical engineer, ran operations at the fortune cookie plant for much of its existence. Because of him, the company builds and repairs all of its machines on-site. "He started it all," Wong told me. "But now he's retired and back in Guangzhou." Downstairs from the battering area, fourteen machines do the bulk of the work on the factory floor. Batter gets piped into each machine from lines in the ceiling, and workers dressed in white uniforms and caps monitor the cookies' progress, from the moment the perfect doughy circles leave the ovens to when they are individually sealed in plastic, boxed away, and sent to the warehouse. "All our cookies need to be shipped every day—it has to be in and out, in and out, right away," Wong says. "The whole inventory only lasts us about thirty-six hours. If we stop production for thirty-six hours, we have nothing to sell."

Over the last forty years, cookie production has become largely automated, but manual labor remains part of the job. Wong still has chronic back problems from his earlier years spent hoisting boxes of flour and other cookie ingredients. These days, the temperature on the factory floor normally exceeds the outside temperature by at least ten degrees. On my first visit, the arrow on the circular thermometer by the ovens hovered somewhere in the colored region above 100 degrees. But no one seemed to mind—for once, the temperature inside wasn't much different from that outside.

THE PLANT MANAGER, Mr. Lui, is from Toisan. When we met, he asked, in Toisanese dialect, where my family was from. When I told him that my mother and her family come from Toisan, he nodded vigorously. "I knew it," he said. "You look like a Toisanese person."

I grew up speaking Cantonese. To my child's ears, when we visited my grandparents every Sunday in Flushing, their Toisanese ran seamlessly into the Cantonese that the rest of my family spoke. It was only when I got older that I realized that they were two separate dialects—someone who speaks one doesn't necessarily speak the other.

When Wong's family first started up the business in the seventies, all of their employees spoke Cantonese. Now, Wong says, it's different. The office and mechanical staff speak Mandarin and English—their training today demands it—and 90 percent of Wonton Food's production workers are from Toisan. Many of them live along Eighth

Avenue in Sunset Park, the recently settled Chinatown in Brooklyn that attracts newer immigrants. Dong Ming Huang, one of the shift managers, told me that he lives in a house in Sunset Park with his wife and two teenage sons. He disagrees with John Tan's assessment of New York's satellite Chinatowns; Sunset Park, he says, is "pretty much Chinatown to me."

Since so many new immigrants now come from other regions of China, I was surprised to find an almost exclusively Toisanese employee pool. But, as Wong explains it, "Chinese people go where they know someone." The company is not exclusive in their hiring, but the production environment breeds a self-selecting pool; though there are occasional non-Toisanese-speaking workers taking jobs on the factory floor, most don't stay very long.

Peter Kwong, a professor at Hunter College whose most recent research has focused on the changing character of Chinatown, labor issues, and the movement of Chinese-American workers, finds that worker patterns in Chinatown have shifted so that jobs with extremely low wages are now being filled by new immigrants from areas like Fujian. But "factories that are older, needing people with a bit more skill," Kwong says, still tend to have workers coming from Hong Kong and Guangdong Province. Worker patterns in specific places like Wonton Food are also heavily influenced by family and friend networks. "It could be who the employers know, who they tend to hire," Kwong says. "And also the training—if a job requires training, language is an issue. So Cantonese tend to hire Cantonese, and so on." The labor patterns, then, have changed because the skills required on the job have changed, and the Toisanese are no longer last on the worker totem pole.

On one of my visits, Wonton Food's newest worker was Wen Hing Feng, a baby-faced young man in his thirties who had arrived in the United States less than a year before. He lives with his wife and seven-year-old daughter in Chinatown, in a rented apartment on Madison Street that they share with his wife's aunt, who has lived there for many years. Because of his resemblance, in counte-nance and disposition, to a smiling Buddha, Feng's co-workers have good-naturedly bestowed upon him the nickname of "Fatty."

In Toisan, Feng was a middle-school teacher for ten years. "It was a living," he said, crinkling his eyes in a smile. "In China, it can be hard to find a job. Even if you apply, it's easier if you know somebody—if you have connections. It's better living here, because you're freer to do different things."

Feng got his fortune cookie job at Wonton Food through the Chinese newspaper. "They teach me everything—I didn't know any-thing about this business," he said, keeping one eye on the machine rumbling next to him. "Everything here runs around the clock, and you learn as you go."

On Saturdays the factory is closed and everyone gets a day off. Feng takes the time to go on adventures. "I'm new here, so I like to explore the city," he told me. "I'll take my daughter, get a subway map, go see landmarks. Last week, we went to City Hall. We're not in a hurry—we'll just walk around a little bit and look at things." His daughter has slipped easily into their new life. She started speak-ing English almost immediately, he says, to fit in with the other kids. Already there are things she babbles on about that Feng doesn't understand.

Feng himself doesn't speak much English, but he says it hasn't mattered much: he lives in Chinatown, and the company provides a shuttle back and forth from the Grand Street subway station nearby. "We're taking it day by day. I have a job, the company gives us transportation and meals, and it's clean and not stressful. I don't have to struggle with English because everyone speaks Toisanese. It makes the job easier."

What you see in the fortune cookie factory today is not like twenty years ago, Derrick Wong says. Most of the early factories were tiny basement affairs in Chinatown, employing low-wage workers and using primitive machines that cranked out dough but still required hand-folding. "The small factory that we took over in 1983 used a very traditional type of fortune cookie machine, the rotary type," Wong said. "The cookie rate was low."

Tsun Mei was the factory that launched Wonton Food's cookie business, and it was at Tsun Mei that my grandfather Suey Lin Dong began a twenty-year career in fortune cookies. He worked at three of those mom-and-pop cookie plants in Chinatown, starting at Tsun Mei in the late 1960s. With fingers bandaged to handle scalding dough more deftly, he and the other workers each averaged two buckets an hour. Five hundred cookies a bucket, two buckets an hour, eight hours a day, five or six days a week. It was the very definition of manual labor, since they used their fingers to fold each and every cookie.

"Factory" might be an optimistic word for Tsun Mei's cookie operation, since there were only two machines on the premises, and two shifts to occupy them—two people working during the day, and two changing in to work at night. My *gung-gung* worked the morning shift for five years before moving on to Duk Hing, on Bayard Street. Duk Hing was also small, and also in the basement, but it had three machines. To earn spending money as a teenager, my uncle John joined my grandfather for summer stints folding cookies in Duk Hing's subterranean workspace.

He hated it. "It was so hot, and we always got burned and had to tape our fingers," he says. He only lasted two summers, and still grimaces and shakes his head whenever I wave a fortune cookie at him.

My *gung-gung*, on the other hand, kept at it. The third factory he worked at had an auspicious name: Lung Fung, or dragon and phoenix. It was located on Centre Street, near City Hall, and he stayed there for twelve years. By the early eighties, he told me, fortune cookies were *ho sang-yee*—extremely good business. There was a lot of demand, and despite all the shops that had sprung up in Chinatown, they couldn't make enough, since New York's fortune cookie operations had begun supplying other states as well.

"When we folded them by hand, none of the cookies were the same," my *gung-gung* says. "You could speed up or slow down, and they would look different depending on how much time and care you took to fold them." When the cookie mixture was good—when all the ingredients struck the right balance—his days were better; the cookies almost made themselves. When the mixture was bad, it produced gloppy, wet messes or a burned char—nightmare cookies that hardened and broke before they could be properly folded. As my uncle and grandfather describe the process to me now, I think of that famous episode of *I Love Lucy* where Lucy works the assembly line in a chocolate factory, shoving chocolates in her mouth and down the front of her shirt to keep up with the machine. Instead of shoving the reject cookies down their shirts, my relatives tossed them into a can at their feet. Reject canisters eventually got filled, and the bosses got angry and clicked their tongues. The error-ridden cookies were wrapped up in plastic bags and brought home to my brother and me. It was how my *gung-gung*'s life in the fortune cookie business began to bleed into my own life as a Chinese-American kid growing up on Long Island.

Fortune cookies occupy a complicated place in the American imagination. "For Asian Americans, the fortune and the fortune cookie can be a little bit of an embarrassing stereotype—that there is this stupefying thing," says Peter Kwong, the Asian-American-studies professor. But he admits that while the cookie's flavor doesn't interest him much, his wife, the writer and translator Dusanka Miscevic, still always asks for them in a restaurant.

Often the first introduction to Chinese culture for many Americans, Chinese restaurants and their ambassador, the fortune cookie, have been an important influence on American dining over the past century, according to Cynthia Lee, the curator of the Museum of Chinese in America in New York. "Chinese restaurateurs acted as cultural brokers by introducing and accommodating Chinese food traditions to American culture," Lee said. In the process, they invented distinctive Chinese-American fare. "The fortune cookie is one example of this balance between the exotic and the familiar."

For the museum's 2005 exhibit on the Chinese restaurant in America, Lee researched the fortune cookie and its disputed origins. She says that it became widely popular in the U.S. during the post–World War II era: "American GIs, who encountered the cookie while on leave in San Francisco, began asking for them in Chinese restaurants in other parts of the country." The cookie's infiltration of American pop culture took off from there; in the cookie manufacturing of the 1950s, fortunes were written as exotic Chinese "proverbs," establishing the common stereotype of "fortune cookie wisdom."

For me, fortune cookies are tied explicitly to my family's history in America. My nostalgia for them has to do with the simple fact of their existence in my everyday life as a child. My brother Andy and I found the misshapen reject cookies my grandfather brought home funny. They were flat and round, or half-folded, or filled with multiple paper fortunes grabbed by hasty hands on the assembly line. We gobbled them while we watched cartoons, mining the cookies for favorable fortunes and throwing away the rest, the paper slips scattering around the room like so many unwanted peanut shells.

The cookies also showed up in my lunch bag at school. Though I sometimes wished my mother would slip Oreos in with my sandwiches instead—in the way that children are, I wanted to be like everyone else, and fortune cookies seemed conspicuously exotic to my peers—I didn't mind too much. In our house, they were as common as the breakfast cereal in the pantry.

At my grandparents' house in Long Island today—paid for in large part by America's predilection for the fortune cookie—I find Golden Bowl cookies on the kitchen counter, evidence of a visit to this or that Chinese restaurant, on Main Street in Flushing or in a nearby suburb. A quarter of a century later, the cookies are everywhere, and no longer exotic.

■ ■ ■

THE DISPERSAL OF cookies has been largely paralleled by the diaspora of those who make them. A few of Wonton Food's staff live
in Flushing, at the end of the 7 line, but, as Wong says, the neighborhood today is for older immigrants who have been here longer.
Workers will make their way from Sunset Park to Grand Street in
Manhattan's Chinatown, where Wong sends a shuttle to take them
to the fortune cookie plant. The rent there is getting too high for
many new immigrants, but Chinatown is still larger now than it has
ever been, with roughly 1,000,000 residents and workers, and it
remains the major hub for much of the Chinese community. Everyone knows how to get there, even if they have moved elsewhere.
The pattern in New York, where the population has followed the
work to sprout new Chinatowns in more disparate locations, has a
precedent in San Francisco's Chinatown.

"Historically, the Chinese factories and residents have slowly
dispersed over the years to other parts of San Francisco," Kwong
told me. "That happened a lot earlier than it did in New York. In
New York, this dispersal has only been in the last twenty years, most
intensively during the last ten years. The same factors are pushing
people out, economically, rising real estate. You go to Brooklyn, you
go to Queens. A lot of factories are moving to Queens and Sunset
Park so people who live there can also work there. They take the
7 train to get there, and they can take it home—the movement has
that kind of character."

Kwong adds that a lot of professional and middle-class Chinese
are moving to the suburbs, with working-class Chinese following
to service them. "In some of the suburban areas in San Francisco,
you have a cluster of places with Chinese restaurants and services.
In L.A., you have what is called an ethnoburb: it imitates everything
that a traditional Chinatown used to have."

Another major factor in the movement of Chinese Americans

from traditional Chinatowns to create newer Chinatowns is the lack of employment. Because of rising real estate values and spatial constraints, business growth has been significantly restricted. "Chinese communities do not create enough jobs," Kwong says. "The standard restaurant and garment small-business jobs"—and mom-and-pop fortune cookie plants—"don't grow fast enough for all the Chinese-speaking workers within the Chinatown. So they have to move outside, work outside, find other businesses all over the place. The Chinese now are like nomads. In Nevada, in a little tiny town, you'll even have a small Chinese community there."

Wonton Food did not become the major producer in the business of fortune cookies until the company moved its operations out of Chinatown. On his daily commute, Wong dons a Bluetooth wireless phone headset and fields calls from the office as he navigates the clogged, warehouse-lined streets of Queens. He himself now lives in Long Island; like my own parents, he moved out there for the schools. His two children are elementary-school age.

But though he rarely goes into Manhattan's Chinatown anymore—"It's too hard to park there"—he has not gotten away from Chinatown entirely. Many of his distributors are located in Chinatown. His favorite Cantonese seafood restaurant is Duen Wong, in Flushing's Chinatown. And on a recent business trip to Las Vegas, he gravitated toward the city of glitz's unique, master-planned Chinatown, the brainchild of a Chinese immigrant businessman named James Chen.

"It's a good Chinatown," Wong told me. "It's in a mall—just like Toronto."

THE LARGEST FORTUNE cookie manufacturer in the world may have moved out of the traditional Chinatown where it began, but so has its cultural reach. A few years ago, a funny thing happened to Wonton Food—it became famous. After a Powerball lottery drawing in March 2005, 110 people came forward with five of six winning numbers to claim a total of over $19 million in prizes. Usually, there are only about four or five second-prize winners. What did this round of winners have in common? They'd all played numbers printed on a fortune in a cookie manufactured by Wonton Food. A glut of media attention followed, and everyone from Martha Stewart's daughter to the *New York Times* came to pay a visit.

"Before the lottery, everyone knew fortune cookies, but no one knew Wonton Food," Wong says. "Now everyone knows Wonton Food."

Part of the appeal of fortune cookies for Americans is the mystery behind it. "People really want a fortune-teller," he says, with a note of surprise in his voice. The company originally started printing "lucky numbers" on the back of its fortunes to separate itself from competitors; the numbers are selected by computer.

The fortunes themselves are now printed in English, Spanish, and French. In the front office, a member of Wong's sales team shuffled fortunes in a folder and showed me a stack of orange plastic printing plates. "This is the fortune database," he joked. Every two years, new batches of fortunes are written and rotated in. Wong is deliberately vague about where the fortunes come from, saying only that they are "outsourced." But on a recent visit I made back to the factory, Wong informed me that Wonton Food is trying "something new" with its fortunes. "We brought in a Chinese guy," he said, "to do Chinese sayings."

Wong receives hundreds of e-mails a week asking for the coveted job of writing the company's fortunes. Everybody, it seems, wants to be the writer of other people's destinies. Some applicants even send résumés. "All kinds of people want to do it—full-time, part-time, freelance. They all offer themselves for the job. And it's not like we even posted a job officially! Writers, teachers, artists. All kinds of people want this job. People have it in their heads that this is real fortune-telling."

And if they want to continue thinking that, Wong is okay with it. He gets it. He likes eating fortune cookies—"especially when they're warm and fresh, the texture and mouth feel are a big difference to those already packed"—and reading the fortunes. Some fortune messages, he says, are inspiring. He has never tried to write one himself.

Though the fortune cookie industry is still tied to Chinatown in terms of history, location, and distribution, it is quickly being mainstreamed—and in some ways it's already there, with regard to consumption and marketing cachet. The addition of customized messages has, in recent years, turned the cookies into a popular sales gimmick, and what could be more American? They come dipped in chocolate, perched on martini glasses, encrusted with sprinkles, baked around bawdy fortunes or engagement rings; they're found in the context of a party, an election campaign.

Fortune cookies are a big part of the identity construct that follows the Chinese in America. Like the American Chinatowns where its basement manufacture grew over time to become a worldwide industry, the cookie smacks of self-invention. Heed its advice, and you might win big. You can be whoever you want to be. That's not one of Wong's fortunes, but it could be.

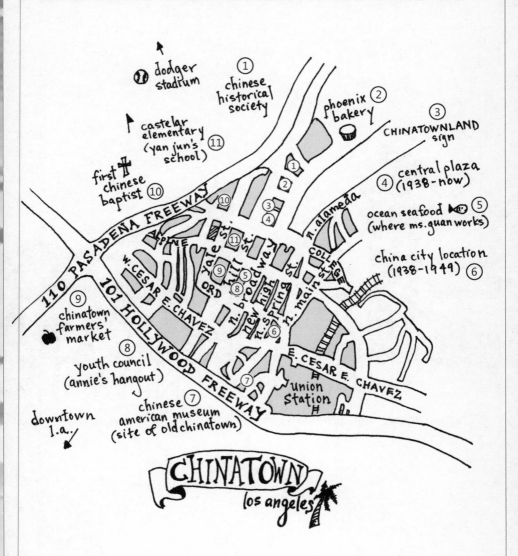

dodger stadium

① chinese historical society

phoenix bakery ②

③ CHINATOWNLAND sign

castelar elementary (yan jun's school) ⑪

④ central plaza (1938–now)

first chinese baptist ⑩

ocean seafood (where ms. guan works) ⑤

china city location (1938–1949) ⑥

110 PASADENA FREEWAY

101 HOLLYWOOD FREEWAY

W. CESAR E. CHAVEZ

PINE

YALE ST.

ORD

HILL ST.

N. BROADWAY

NEW HIGH ST.

N. SPRING ST.

N. MAIN ST.

COLLEGE

N. ALAMEDA

⑨ chinatown farmers' market

⑧ youth council (annie's hangout)

downtown l.a.

chinese american museum (site of old chinatown) ⑦

union station
E. CESAR E. CHAVEZ

CHINATOWN los angeles

CHINATOWNLAND sign, Los Angeles. *Bonnie Tsui*

SEVEN

CHINATOWNLAND

*The longtime partnership between
Hollywood and Chinatown.*

In a darkened Maryland movie theater in 1951, during his deployment for the Korean War, thirty-year-old Ben Fong sat in the audience during a showing of a potboiler called *Peking Express*. The black-and-white film stars Joseph Cotten—famous in the period for his prominent roles in Orson Welles' *Citizen Kane* and *The Third Man*—as a U.N. doctor, and French actress Corinne Calvet as his old flame. The two characters chance to meet again aboard a train, the Peking Express, en route from Shanghai to Peking. The good doctor is on his way to perform an operation on a Chinese Nationalist leader fighting against the Communists. A gang of bandits boards the train to rob and hold its passengers hostage. As the first action-packed sequence played across the screen that evening in Maryland, Fong was engrossed in the melee. The camera panned suddenly to a young Chinese robber wielding a machine gun, raining a fearsome hail of bullets down on the scene, and Fong couldn't believe his eyes. He stood up and pointed at the screen.

"Hey!" he shouted. "That's my kid brother!" The audience responded with wild clapping and cheers.

Back in Los Angeles, unbeknownst to Ben Fong, his youngest brother Tom had tapped into a booming local business while hanging out with his high school friends and trying not to think about

113

being called up in the draft. "We were caught up in make-believe land," Tom told me recently. He referred both to the movie industry culture and to the unsettled feeling among draft-age men like him during the war. At the beginning of the Korean conflict, he was enrolled at the local community college and could often be found in Chinatown. One night, he was approached by casting agents at a downtown bowling alley. "They said, 'Hey, we need some Oriental extras,'" Tom recalled. "They paid twenty-five dollars a day—it was good money. Half the time we were all broke, you know? I got an extra twenty-five because I said I knew how to handle a machine gun." He chuckled at the memory. "Which I didn't."

Though postwar America had demonstrated interest in the Far East as friend and foe, Hollywood wasn't filming on location in China or Japan in 1950. So it brought its cameras, and its scripts, to Los Angeles's Chinatown. In the American moviegoer's imagination, both China and Chinatown have long been the scene of danger, excitement, and mystery. Who can forget the enigma of *Chinatown*, even as Jack Nicholson is told to do so at the end of Roman Polanski's era-defining 1974 film? In actuality, the partnership between Chinatown and the pictures goes back to a much earlier time in Los Angeles. From the 1920s on through the 1950s, the city's Chinatown was where Hollywood went to cast Asians for their movies in large numbers. "You couldn't be in Chinatown at that time and avoid being involved in the film industry," Eugene Moy, a longtime member of the Chinatown community and a program director at the Chinese Historical Society of Southern California, told me. It was in the historical society's library where I met Ben Fong, and where he told me his brother's Hollywood tale; a frequent visitor to the society, he recently moved into a Chinatown apartment so he could be closer to his community.

If a film needed an exotic backdrop, it was going to be Chinatown, a neighborhood in the northeast corner of downtown Los

Angeles. Charlie Chaplin filmed here, as did Buster Keaton. With its winding alleys and Chinese denizens, the neighborhood was the perfect "ready-made set, complete with actors and actresses," Pauline Wong, the executive director of Los Angeles's Chinese American Museum, told me. And on celluloid, Chinatown could be made to represent itself or any other Chinatown in the world. Even today, it stands in for the ambiguous Asian "anywhere" Hollywood producers want it to be.

The Chinese American Museum is housed inside the historic 1890 Garnier Building, the last remaining structure of Los Angeles's first Chinatown. In 1933, demolition began in the original neighborhood, now referred to as Old Chinatown, to make way for the building of the opulent, Mission-style Union Station railroad terminal. Two other Chinatowns—China City and New Chinatown—were erected nearby, both opening in 1938. The new communities had a continuing involvement with Hollywood, with residents who not only acted in films but ran curio shops—with names like "Asiatic Rentals"—that lent props. Chinese restaurants also catered to the Hollywood crowd, which liked to entertain guests with what it called "those famous Chinese dinners" in a festive, colorful atmosphere. As New York had an industry-specific use for Chinatown, so did Los Angeles. For decades, the Chinese-American community served, in a way, as the Asian home office of Hollywood.

IN AN OVERGROWN, abandoned lot behind a chain-link fence on Hill Street, the main drag of Los Angeles's Chinatown today, there's a sign that reads CHINATOWNLAND. Large white block letters are set in a scaffold on the ground as a nod to the famous HOLLYWOOD sign (which, when it was first unveiled in the hills as a real-estate ad in 1923, originally read HOLLYWOODLAND). The Chinatown sign has an odd, derelict quality to it—an art installation created in 2002 by Andre Yi, the sign was originally meant to stay up for just a few months—but in that vacant lot, it has become its own Los Angeles landmark. Most people in the neighborhood don't know where the sign came from, or what it's supposed to mean. To me, the relic is as ideal a representation as you can get of how the city's Chinatown has been tied to its film industry since the early days, in ways that are significant but little known, and increasingly forgotten.

The 1930s was a pivotal time for the Chinatown community in Los Angeles. Will Gow, a community historian at the Chinese Historical Society of Southern California, whose recent oral history documentary project, *Chinatown Remembered*, interviewed old-time residents who lived in the neighborhood in the 1930s and 1940s, told me that the intersection of a booming film industry and neighborhood upheaval made it a ripe era for Hollywoodized versions of Chinatown to form. It was a decade when Chinatown figured prominently in the Hollywood gossip pages of the *Los Angeles Times*—not least because the Chinatown-born film and stage star Anna May Wong entertained there. The "foreign quarter" was also a hangout for other actors and movie people. A 1935 column by Read Kendall titled "Odd and Interesting Hollywood Gossip" included this juicy item: "Una Merkel took a group of friends to Chinatown for a feast and made them finish the banquet with chop sticks . . ." Chinatown was a scream, a hoot, a hopping, escapist nightlife draw. And when Old Chinatown was razed, proposals were put forth for a new Chinatown settlement that would maintain its coveted status as a tourist attraction for the city—as well as house a displaced population of over 2,500 Chinese.

The June 1938 openings of the competing New Chinatown and China City projects set up a sort of "Battle of the Chinatowns." In one corner was New Chinatown, spearheaded by Chinese community members, including prominent business leader Peter Soo Hoo. Its Central Plaza was established where the old Italian neighborhood used to be, bounded by North Broadway and Castelar (now Hill Street). The force behind New Chinatown was the Los Angeles Chinatown Project Association, whose mission statement was an exercise in self-reliance: "We cannot make ourselves go back into slums and tumbledown shacks. We are able to pay our own way and stand on our own feet." New Chinatown was arguably the first planned urban Chinatown in the country, intended to house businesses and residents that had been forcibly removed from the traditional Old Chinatown. Its developers were careful to address locals' concerns with clean, modern streets, restaurants, and shops, but it was also designed to appeal to tourists. There was an East Gate and a West Gate, and narrow lanes with names like Gin Ling Way. On June 25, 1938, a full-page ad in the *Los Angeles Examiner* invited readers to enjoy "The Enchanting Charm of Old China in Los Angeles." Opening-day festivities included Chinese opera singers and lion dancers and remarks by former California governor Frank Merriam and Chinese consul T. K. Chang.

Situated just a few blocks away, between Main and Spring streets, was the rival: China City. Its development was led by social activist Christine Sterling, whose vision of a romanticized Orient included props donated by Cecil B. DeMille from the Oscar-winning 1937 film production of Pearl S. Buck's famous novel, *The Good Earth*. China City had opened three weeks earlier than New Chinatown, on June 7, and was far more outrageous than New Chinatown in its depiction of a film-set Chinatown—for one thing, it actually included a replica House of Wang set from the DeMille picture (entry fee: five cents). China City was also designed and built in consultation with an architect, a set designer, and a construction superintendent from the Paramount lot. It featured rickshaw rides for tourists and numerous curio stalls that employed Chinese merchants in costume. Local Chinese children were also dressed as rural peasants by day to add to the ambience; by night, they changed back into their normal Western clothes. It was in the construction of this place that reality and fiction really began to blur. One of the most carnivalesque "Chinese American" inventions for sale in the China City theme park was something called the Chinaburger.

"It had bean sprouts on it," Esther Lee Johnson told me. "Other than that, it was just a regular old hamburger." Johnson, a Chinese American who grew up in Old Chinatown and lived on Los Angeles Street through the thirties and forties, worked in a bakery in China City when she was a teenager. Over a half-century, she also worked as a stand-in and extra in over a hundred movies and television episodes alongside Hollywood stars like Gregory Peck, Betty Grable, and John Wayne. To the studios, she was known as Esther Ying Lee (Johnson is her married name). What stands out to me most from my conversations with former extras like Johnson and Tom Fong was how *ordinary* the show-business experience was for them and other people in the Chinatown community during those years.

The ease of it all was due partly to people like Tom Gubbins, who worked as a Chinese-casting agent and prop furnisher for numerous films in the thirties, including *The Good Earth*. "He was a white guy, but he spoke fluent Chinese, and he was up one corner of Los Angeles Street from where my family lived," Johnson recalled. Born in China to an English family in the diplomatic service, Gubbins lived in Chinatown and cast a lot of neighborhood kids in "refugee" or "coolie" roles; Johnson's first role was that of a young Chinese peasant girl in *The Good Earth*. "He had buses parked in front of his shop. We'd get on his bus and they'd take us to the studios. When we were young, it wasn't as strict—you didn't have to have a guardian. They'd scoop up everyone in Chinatown and bring them to the studio."

For a decade, China City was a popular tourist attraction and marketplace. Dubbed "Chinese Movie Land," it was a place where Hollywood physically shaped the image of what it thought an

American Chinatown should be. And through the recruitment of Chinese residents as extras in its film portrayals of China, Japan, Korea, the Philippines, Hong Kong, and Chinatown itself, Hollywood also shaped the way Americans viewed Asia—and Asians *in* America. War pictures featuring Asian faces proliferated from the time of the Second Sino-Japanese War—which began in 1937 and bled into World War II—on through the end of the Korean War, in the mid-fifties. The 1938 film *The Adventures of Marco Polo* needed 600 Chinese extras for palace and battle scenes alone. For other big productions, like *Love Is a Many-Splendored Thing*, which takes place in Hong Kong during the Chinese Communist revolution, or the Bogart picture *The Left Hand of God*, which is set in China during the same period, Esther Lee Johnson remembers that "practically the whole Chinatown was in there." Both movies came out in 1955. She and her friends worked regularly as extras, and they would round up whomever they could think of to help out the casting agents. There were never enough people. The entire community, it seemed, was involved with Hollywood.

By the fifties, however, China City was gone. Two fires, the first during Chinese New Year 1939 and the second in 1949, eventually wiped out the quarter's wooden stalls, restaurants, and shops, and it was never rebuilt. It is now a parking lot. New Chinatown, with its modern look and financial and cultural investment by the Chinese community itself, emerged as the enduring enclave. After World War II, a West Plaza section of New Chinatown was added, with apartments situated on the second floor of each business. New Chinatown still makes up the heart of Chinatown today. The World War II–era Grand Star Chinese Restaurant survives as a jazz club, and one of Central Plaza's first gift shops, K. G. Louie Company, remains open for business. But a new generation of establishments, including art galleries and clothing boutiques, has begun to edge its way in. By the time China City burned to the ground, people had already begun to settle in other pockets around L.A. To the south, Chinese produce workers and distributors had increasingly clustered around City Market, a wholesale marketplace established some years earlier by local vegetable growers. Some Chinese residents ended up on the edges of Old Chinatown. The dispersal would eventually lead to the establishment of new suburban communities like Monterey Park, Alhambra, and other enclaves in the San Gabriel Valley around Los Angeles. The distinction between the original Chinese American settlements—Old Chinatown, China City, and New Chinatown— and the more recent ethnoburbs, however, is an important one. While the older neighborhoods were formed under the pressures of racism and economic and cultural survival, the new were established by choice, reflective of the considerable advantages of wealth and mobility in the Chinese-American population today.

FOR ALL ITS CONVENIENCE, extra work was not a career-making turn for Chinatown residents. Even the biggest Chinese-American stars of the era—like Anna May Wong, Keye Luke, and Benson Fong—had trouble getting lead roles because of their ethnicity. Despite all the Chinese extras toiling in the background as rural peasants in *The Good Earth*, the film's principal roles were played by white actors with taped eyelids and heavy makeup.

"It was really something you just expected," Esther Lee Johnson says of the "yellowface" practice. "In the old days, they'd have Myrna Loy playing a Chinese woman, or a white actor playing Charlie Chan. It took a long time for them to make the change. That's why even the top actors all owned restaurants or had little shops in New Chinatown or China City, because they couldn't make a living on just the movie work."

Anna May Wong is widely known as the first Asian-American Hollywood star. Born in Old Chinatown in 1905, she loved movies from an early age. She played hooky from Chinese school to go to the five-cent neighborhood theater, and recruited her brother Jimmy to help her put on plays of her own creation. She hung around film sets in Chinatown. Her parents' friends were among the hundreds of Chinatown residents often recruited for background work, and one day Anna May slipped aboard one of the buses to the studios. After she shone in her first lead role as Lotus Flower in *The Toll of the Sea*, a 1922 version of the Madame Butterfly story set in China—and the first wide-release color feature made in Hollywood—she quickly became famous. Not long ago, I sat down to watch the fifty-minute film. Despite the melodrama of the era's silent pictures, Anna May's delicately expressive face and restrained performance contributed a sense of genuine tragedy and emotion; she was clearly the most talented of the film's cast.

In 1928, the leading role of a Chinese slave in *The Crimson City* was given to Myrna Loy over Anna May Wong, who had to resign herself to a bit part. The slight was widely seen as the trigger that sent her looking for more sympathetic and realistic Chinese roles in Europe. Anti-miscegenation laws in effect in the United States meant there could be no on-screen kissing between Asian and white actors—even if they were both playing Asian characters. (Ultimately Anna May was allowed one kiss, in a 1934 British B-movie called *Java Head*.) Her tribulations served as the inspiration for a poem entitled "No One Ever Tried to Kiss Anna May Wong," by the award-winning poet and critic John Yau, in which she is "annoyed at all the times / she's been told to be scratched, kicked, / slapped, bitten, stabbed, poisoned, and shot."

According to Shirley Jennifer Lim, a historian who wrote a recent book on Asian American women's culture from the thirties to the sixties, Anna May Wong was seen as embodying an "'authentic' Chineseness" as a product of Chinatown. "However, given the 1882 Chinese Immigration Exclusion Act, Wong and the Chinese Americans who inhabited Los Angeles's Chinatown did not have personal knowledge of China but gained it through their work on Hollywood movie sets," Lim writes. The restrictions on Chinese immigration ensured that by 1940, more Chinese in the United States were American-born than foreign-born. Anna May and her fellow neighborhood actors were pretty much as American as anyone—despite the fact that they weren't treated that way.

Anna May found success in the U.K. and Germany, in films like *Piccadilly* (in which she played a scullery maid who eventually becomes a nightclub star) and onstage in a German operetta (she performed in fluent German, to rave reviews). Returning to Hollywood in 1930, she struggled in the ensuing decades to find better roles, speaking out against negative Chinese stereotyping. "Why is it that the screen Chinese is nearly always the villain?" she asked in a surprisingly blunt interview with Doris Mackie of *Film Weekly* magazine in 1933. "And so crude a villain. Murderous, treacherous, a snake in the grass. We are not like that. How should we be, with a civilization that is so many times older than that of the West?" Her biggest disappointment was MGM's refusal to cast her in the role of O-Lan, the main female character in *The Good Earth*; a white actor, Paul Muni, was to act in yellowface as O-Lan's husband, Wang Lung. Anna May Wong died in 1961, just before she was to perform in *Flower Drum Song*. Ironically, *Flower Drum Song*, which takes place in San Francisco's Chinatown, would be a pioneering Hollywood film in its casting of Asian actors in almost all roles. Esther Lee Johnson, who worked as the stand-in for lead actress Nancy Kwan in the film, told me that she remembers just one white actor of any note, who was cast as a lowly gardener.

Anna May's obituary in *Time* magazine read as follows: "Feb. 10, 1961: Died. Anna May Wong, 54 [actually 56], Los Angeles-born daughter of a local laundryman, who became a film star over her father's objections that 'every time your picture is taken, you lose a part of your soul,' died a thousand deaths as the screen's fore-most Oriental villainess; of a heart attack; in Santa Monica, Calif."

"*ROARING THROUGH CHINA TODAY! Adventuress, doctor, thief, clergyman . . . they all ride the peril-laden Peking Express . . . rushing through the intrigue and the terror of the strife-torn Orient!*" These stylized, sensationalist lines run across the movie poster for *Peking Express*, set in a forward-leaning font designed to intimate speed and thrills.

As in other films of the period, the background actors and extras in *Peking Express* were largely Chinese, but the main Chinese bad-die was played by a white actor, Marvin Miller. It was a sign of the midcentury times, as were the "perils" and "terror" associated with villainous China and its Chinese characters. Recently, I visited Tom Fong, the extra who played the Chinese bandit, at his home in Alhambra, where he lives with his wife of fifty years, Bonnie. Located seven miles east of Los Angeles's Chinatown, Alhambra is a suburban community, with pretty, tree-lined streets, white stucco houses, and big-box stores on the main avenues. After his 1951 film appearance—his first and only role—Fong spent many years working as an aerospace engineer. Now well into his retirement at seventy-eight, he has a second career as a successful watercolor painter, teaching at local colleges and holding regular workshops across the country, including a summer art session at Yosemite National Park. Over a half century later, he remembers his stint as a Chinese gunner in sharp detail.

"Yeah, I was the bad guy," Fong told me, laughing, as we sipped tea in his living room. "At Paramount Studios, they even had a moving train all set up. My buddies and I, we went there early in the morning, and they told us to change into these uniforms. Most of the time, we just hung around playing cards until we were called.

When the day was over, you might not have done anything, but you were still paid your twenty-five bucks."

For his day's work on the set, he got his fifteen minutes of fame. "I killed a lot of people onscreen, because they kept repeating that sequence over and over again." He sighed wistfully. "I only saw that movie one time. I wish I had a copy of it today."

Though he himself only worked on one film, Fong had many Chinatown friends who were extras. He can chant a litany of names: Betty Wong, Albert and Rosie Jue, Larry Chan, Ruth Lung, Esther Ying Lee, the Soo Hoo brothers. It was a close-knit community. If you were in the right place at the right time in Chinatown, he said, they would just call you up. He remembers going to a lot of war pictures, but unlike his brother Ben, he wasn't surprised to see his Chinese buddies up on the big screen. "If I went to the movies, I'd be like, 'That's Walter,' or 'That's so-and-so.' A lot of them played the part of the bad Japanese. We would recognize them, and then we'd start laughing."

I talked with Fong's friend Rose Jue, who worked as a children's talent manager for many decades. She, too, recalls a Chinese-American community where everyone knew everyone else, in which casting calls were broadcast around largely by word-of-mouth. It was a chance to meet people and make a few extra dollars in the process. "You didn't have to be an actor or an actress, you just needed to have a head count," she said, especially when they were doing a war picture and needed Asian faces. Her husband often helped fill the quota, and when he heard about a film that needed children, their kids got involved. When her son Craig was eight years old, he starred in a 1968 John Wayne picture, *The Green Berets*, about two crack Special Forces teams who are sent into Vietnam. The experience of filming with John Wayne in the hills of Georgia still ranks high on his list of life moments.

For all the fun of playing in the pictures, I wondered if Chinatown's extras felt put off by the "exotic" and "evil" stereotypes that so riddled their roles. Born-and-bred American-Chinese actors were told to play opium-smoking criminals and kowtowing servants, and to put on pidgin-English accents. To Fong, sometimes the representation was plausible—"maybe for the acting part of someone in China, it's okay"—but for the roles set in America, the exaggeration felt a bit ridiculous. "Here in the United States, not all cooks will speak with an accent, you know? They sometimes overextend that, even today," he told me dryly. "We all speak properly here."

On the set of the television series *Ben Casey*, which aired in the early sixties, Esther Lee Johnson was called Egg Roll by her fellow cast mates because she was the only Chinese under employ. But she doesn't resent it. "It was the way it was in the business," she said, her voice unsentimental. "I got to travel. I worked hard. I had a lot of opportunities. We did a lot so that the kids these days can do more. Before you could only be a laundryman or a refugee. Now there are parts as attorneys, as doctors. We opened the doors."

Local historian Will Gow estimates that there are roughly a hundred people still alive from that era, of a Chinatown community that was approximately 3,000 to 5,000 strong in the thirties and forties. Arthur Dong, a filmmaker born and raised in San Francisco's Chinatown, touches on the early relationship between Los Angeles's Chinatown and Hollywood in his 2007 documentary, *Hollywood Chinese*. "There was a real synthesis of Chinatown's working people and the film industry in the thirties and forties," he told me. Those historic players—whom Dong describes as a largely ignored and untapped "gold mine"—have a unique view of the changing iconography surrounding the Chinese in America.

Chinatown's extras also have a rare perspective on the various forms that the neighborhood came to take as it reincarnated itself over the decades. Johnson says that going to Chinatown used to be "a treat, real entertainment." Bustling with activity and people, Chinatown was where you went when you had visitors and wanted to show them a good time. These days, she recognizes the limitations of what Chinatown can be.

"I go there once in a while to see my friends, but there's not too many left," she told me. "Nobody wants to be locked there anymore, and at the same time, you can't blame them. They better themselves. You don't have to be locked in a curio shop in Chinatown anymore." In the same way there are more acting opportunities for Chinese Americans, the world at large has opened up beyond Chinatown. "It's progress."

I asked Johnson what she remembered most about being an extra in Polanski's *Chinatown*, which filmed on location on Spring Street and Ord—the Los Angeles streets on which she grew up. "Oh, it was a long shoot," she told me. On one particularly tiring day, she put her head against a restaurant window, where she could see the cooks working. And she fell asleep.

As New Chinatown celebrated its seventieth birthday in June 2008—restoring the original, quintessential look of neon lighting along the pagoda rooflines of its buildings, and throwing a 1930s-style, big-band party featuring a montage of film clips shot here—I considered the special relationship Chinatown has had with Hollywood and, through the camera lens, with America at large. Chinatown was the complicated site of fiction and reality, a "Little China" right at home, where the local Chinese were cast in movies that outlined ideas for America about the Orientals in their midst. Chinatown as an idea existed in part because America needed it—to play the role of the villain, to be the exotic other, to entertain, to inspire patriotism, to tell a story of good and evil. It was out of this enforced play-acting that real self-invention and self-representation for Chinese Americans would become possible, but only decades later. It wasn't until Steven Spielberg's 1987 film *Empire of the Sun* that a major American studio returned to shoot in China—and it was the first to film in Shanghai since the 1949 Communist revolution. Despite the conflicts of the era, Tom Fong takes pride in being a Chinese American. His father came to California from Toisan as a fourteen-year-old boy, alone, seeking his fortune. Fong feels lucky that he did. "We as his kids live in the best of two worlds," he told me, suggesting an alternate reality of his own to make the point. "Heck, I could have been born in China and become an officer in Mao's army, instead of just playing one in the movies."

Chinatown Youth Council meeting. *Bonnie Tsui*

EIGHT

HOMETOWN CHINATOWN

In an increasingly disparate community,
it's where the kids hang out.

When Annie Luong was a junior in high school in Echo Park, an L.A. neighborhood just northwest of downtown, she and a friend decided that they would embark on a mission to go to every shop in Chinatown. It took them about a year. Even though they had grown up with the neighborhood, just a couple of miles from home, there were surprises. As she put it, "We found things. Like, oh, I never knew there was a bookstore on this corner. And one day, just walking, we found nine art galleries." The day she realized that art galleries had arrived in Chinatown was the day she walked up to a store window and saw a room full of sand, five fans blowing it all around, and a price tag for the whole thing that read $2,000.

Like many in the disparate Chinese-American community of Los Angeles, Annie didn't live in Chinatown. But she had spent her whole life here, and knew its streets better than any other neighborhood in which she'd actually resided. She was born at the hospital right in Chinatown. Her parents were ethnic Chinese born in Vietnam, and Cantonese was the language of the family household, with a few Vietnamese words sprinkled in. "My parents, they didn't really know English, so we always came here to Chinatown for everything," she told me. "I liked it a lot, even when I was little. Except for the crowds. I hated the crowds. You're at that knee level, and you can't breathe." She laughed, shoving a thick mop of black hair from her eyes.

Annie viewed Echo Park as an "extension" of Chinatown. A five-minute drive is all that separates the two. But it was the language she used to describe her relationship to Chinatown that was particularly evocative to me. As in the San Francisco Bay Area, the Chinese here are an extended family—an extended community that is forever stretching outward from Chinatown. Immigrants come and settle in the Chinatown, around the Chinatown, sometimes a significant drive from the Chinatown. These days, the population has scattered all over, and there are plenty of other places to get the familiar foods and products they want. But for their Chinese-American kids, Chinatown *is* necessary, as a place to reconnect with their Chineseness, in a way that is more meaningful than going to the mall in Monterey Park.

"When you go over to Monterey Park or San Gabriel, there are huge stores and Starbucks—it's more about buying stuff," Annie said, when I asked how the other Chinese-American enclaves stacked up against Chinatown for her. "Even if it attracts new immigrants, it's still really commercial. You walk around there, it's nice and new, but it's not the same feeling. Here in Chinatown, I feel like I'm going home. I like to walk around and see how the neighborhood changes." To Annie, exploring Chinatown is a social thing she does with her friends, but it is also a way to figure out her identity—to parse out the meaning of the community and its significance for her as an eighteen-year-old getting ready to go to college. It's a way of figuring out how to leave home for the first time.

FOR ME, an outsider, a walk in Los Angeles's Chinatown isn't quite so personal. But still it has a compelling narrative: shared stories of vibrant worlds as told to me by ordinary people. It's a pilgrimage through the neighborhood's past to its present, all of its old parts linked up today by the modern connective tissue of concrete mini-malls and the heavy car traffic filtering through its four- and six-lane streets. Chinatown itself has a bit of the L.A. urban sprawl. At the southern end is Old Chinatown's Garnier Building, considered at the turn of the twentieth century as the Chinese City Hall. One afternoon, I headed north from there, passing Union Station, the reason for Old Chinatown's demise, and strolling through the vast parking lot that was once China City. By the time I got to the Central and West Plazas, on the northern edge of the neighborhood near the entrance to the 110 Freeway, I'd encountered plenty of the bi-level shopping centers and marketplaces—Bamboo Plaza, Dynasty Center, Far East Plaza—that filled in around New Chinatown in the decades following the momentous arrival of Central Plaza.

In this jumble of eras, I saw the children of Chinatown, and how their lives intersected with neighborhood history. In the Chinese American Museum, schoolkids were invited to peruse exhibits that described the Chinese Massacre of 1871, in which the accidental shooting of a white man led a mob of five hundred Angelenos to attack Chinatown, killing nineteen Chinese men and boys. On week-ends, packs of teenagers roamed the streets, sucking down bubble teas and sifting through cheap trinkets in outdoor shop bins. In Central Plaza's main pedestrian square, I sat in the shade of a bearded palm tree and watched young martial-arts troupes in blazing-orange garb prepare to perform for tourists, while elementary-school kids rode their bikes in circles and flung gunpowder snaps—gleefully, if somewhat viciously—at passersby. One block over, I walked behind a young couple strolling hand-in-hand into Phoenix Bakery, a kitschy, powder-blue landmark that has been advertising "Chinatown Famous Birthday Cakes" for seventy years. Not everyone wonders about the formative events that shape the place where they live, but the lure of lore has always been an insistently powerful part of Chinatown's draw.

Annie, for one, has found ways to link up to those stories. When

I first met her, she was working at the front desk of the city's Chinese Historical Society of Southern California, which is housed in a blue-and-red-painted Victorian house on the north side of Chinatown. On a bright spring afternoon, I stood outside on the front porch with Eugene Moy, a program director for the society and a wonderful raconteur. A mass of unruly rosemary bushes lining the porch railing was fragrant in the sunshine. Moy recalled that his parents ran one of the many Chinese mom-and-pop grocery stores in the city during the 1940s. To him, Chinatown was the place the family came for weddings and banquets, where he visited his grandparents. "Here I am fifty years later, still here," he mused, as we watched teenagers across the street walking home from school.

Annie's friends often came by to visit her at the historical society. When they did, she shared tidbits of the Chinatown history she learned from Moy. She admitted that she didn't know much when she first started. "I was scared when Eugene and the other guys here first asked me what I knew about Chinatown," she told me one day after school. Next to the floridly named Best Western Dragon Gate Inn, we drank tea and strawberry soda at an outdoor café table hidden in a side courtyard. "I didn't know about all that history—that there were three Chinatowns. It's been interesting to be here my whole life, and then suddenly to see it totally differently."

When Annie learned that the Central Plaza area was built as part of New Chinatown in the 1930s, she was confounded. "I said, 'Wait, isn't that *Old* Chinatown?'" She laughed. "Kids my age, we always called it Old Chinatown, because we always thought that it looked old and the old folks hung out there." Working at the historical society, she said, helped her to clarify her terminology. It also clarified her understanding of the place of the Chinese in America.

Annie pokes fun at her response to learning about Chinatown in the thirties and forties. "What?! There were Chinese here?!" she said, in mock amazement. In school, she had learned about the railroad workers in California, but not much more. "You know how in the history books Chinese people disappear?" she asked me, her words startlingly poignant. "You don't think about it. Now you realize, 'Oh, we've always been here, huh?'" Similar to the way the alleyway kids of San Francisco combined neighborhood research with their own stories, Annie found that knowing the past led to useful realizations about her own place in the community. Her perspective: Here, we belong. We're caught between the Chinese and the American culture. This is our hangout. And the more we know, the more we see that the community is changing faster than ever.

Even in her own brief lifetime, she observes that the resident population has aged—it is now mostly elderly, plus the new immigrants who have come straight from China. "We started noticing that there are more tourists than Chinese on the weekends," she said. The gift shops now outnumber the "regular" stores that sell useful household items. "Some of the restaurant owners, they remember me from when I was little. And so it's that kind of community, where it's all close. Everyone knows each other. But now, new people are coming in, and the longtime people are leaving, so it's kind of not the same."

When Annie was little, she barely saw tourists. In a crowd of Chinese, a tourist with a hat in the crosswalk stuck out like a sore thumb. "You'd be like, 'Somebody's from out of town!' But now, they're like everywhere. One time, I saw a family in Chinatown. They all wore the little tour hats. They were taking a picture. And they said, 'Okay, one-two-three, say, "Chinese!"' And I was like, 'What?!' And me and my friends started mimicking them: 'Can we say, "Tourist?!"' We weren't offended. It was more like, 'Wow . . . people do that?' Well, some tourists, they just want to get to know the culture. But others, they're not really getting it. They're getting the fans, and the lanterns." The cheap surface clutter of fans and lanterns is designed to make visitors feel like they've been somewhere special—Chinatown—but in truth, it's a place they haven't really seen at all.

Chinese New Year is a time of year when the commercialization of the neighborhood is most obvious to Annie. She remembers streets packed with locals all dressed up to see the firecrackers, the dragon, and the parade. Now, she says, it's almost all tourists. "There's not that feeling of culture," she explained to me. "When I was little, they didn't need all of those sponsors. It was just something that the community did to celebrate itself and come together. It felt more meaningful." She paused, taking a sip of strawberry soda. "Now, you do it for the show."

EVEN THOUGH ANNIE and her friends mostly live outside Chinatown now, it's in Chinatown that they find what they need: a place to hang out. On Fridays after school, they go to the weekly meeting of the Chinatown Youth Council. It's less of an agenda-driven meeting than a certified hangout session, but for these students, having a place to hang out isn't a thing to be taken lightly.

Danee Prasert, a young afterschool program assistant who grew up in Chinatown, told me that the kids show up at the youth council largely to have a peer group. "It's the same problems that other inner-city youth face: boredom, not really having any choices out there," she told me as we watched the teenagers fall into their little cliques. There were snacks set out; while the high schoolers held their meeting, middle-school kids could work with Danee on the computers. "Just having a social group they're comfortable with here, that really helps. They feel comfortable with other Asian kids." Danee is Thai; when she was small, her family moved to Chinatown to be among other Asians. She still lives in the neighborhood, which has progressively become more mixed, with increasing numbers of Southeast Asians and Hispanics. She is clued into the difficulties faced by kids in the area.

"You don't want to go out, because there's nowhere to go. And the gangs—we call them Wangsters now," she said, laughing. "Now that I'm older, I'm not scared of them. But it was menacing to be out when I was younger."

Nearly all the students I met were the first generation in their families to be born in America. Some of their parents worked construction and other blue-collar jobs; most had to help their parents with English. Almost all were of Chinese descent; a couple had families who came through Vietnam; all agreed that for them as Asians, Chinatown was a comfort zone.

At the meeting, I sat, and listened, and asked questions, and what I heard was by turns hilarious, poignant, and outrageous. I'd listened to teenagers across America talk about Chinatown, and the most remarkable thing about them all was their refusal to hold back on what they saw or felt. The narrative of their lives was an open tap: unfiltered, tainted with occasional misunderstandings, but always flowing honestly.

Joey, a perky, chatty sophomore who lives with her aunt and uncle across the street, told me that though she loved Chinatown, she didn't like where she had to stay. "Since I live right next door to a liquor store, there are a lot of drunken people," she said. "I've lived in Chinatown ever since I was two, so I feel pretty safe, but it's just that things like that are annoying."

"When I was a kid, I used to think everything you buy here was cool, all the toys and action figures," a boy named Marvin said. "But now that I've grown up, I see that those are all low-tech things—people will just sell those to get by. And I'm like—oh, that's kind of sad." He tugged on the strings of his gray hooded sweatshirt.

Another boy named Albert spoke up. "Yeah, I think most of the stuff here is for tourists. Not for people in the neighborhood, except for a few shops and restaurants. You go over to places that are selling slippers, like handmade slippers for two dollars each." He shrugged. "Who wants those?"

But he is savvy enough to recognize that a lot of people in Chinatown depend on the tourists for business. "In a way, it's good for the place, but it also gives it a feeling that it's not a real place—that it's cheap and cheesy, and just a place for money," he added. The tension between the two ideas—that tourists come here more than locals now, but that the locals need tourists—raises the complicated issue of whether or not anyone has real ownership of Chinatown.

When it came to why they were in Chinatown, Albert put it simply: "To hang out." A girl seated next to him agreed, adding, "School's close by." She explained that she lived in Echo Park. "And it's not fun to hang out there. It's not nice at all." Other kids piped up; they came to Chinatown to go to Chinese school, to eat in the restaurants, to buy books or groceries.

Annie said she thought of Chinatown as her downtown: it was where she went first if she needed anything. The other kids echoed her sentiment. "If you need small groceries, you can always come here, and it's convenient," Albert said.

"Like Chinese food," Joey said.

"But it's bad for you," a skinny boy with glasses said. "Isn't it fat you can't burn off?" The entire room cracked up.

"Wait, haven't you been eating that your whole life?" Albert asked. "What does your mom cook?"

"Vietnamese food," the boy answered. Another huge laugh. "There's a difference. Asian food isn't all the same." There was a murmur of agreement.

"The only thing my mom says about MSG is that it makes your hair fall out," someone else added. Another roar.

"I *shave* my head," Albert said, laughing good-naturedly and running a hand over his buzz-cut head. "That's by choice."

Beyond the surface hilarity, behind the discussion of shopping and food and tourism, they offered serious insight. They recognized Chinatown as a place that was necessary to new immigrants most of all—the garment sweatshops and souvenir stores and restaurants that employed them, the cheaper apartments that housed them. But still, despite their complaints about the neighborhood's touristy stretches and lack of cleanliness, something about Chinatown drew them as children of immigrants. They felt safe; they liked it there. It was familiar, they said, in a way that nowhere else was.

Albert's family had sent him back to China a few times so he wouldn't "lose his culture." Or that was how they explained it to him. "I visited relatives and ate food that I never ever heard of before," he said of his time there. To him, the trips only underscored the fact that his parents stuck stubbornly to Chinese ways of thinking, while he himself was something else: Chinese American. "When I speak English in the house, they scream back at me in Chinese," he said, wryly. A girl named Ling said her parents had already given up on getting her to speak Chinese to them, even though they continued to speak to her in Chinese. Marvin said his dad wanted him to speak Mandarin, but their conversations were almost always half-English, half-Chinese. Broken English was a mark of being a Chinese immigrant. Broken Mandarin, he said, was a mark of being Chinese American.

ONE THING ANNIE found in her quest to go to all of the stores in Chinatown was a lot of old bookstores. She had never gone to Chinese school, so while she spoke Cantonese well, she didn't know how to read or write any Chinese characters. Browsing through the bookstands awakened something in her. "Last year, I started to go through this thing," she told me. "I said, 'I don't know any Chinese.' And my friend offered to teach me, because she's still in Chinese school and her Chinese is pretty good. I learned how to write my name, and a few other things." They took a hiatus from the impromptu lunchtime lessons when schoolwork started piling up and A.P. exams loomed on the horizon. But she hasn't lost interest.

"You know what sucks?" she asked me. "My school, next year they're having a Chinese class. But I'm graduating this year! I took

Spanish for three years. But I want to learn Chinese really bad. I want to learn it in college, so I can write to my mom."

Chinatown is a physical place, but it's also an idea. It presents the question of how an immigrant cultural heritage can survive in a life otherwise lived in mainstream America. Annie says that if she didn't live in and around Chinatown, Cantonese wouldn't have been as present in her life. As it is, she finds it frustrating when she doesn't have the Cantonese vocabulary to communicate with her mother. "Like, if I talk about school, and I say 'history'—I just say, 'the class that talks about a long, long time ago.' I don't know all the exact terms. My mom asks me questions about my studies sometimes, but she only knows doctor, lawyer, or accountant. So if I try to say, 'engineer,' or try to describe science, it doesn't really work. And then you don't try after a while. Because you can't figure out how to say it."

Annie has a close relationship with her mother; when we met to chat at a Chinatown café, it was her mother who dropped her off and picked her up. I asked Annie if she ever identified with her Vietnamese roots. "I don't feel Vietnamese, because I never went towards that culture," she said. "My mom always brought us toward the Chinese culture. I think the way I think is American. But then I like Chinese things more than I like American things." She laughed at the contradiction. "So I think I'm in between. The way our mind-set is—in our group of friends, I mean—we're American. When we see everyone running across the street in Chinatown, we think, 'You shouldn't jaywalk!' And my mom will say to us, '*Aii-yah*, you Americans!' But then sometimes we're really like Chinese people, and we're like, 'Damn Americans!' Which is funny, because *we're* American. So we're caught in between. We're like both cultures, basically. I'm kind of glad my friends are into it, too."

Annie and her twin sister, Joanie, were both bound for the University of California at Berkeley in the fall. They had not yet visited the campus, and Annie admitted to being a little scared—she and her sister are the first in her family to leave Los Angeles. The only place she'd ever gone outside of the L.A. metro area was Las Vegas, when she was ten. What made the move to the Bay Area a little less frightening, though, was the excitement of finally visiting the "real Chinatown" in San Francisco.

"My sister and I, we're really into Chinatowns, and we really want to go to the New York one, and the San Francisco one. I want to go to the Mexico one, too. Because Mexico City has a China-town—my friend in Mexico told me." She grinned at me from under her thick mane of black hair. "He said it was weird to see Chinese people speaking perfect Spanish." Her curiosity about where the Chinese diaspora had taken others made San Francisco a captivat-ing destination in her mind.

"I want to go to San Francisco mainly because I want to see the Chinatown," she said wistfully. "In a way, it's like a familiar place that I know I won't be too lost in even if it is in another area." At the same time, she said, she also knew there would be surprises beyond those she'd already found in her own hometown China-town. "We've heard so many stories of how different it is there—that it's almost like being in the China outside of China," she told me. "That's what they say." For a certain generation of Chinese Americans, Chinatown is a way to find something familiar in a strange place. An ethnic identity can be a passport to other destina-tions within America—and outside of it, too.

Principal Cheuk Choi and students at Castelar Elementary. *Bonnie Tsui*

NINE

PREACHER MAN, TEACHER MAN

Neighborhood anchors for the new arrival.

One spring night in Chinatown, a fire started in eight-year-old Yan Jun Deng's bedroom. An electric spark from the socket near her bed caught on the mattress; the smoke from the fire deepened her slumber. It wasn't until the flame reached her bare right arm that she awoke with a start, bolting through the connecting bathroom to her parents' room, which they shared with her three-and-a-half-year-old sister. The smoke alarm finally sounded.

The family was lucky—though Yan Jun's arm had third-degree burns that would require a series of skin grafts, they all got out of the apartment alive. The incident made Yan Jun's mother, Hui Yan Guan, feel terrible. How could she have brought her child to America, only to have this happen?

Guan and her husband had a comfortable life in their village in southern China, where she taught elementary school and he worked as an office manager in a textile factory. But her mother-in-law had lived in Los Angeles's Chinatown for a long time, and she wanted her son and his family to come to America. "Your whole family is here," she told her son. "You should move here, too." In 2003, they did.

From phone conversations she'd had with her mother-in-law, Guan knew that life in America could be difficult. She made it a goal to take English classes right away. But in addition to taking care of Yan Jun, who was only three years old and not yet old enough for kindergarten, she had to look after her mother-in-law, who, it turned out, was in poor health and frequently in and out of the hospital. Her husband began a job as a long-haul trucker, crisscrossing the country to deliver dry goods for a Chinese-owned company. He often spent a week at a time on the road. Together with his parents, they moved into a three-bedroom Chinatown apartment. A year and a half later, their second daughter was born. They gave her an American name, Tina.

One of the busiest times in Los Angeles's Chinatown is Sunday, when 2,000 people from around the city come to the First Chinese Baptist Church. Congregants drive from as far as Bakersfield, almost two hours north through the Santa Susana and San Gabriel mountains, to attend various services in Cantonese, Mandarin, and English; the sidewalks and streets stream with families chatting in all three languages. As scattered as the Chinese-American community has become in Los Angeles, Chinatown still has a large cultural footprint. And services helpful to newcomers are concentrated here. Guan began taking Yan Jun to the church's preschool. There, she met other young families and got to know Warren Ng, a pastor who ministers to the Chinese-speaking immigrant population. "Where new immigrants go really depends on their economic status, and where their relatives are," Ng told me when I visited the church. The Chinese are accustomed to relying on strong kinship networks—he knows one congregant alone who eventually drew in thirteen separate families. "If they come in with a load of cash, they will probably buy a house somewhere in San Gabriel. They have plenty of options. If they are not as well-to-do and don't know English, and they need to assimilate into American society, then Chinatown is the first step."

To Guan, Chinatown was that first step. "China is so far away, but to come to a place where you see some of your own people, it makes you happier," Guan told me. A block away from the church is the school, Castelar Elementary. The ladies in the school's main office speak Cantonese, and so does the principal, Cheuk Choi. An immigrant himself in the post-1965 wave, Choi grew up in Chinatown and also speaks Toisanese and Mandarin. Because of this, neighborhood parents feel a certain closeness with the school. "If they want to yell at the principal, they can yell at the principal," Choi, a lively, easygoing man in his fifties, observed. He chuckled. "And the principal will understand what they're yelling about."

Even after Yan Jun began kindergarten at Castelar, she kept up with her friends in the church's after-school programs and at Sunday school. When her sister Tina got old enough, she enrolled in a preschool program right next door to the elementary school. On some mornings, after Guan dropped the girls at school, she went to school herself, squeezing in English lessons at the adult school down the street. She also started working part-time as a dim sum server at a popular Hong Kong-style restaurant called Ocean Seafood.

Though life in America was still challenging, the days had acquired a rhythm and a routine. Then the fire happened, and the family's hard work seemed to go up in smoke. Despair began to creep in.

Here was a chance to move out of Chinatown. But they did not.

To her surprise, Guan found that her daughter did not want to leave Chinatown. "After the fire, I asked Yan Jun, 'Do you want to go live somewhere else, maybe go to a different school?'" she told me. The incident had given Yan Jun—normally a relaxed and bubbly girl—an anxious air. "But she said, 'No, I like it here. I want to stay.'"

When I asked Warren Ng about Guan, he said that her family situation epitomizes the new generation of immigrants in Chinatown. "There are reasons for her to stay in Chinatown," he said. Since there is no set system for settlement assistance once people arrive in this country, it's no wonder that new immigrants rely on ethnic community and family ties, if they have them. Guan's in-laws live in Chinatown, and her mother-in-law's own mother lives in China-town's senior housing. One generation pulls in another—that is the strength of traditional Chinese family ties. But once in Chinatown, it's not so easy to leave. Everyone depends upon each other and the long-standing community network for their needs. And so, for now, Guan stays.

ON THE SURFACE, what brings a recent immigrant like Guan to Chi-natown seems to have little to do with why second-generation kids like Annie Luong come to Chinatown. But their lives do intersect. Like Guan, Annie's parents were drawn into Chinatown as newcom-ers by the comfort and convenience of a place that recognized and understood them. Though they moved away, the connections still exist for their daughter. Kinship ties—the word-of-mouth recom-mendations, the chain migration settlement patterns—have created a remarkably connected community for the Chinese in America. It's why even today, as historian Peter Kwong explains, "new Chinese immigrants still favor the three main cities and their surrounding suburbs—San Francisco, Los Angeles, and New York—that were the oldest and earliest Chinese settlements in the country."

In Chinatown, Annie sees the connections all around her. Her brother plays basketball on the courts at the church, and she has a friend who volunteers there as a tutor. They view the institution as yet another Chinatown hangout. Everybody knows somebody, and that somebody knows you—that's the connectivity of Chinatown. "It's more community than religious," Annie told me. "For a lot of people, it makes them feel better that the church speaks their own language. I mean, I would join if I were in their shoes as a new immi-grant. It's a place to meet new people."

Chinatown persists because of the community network. And because L.A.'s upwardly mobile Chinese have created other heavily Chinese enclaves outside of Chinatown, like Monterey Park, the San Gabriel Valley, and Alhambra, a life begun in Chinatown can lead to those places as well. For the Chinatown Chinese, they are neighborhoods to aspire to, and their residents remain connected to Chinatown through institutions like the church and other kinship ties. In San Francisco, the network stretches from Chinatown to the Richmond, Visitacion Valley, and Oakland across the bay; in New York, it connects Chinatown to Flushing, Sunset Park, and other pockets of Queens, Brooklyn, and Long Island.

How much she had become part of the Chinatown community wasn't actually apparent to Guan until after the fire. She was startled by the response of the people in the community when they heard about her family's plight.

One morning after she'd dropped Yan Jun off at school, Guan and I met in the busy and brightly lit main office, where flowers and colorful paper animals from the Chinese zodiac served as cheerful decorations. Her close-cropped hair and glasses were conservative, but it was the serious expression she wrote that gave her the look of someone older than her thirty-six years. We sat on a bench along one wall of the office, and she told me about some of the things that happened in the aftermath of the fire. That day, she was wearing clothes that were too big for her. They were garments donated to her by friends and acquaintances, since all of her own belongings were choked with smoke and soot from the fire.

The pastors and the Sunday school teachers at the church held a collection for Guan and her family—a big financial help. "They came to visit my daughter at the hospital a lot," Guan said, in Cantonese. "And when we couldn't find a place to live, when we were living in a hotel, the Sunday school teachers were still visiting us, visiting Yan Jun."

Two visitors in particular moved Guan—a husband and wife who are members of the church. The husband is a fireman, and the wife a former teacher. "They both work with youth," Guan explained. When the couple found out about the apartment fire, they drove from Orange County to visit Guan and Yan Jun in the hospital. They were stuck in freeway traffic for hours, but they still came. The most recent trip they'd made was just the week before, to see the new apartment and talk to the family about fire and electrical safety precautions. They also offered to help with "English things"—to talk to the landlord, lawyer, or insurance people, if the family wanted. "They live in Orange County, past Newport Beach—it's a far way from Chinatown," Guan said. "To drive here on the freeway, it's a long drive and the freeway is always jammed. But they still got to us somehow. Even though gas is so expensive now, they are willing to sacrifice time, and money, and energy to visit us. The woman had a brace, from a past car accident, she had her arm put up in a sling like my daughter. She was in pain, but she still came. She used to be a teacher, and she got these two big language arts and math textbooks, and she offered to teach Yan Jun when she was at the hotel, for a couple of hours at a time. Yan Jun was out of school for almost a month, and she didn't want her to fall behind." Her eyes widened in emphasis. "She really wanted to help her."

Cheuk Choi, Castelar's principal, also came to visit often, as did Yan Jun's teachers and school friends. They wrote letters, drew cards, and made signs that read "Get Well Soon." When I asked Guan how all the attention made her feel, she became quiet.

"Normally, in this day and age, this society seems to me not that kind," Guan said hesitantly, struggling to articulate her thoughts. "The world is practical—when people have money, they can do what they want. If you don't have money, maybe they make fun of you. But sometimes when you're down and out, people really come together and help you." She pointed to her clothes. "The clothes they give you to wear, it doesn't fit you exactly, but you see that they have the heart, they care to bring you things to try to help you. It made me see that this community cares about us. It showed me that people are not so cold after all."

■ ■ ■

ONE OF THE neighborhood pillars Guan leaned on was Cheuk Choi. Choi began working at Castelar Elementary School as a teacher in 1978. From his high school years in Chinatown to his most recent decade spent as principal, Choi has observed a shifting population move through the community. After the early wave that populated Los Angeles's three Chinatowns with Toisanese and other Cantonese immigrants, the next generation continued to establish businesses and raise their own families. In the late sixties and seventies, most Chinese came through Hong Kong as refugees from Communist China, as Choi did, since the United States had no relationship with China itself. After the fall of Saigon in 1975, ethnic Chinese from Vietnam began streaming into Chinatown. "A lot of them found their way West—I think the weather was more familiar," Choi told me. Many also ended up in Hawaii. In the eighties, there was another wave of refugees, this time from Cambodia. In his school, he began to see names no one could pronounce, and he held sessions to familiarize his staff with the students who were coming in. He had to give some of the students American names just to get them out of trouble. In the early eighties, due to overcrowding—there were more than 1,300 students for a school meant to hold only 800—Castelar moved to a year-round schedule.

Choi had the unenviable task of keeping track of all the students. "I put everyone into the one computer we had, and I found that a lot of them were sharing the same address—a *lot* of them," he recalled. "It was really amazing. I know we have limited housing here in Chinatown, but we had thirteen hundred students here. And we never checked the addresses before. So we went and visited some of the homes. It really surprised us, how people were living. There was one three-bedroom apartment, which was quite luxurious at that time. But the owners had converted it into a four-family apartment: three families would get a bedroom, and the unlucky one would get the living room. So you had tons of people in there. That was really an eye-opener." Choi and other school staff looked in on several more students' homes, and found the same situation. "Most of them were refugees—they couldn't afford it, so they shared. They said, 'This is a lot better than the refugee camp. We got running water with a bathroom. At least we have a room of our own. We got privacy.' To them, it was much better than where they were."

After 1985, Choi saw the numbers from mainland China go up, first gradually, then at a rapid-fire pace, as China began to open itself to the world. "The names have all changed to Mandarin-style English spellings—no more Hong Kong spelling, no more Vietnamese spelling," Choi told me. "They're all from the mainland. So again we had to deal with the names." He remembers one incident in particular about a decade ago, when one boy, a brand-new immigrant from the Toisan region, raised a ruckus in class and was sent to his office. "I asked him, 'What's the problem? Sit down, I don't bite. I speak your language.' He said, 'Well, they're making fun of me. They're making fun of my name.' So he was having, in a way, an identity crisis. Just like me. The first day I stepped into a local school here. The teacher looked at my pink slip, and I knew, he had a difficult time. I did not have an American name—I had a Chinese name. Cheuk. He didn't know how to say it. Because in my native tongue, Toisanese, it was very different. Different in Cantonese, and also different in Mandarin. Mandarin in my day, it was not an issue. But now it is. So the boy said, 'Well, they're calling me all kinds of names.' His classmates were a mix, not just Toisanese. You could have ABCs here, you could have Vietnamese Chinese, you could have Mandarin Chinese. Everybody said his name different. So he was totally uncomfortable with whatever they were calling him. The teacher didn't know, either. So I said, okay, I understand what the problem is.

"I took him back, and I talked to the whole class. 'This is the way his name has been since he was born.' In Toisanese, it's Git Bong.

But in Hong Kong Cantonese, it's Geet Bong. And in Mandarin, it's Zhe Bong. So what do they call him? Gee Bang! Well, you've been raised Git Bong, and they are calling you Gee Bang! So I explained to the class, 'This is the name he's been known his whole life, he's eleven years old. And you guys have been calling him something totally different. Wouldn't you be upset?' And they said, 'Oh, yeah, you're right, Mr. Choi.' So I assigned some of them to work with him. And now he's fine. I saw him maybe three years ago, he was graduating from high school. I played against him in a basketball game." He grinned. "They always want to beat the principal."

Out of the 760 kids currently enrolled in the school, about 600 were born in the United States, and more than a hundred were born in China. But Choi says that though the numbers from China to Chinatown are still high, it's not as high as it used to be. "Many immigrants have more options," he told me. "They go away from Chinatown. If they have any money at all, they will go to Arcadia, or San Marino." His voice dropped to a comical whisper, and he confided that a lot of Chinese government officials have been buying up houses in Arcadia with piles of cash. "But Chinatown is still the working-class neighborhood. These kids, their parents are restaurant workers, garment workers, handymen. It's still that gateway."

The family and friend connections, he says, are a balm for new immigrant families. "It's scary to venture into someplace you totally have no knowledge of," Choi said.

When I first visited him one afternoon after school had let out, Choi was chatting in Cantonese with a mother and a young daughter in a Dodgers baseball cap. He later told me that the mother was one of his students from his first year of teaching at Castelar. "This is the third child she has who is coming through the school," he said. "She and her husband, who's Caucasian, actually moved *back* to Chinatown, because she wanted her kids to go to school here . the way she did." Here in Chinatown, longtime connections and trusted relationships carry weight across the generations. Newer immigrants like Guan are at the end of a kinship chain that can stretch back decades, to people like Choi.

"I stayed here in Chinatown because I came as an immigrant," Choi told me. "I struggled through. I went to the local high school here. In those days, there weren't that many Chinese. You could count them. You knew who everyone was. In high school, I saw a lot of issues with gangs here. I saw a hopelessness. They didn't want to go to school. I saw that problem. We were all immigrants. All of our parents were struggling the same way."

GUAN DIDN'T WANT to come to America at first, but she saw that it would be better for her children here. "I want them to have more," she said. "It's tougher to come here as an adult, but one day, my daughters will be able to do whatever they want—they will know English, they can study, they can find good work. They can do it on their own. In China, if you don't have money, you don't have a chance."

It was time for her to begin her shift at the restaurant, so we walked the few blocks from the school together. She told me that her favorite dim sum dishes are *shumai*—pork and mushroom dumplings—and *ha gow*, steamed shrimp wrapped in a thin, translucent dough. When she sees Americans come to the restaurant, she is proud that they like Chinese food—that they appreciate and seek out her culture.

Guan continues to experience new things herself. "When my husband first saw snow on the road, he took a photo of it with his cell phone to show us," she told me quietly, with a smile. "He's been to a lot of places. So whenever he sees something special, he takes a picture of it so we can see it, too."

As we walked, Guan told me that even though her husband finds his job tough—he sleeps inside the cab of his truck and keeps a rice cooker there to save money while on the road—he enjoys the things that it allows him to see. "The accident—I never dreamed that when we came to America that this would happen, that my daughter would be hurt," she said. "It has become for me—I feel very sad, very unhappy that she is scared at night when the phone rings and cannot sleep without me near her. And that she will always have a scar, on her arm, and on her leg, where they took her skin." Tears came to her eyes.

What Guan does not want is for Yan Jun to become afraid of life here. More and more, their extended network of friends and family leads them outside of Chinatown. Friends have taken Yan Jun to places like Disneyland, while Guan and her husband have begun to drive to other cities, go to parties, and visit friends. Guan drew concentric circles with her hands. "I feel that after you live here for a little while, and this becomes familiar, you need to slowly go outside. See other things, get to know other things." She paused, and remembered a well-known Chinese saying. "You can't be like a frog at the bottom of a well. When he looks up, the sky is only as big as the opening at the top. It's the same sky, but if you're at the bottom of the well, the sky is very small. There's more to what you can see, if you open your mind. The sky is very big. You should go out there, stick your neck out, see things that are further." With her hands, she indicated a widening horizon of where they can go. "I know America is bigger than Chinatown. I want my daughter to feel that, too."

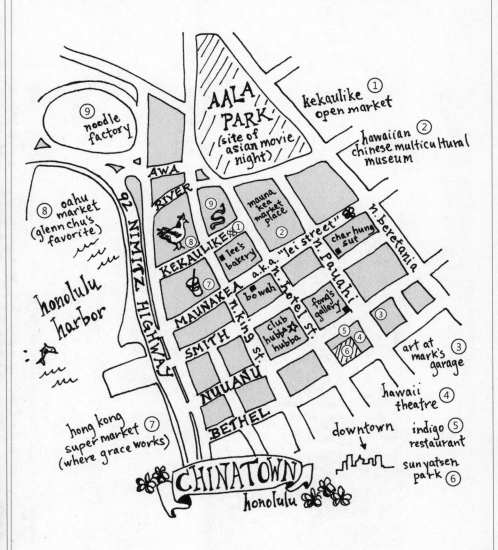

noodle factory ⑨

AALA PARK (site of asian movie night)

kekaulike open market ①

hawaiian chinese multicultural museum ②

oahu market (glenn chu's favorite) ⑧

AWA RIVER

92 NIMITZ HIGHWAY

honolulu harbor

KEKAULIKE

⑨

⑧

①

lee's bakery

mauna kea market place

"lei street" a.k.a. N. hotel st.

② N. pauahi

char hung sut

N. beretania

MAUNAKEA

⑦

bo wah

N. king st.

fong's gallery

③

art at mark's garage ③

SMITH

club hubba hubba

⑤

④

⑥

NUUANU

hawaii theatre ④

BETHEL

downtown

indigo restaurant ⑤

sun yat sen park ⑥

hong kong super market (where grace works) ⑦

CHINATOWN honolulu

Fong Chan and Lum Bok, Honolulu. *Bonnie Tsui*

TEN

KAPAKAHI CHINATOWN

Where "all mixed up" is the enduring story.

Hawaii's famously fusion culture owes a lot to its location. Smack in the middle of the Pacific, the archipelago has always served as a crossroads between East and West, first visited by the Chinese in 1789. In Honolulu, Chinatown touches the water where the first shiploads of Chinese laborers disembarked in the 1850s, destined for the sugar plantations. As the neighborhood took shape along Honolulu Harbor, closely tied to the industry of the sea—in fact, heavy granite blocks used as ship ballast from China became paving stones for the sidewalks of Chinatown—it continued to serve as the gateway for a flood of Asian immigrants over the years. It was not just the Chinese but Japanese, Koreans, Filipinos, and Vietnamese who found a home in Chinatown. Like the rest of island culture, the neighborhood became a jumble—*kapakahi*, Hawaiian for all mixed up.

Honolulu was the first place I remember feeling at home as a Chinese American, within and without Chinatown. A close friend who grew up along Oahu's shores and knew my love for all things aquatic introduced me to life here. With my brown skin and Chinese heritage, I blended in. More than half of Honolulu's population is Asian. Everywhere you look, Chinese traditions have made their way into Hawaiian life. *Li hing mui*, the preserved, salted plums that the Chinese ate with rice on the long journey to the islands, evolved into crack seed, the mouth-puckering snack that every local kid is weaned on. Chinese New Year is a monthlong affair that involves the entire city in its celebrations. Sweet red bean paste ended up at the bottom of the quintessential Hawaiian shave ice, flavored with syrups like lychee and guava. Chinese lion dances entertain at weddings and at baby luaus, held on a child's first birthday. And if you page through the Oahu phone book, there are more Changs than Smiths, more Lums than Joneses.

In a city where the Chinese have been around a long time—and where Chinatown itself has long been a mix of cultures—you might think that Chinatown's glory days have been relegated to the history books. But look closer and you'll see that its story is essentially the story that is unfolding in Chinatowns all over America today: how a traditional Chinese neighborhood can evolve into something else while still staying Chinese. Over the course of the twentieth century, this Chinatown has played many roles: as the thriving social center of 1930s Honolulu; as a red-light district for GI's during World War II; and, most recently, as a downtown arts district. Throughout it all, the neighborhood has somehow endured as a Chinese cultural touchstone. A recent Chinese immigrant still looks to Chinatown as a place of refuge; a fourth-generation local still comes here to fill in the blanks of his knowledge. And when they do, it's not unusual for them to end up in Fong Chan's pristine, art-filled shop, examining a piece of the past.

FONG, as everyone calls him, owns a glass-walled gallery at the edge of Chinatown, on the corner of Nuuanu Avenue and Pauahi Street. As in many urban centers, the alchemy of gritty second- and third-floor apartments, cheap rent, and proximity to downtown have attracted working artists. In high-rent Honolulu, the neighborhood has the unique distinction of being the only place where significant stretches of dilapidated buildings remain. Fong, who immigrated to Honolulu in the late 1970s, was among the early arts pioneers to begin living and working here during the eighties.

The idea of an artsy Chinatown appealed to me. My father, himself a painter, nearly moved our family to Honolulu in the seventies, and as I started talking to people in the streets and shops of the city, I tried to picture an alternative girlhood that saw, in fits and starts, a blighted, run-down Chinatown made over by art. One warm winter morning, I entered Fong's gallery, drawn by the luminous window displays: hanging ropes of pearly, amber-hued beads, delicate jade figurines, firecracker-red bowls with scalloped edges. The first words I heard—"So how come there's a Chinatown here?"—were revealing, and they came from a middle-aged Canadian tourist dressed in khakis and an aloha shirt. He told Fong he was visiting from Vancouver. Fong smiled patiently and adjusted his glasses; he explained to the man how the sugarcane industry in Hawaii started drawing large numbers of laborers from China in the 1850s. The customer's wife, who had been peering into a display case of tiny Hawaiian-style shell earrings designed by Fong and crafted in Vietnam, turned her attention to the proprietor.

"We have a big Chinatown in Vancouver, too—I just love going," she enthused. "I think it's fascinating that there are Chinatowns everywhere." I listened as Fong obliged the couple's request for more commentary, sketching out a broad historical picture: sugar, and then pineapple, brought many Chinese to Honolulu, around the same time that gold and railroads drew other Chinese to California; many sojourners came from southeast China because it was a port region with a long seafaring tradition. There were long-standing ties between China and many countries, he explained, including Vietnam, where he was born. He showed his audience rare objets d'art to illustrate his points: a lipstick-red seventeenth-century Chinese vase that used French techniques for oxidizing gold to achieve its

eye-popping color, eighteenth-century porcelain created for the Vietnamese royal court by Chinese artisans.

"I know about this piece because it has been handed down in
my family for three generations," he said, holding up a ceramic pot
delicately threaded with blue. On the bottom of the Chinese-made
porcelain was the signature red stamp of the Vietnamese royal family. He described the delicate vertical brushstrokes, which revealed
the traditional techniques of a Chinese master artisan. Though
Fong was reared in Saigon—in Cholon, that city's own Chinatown
district—his father gave him a rigorous education in Chinese arts
and culture. As a boy, Fong even studied under a famous Chinese
master painter from Guangzhou. Art, he said, was in his blood.

Later, I asked Fong to tell me more about his connection to
Honolulu Chinatown. In this mixed-up place, he said, he felt at
home. Was it because he was Asian? Or was it because he spoke
Vietnamese, English, and four different dialects of Chinese?

"From the beginning, I was very comfortable here," Fong told
me. He pulled up a high-backed antique chair and invited me to sit
down. "I like the cross-culture. That is what I am. And that is what
Hawaii is."

IN THE WINTER of 1979, Fong Chan arrived in Honolulu with only
his brother and the shorts and T-shirts on his thin frame. Born into
a well-to-do Chinese family in Vietnam, he was a nineteen-year-old
refugee who had barely escaped the country with his life.

Fong's family had moved to Vietnam in the late 1940s from
Fujian, fleeing the Communist takeover of China. Thirty years later,
they were forced to flee again in the aftermath of the Vietnam War,
when the Vietnamese government began to repress the country's
Chinese minority. The ethnic Chinese refugees became known as
the "boat people," and Fong says that 1979 was the worst year for

those who were trying to get out of the country. His parents sent him away first, with one brother and one sister in his care. On the twenty-eight-foot fishing boat that ferried him from Vietnam, there were 270 people piled six-deep on top of one another. The boat was one of five that traveled in a flotilla, and all of the vessels were forced to stop by various military forces on beaches in Thailand and Malaysia. He was robbed thirteen times on the journey. "Men and women, we were all naked on the boat, hoping that raiders would leave us alone," Fong told me. "People were raped and beaten. After so many times, you don't care no more. We just want them to finish so we can get food and drink. All these kinds of things—they are real. My sister was separated from us. It was only two years later that our family found out she ended up in Australia." There were times, Fong said, when he contemplated suicide. Eventually, his drifting boat came ashore in Indonesia, where fishermen rescued the surviving passengers. After some months, a woman with the Red Cross helped Fong and his brother get sponsorship in Hawaii.

When he finally made it to Honolulu, he told me, he was "a jungle man." His skin was dark from constant exposure to the sun; he had been wearing the same pair of shorts for an entire year. All the possessions he had taken with him on the journey from Vietnam had been stolen. "We grew up in a very good family, a wealthy family, and in a good neighborhood, too. But suddenly, everything changed." He motioned to the floor. "I was at the bottom, and I had to raise myself from there."

Fong found something familiar in the warmth of Hawaii. With the help of a welfare case worker, he got a job at a picture framing shop. It was the thing that would eventually allow him to get closer to the work—the art—that he knew. But above all, he needed money. "All the hope I had for my parents, my other sisters still in Vietnam . . . I didn't know what would happen to them," Fong recalled. He kept in touch with his family through frequent letters and worked as much as he could, with the intention of bringing them over to join him and his brother in Honolulu as soon as possible. He learned quickly—the shop manager saw that he had experience handling art—and after a year, he became a supervisor. A year and a half after that, he managed production in five stores. Then he quit and opened his own art gallery, working out of the basement of a house in Kalihi, a couple of miles from Chinatown. Every month, he sent his parents the little bit of money he had saved—first a hundred dollars at a time, then more, as his paintings sold. His brother, who found work as an interpreter for Vietnamese refugees at Honolulu's help centers, did the same.

By that time, in the mid-eighties, Fong had begun living in Chinatown, in a small apartment on Maunakea Street, where he still resides. "I thought, hmm, I am Chinese, and somehow here I feel a part of the culture my family taught me when I was very young," he told me. As a child, he sat down every morning with his father for lessons in traditional Chinese drawing and poetry. As an adult, he began to think it would be useful to work in an environment that felt culturally connected to his roots, so he moved his workspace and gallery to Chinatown, two doors down from where his current gallery is located.

Chinatown was seriously down on its luck. The open-air markets were busy with people during the day, but at night, the area emptied. On Pauahi Street, Fong watched prostitutes, drug dealers, and the homeless congregate outside his door. But he didn't feel threatened. "I was a rock," he said, referring to the changes wrought in his character by the harrowing experiences that had brought him to Honolulu. Life in Chinatown felt easy by comparison. Little by little, he and his neighbors got used to each other.

As in other American Chinatowns during the period, Cantonese was the primary dialect spoken. Fong was fluent in both Cantonese and Mandarin, but the latter was rarely used in Chinatown, and he never heard any Vietnamese at all. Part of the reason for that, he says, was the racism within the Chinese community against the boat people. The larger community looked down on the boat people for being from Vietnam—perceived as a poor and lesser country—even though they, too, were ethnically Chinese. Up until that point, most Chinese immigrants to Hawaii came from Zhongshan, a city in Guangdong Province that, like Toisan, was a source of overseas Chinese. It is the birthplace of Sun Yat-sen; before he founded the Nationalist Party and overthrew the Qing Dynasty to become the father of modern China, he was educated as a boarding student at Honolulu's elite Iolani School. Since 1997, Zhongshan has been designated the Chinese "sister city" to Honolulu.

"There were some Chinese here who discriminated against me for not being Chinese Chinese," Fong told me. "Twenty years ago, I would be in a Chinese restaurant, reading a Chinese menu and trying to speak with the servers in Chinese, and they would speak to me in English." Many Vietnamese immigrants, he said, would pretend they didn't speak Vietnamese. "They don't want people to know that they're refugees, or that they come from a poor country. If people ask them, they say, 'I come from Hong Kong,' or 'I come from Taiwan.' I say, 'No way, I can hear your accent. Please—just be happy who you are.' In fact, I'm more proud that I was poor, I was dead broke, and now I survived. I came up again."

Eventually, Fong says, people in the community came around to something like acceptance. "They can hear that I speak Cantonese, I speak Mandarin, I can read and write Chinese very well. They are surprised, and they say, 'Okay, you are Chinese.'" As was happening on the mainland, the mixing in of newer immigrants into Honolulu's Chinatown began to turn an older, entrenched idea of what was Chinese on its head.

■ ■ ■

AFTER A FEW YEARS, Fong came to be known in Chinatown for his deep knowledge of traditional Chinese art, and more people began visiting his shop, looking for conversation. He showed his own contemporary landscape paintings, many of them portraying Hawaii, alongside antique calligraphy scrolls and wood carvings; despite their differing subjects and styles, all illustrated traditional Chinese techniques. The Honolulu Academy of Arts and the art programs at Kapiolani Community College sent students for talks with him in his gallery. He says he was glad to do it. "As much as I know about Chinese culture, I will share it," he said. "If you keep it all too secret, like was the tradition, it won't grow. You have to discover new things, too, and add to your knowledge."

Some years ago, students from the Honolulu Academy of Arts came to look at artwork in Fong's gallery. Among the group were two older students from Hong Kong. At the request of the teacher, Fong began to explain a few concepts of Chinese history, the origin of Chinese petroglyphs, and how petroglyphs evolved into modern-day Chinese characters. The two students, Fong recalled, would not even look at him out of the corners of their eyes. "They looked at the ceiling, at the art, anywhere but at me. They pretended like they didn't care what I had to say," Fong said. That day, he explained the origin of the two words for "fortune" and "love": *fook* and *oy*.

In Chinese characters, Fong explained, all the pictures are present to reveal to the reader the meaning of a word. He sketched out the pictographs and the corresponding characters on a piece of paper to show me what he meant. In *fook*, a person stands on the left side of the character, with material for clothes to cover the body. On the right side, there is a mark for "one," and a mouth, and a grid to represent land. "Good fortune, then, means that you have clothes for warmth, you have land, and you have food coming from that land to feed yourself," Fong said. "What more do you want? You have fortune already. It's a very simple, very elegant way to show the meaning."

In the word for love, *oy*, the two strokes at the top of the character indicate the roof of a house. Inside the house, there is a heart, as
well as two people, which represents friendship. "So you have under
one roof two people sharing one heart," Fong explained. "That is
love. It's beautiful." On the day he taught this lesson to the students
in his gallery, they listened. When he finished, the two Hong Kong
students came over to shake his hand. They told him they were
impressed by his deep knowledge of Chinese culture—knowledge
that they themselves had never had.

In 1990, Fong was finally able to bring his parents and four sisters to Honolulu. His other sister stayed in Australia, where she
raised a family of her own. Throughout the rest of that decade,
he observed larger numbers of Vietnamese making their home in
Chinatown. On some blocks today, there are as many signs in Vietnamese as Chinese, and the densest cluster of *pho* houses—shops
serving traditional Vietnamese noodle soup—is sometimes called
Little Saigon. Mirroring settlement patterns elsewhere, Taiwanese
and mainland Chinese immigrants also arrived in the nineties, but
many settled outside of Chinatown.

Honolulu Chinatown continues to be made up of people coming
from everywhere: Taiwan, China, Vietnam, Laos, and the Philippines. But even with the intermingling, Chinatown remains the center of Chinese life in Honolulu, with more than 100 organizations
active in the community. The Chinese still have a historic claim on
the neighborhood, and an inclination to stand slightly apart from
the rest. "After all this time, it's still a Chinatown," James Ho, a
local historian, told me. I found this intriguing duality of identity—
a simultaneous inclusion and exclusion—evident in the name of
Ho's museum and archives: the Hawaiian Chinese Multicultural
Museum. "Chinatown is not just Chinese," he said. "But it means
everything to us in terms of Chinese culture."

■ ■ ■

IN TRUTH, Honolulu Chinatown has always been less of a ghetto than other major American Chinatowns. The dispersal of the Chinese community from Chinatown into the rest of society happened early in Hawaii, says Sen-dou Chang, a recently retired geography professor at the University of Hawaii. Honolulu Chinatown acted as a Chinese ghetto only during its first fifty years. "Even in those years," he wrote in a 2003 essay, "Honolulu's Chinatown was not really a ghetto as only a little more than half its population were Chinese." In Hawaii, the Chinese were not prevented from acquiring land, as they were on the American mainland. Chang says that this is a key reason that the Chinese were able to leave Honolulu Chinatown as early as the 1880s; today they have the highest percentage of land ownership among all ethnic groups. Chinatown continued to function as an important social center, as other key American Chinatowns did, but the Chinese community here was unique in its ability to integrate into larger society when its counterparts were still ghettoized on the mainland.

That's not to say that this Chinatown and its people had an easy time of it. The neighborhood endured earthquakes, vermin infestations, and the bubonic plague; fires in 1886 and 1900 burned it to the ground. As in San Francisco Chinatown after the 1906 earthquake, many saw the Honolulu Chinatown fires as fortunate events—opportunities presented by "a higher power" to create a "sweeter, healthier" town. Actually, the 1900 fire was purposely set by the city's department of health, to rid certain buildings in the quarter of the bubonic plague; it raged out of control, burning 5,000 homes and razing a fifth of Honolulu.

James Ho says that Chinatown here has never been like any other Chinatown in the world. Even before San Francisco and Honolulu established their Chinatowns, Hawaii had important relations with China. "The sandalwood trade began in the 1790s—that's what brought the Chinese to Hawaii," Ho told me. Much of the sandalwood was shipped to Hong Kong, hence its name—in Chinese,

Hong Kong means "fragrant port." The first Chinese settlement in the Kingdom of Hawaii was actually in Lahaina, Maui. Since the pioneer Chinese workers were all men, many of them married Hawaiian women. "We all have Hawaiian blood," Ho said. He pointed to himself and to his cousin, the late, popular singer Don Ho, as prime examples of cultural mixing (Ho the entertainer was known to be of Hawaiian, Chinese, Portuguese, and other descent).

After the 1900 fire, Chinatown was rebuilt, and over the course of the twentieth century, it took on different mantles for Honolulu. By the 1930s, it was a thriving downtown hangout. James Ho, also a veteran of World War II, describes the Chinatown of the following decade as a "honky tonk," with brothels, bars, and strip clubs catering to thousands of GI's on leave. Years of decline followed, and the area became a vice zone for drug dealers, prostitutes, and the homeless. In 1973, the federal government listed Chinatown on the National Register of Historic Places, and so began the city cleanup. It was a slow renaissance.

Nowadays, galleries stay open late and serve wine on the first Friday of every month, drawing crowds of young hipsters to Chinatown after dark; the fact that long-established artists, including Ramsay and Pegge Hopper, have galleries here has given the area real artistic cachet. A recent exhibition called "Chinatown, HI" took over the popular Arts at Mark's Garage gallery, borrowing many artifacts—a stunning Cantonese opera costume in embroidered pink silk, a ceremonial drum—from the Hawaiian Chinese Multicultural Museum and showing them alongside prints and Chinese landscapes of modern Honolulu by artists like Guo Liang Cai; performance artists from the neighborhood also put on shows. Lounge rooms and bars with boudoir décors and names like Opium Den give a nod to scandalous attractions of years past (like Hotel Street's World War II–era Club Hubba Hubba, now boarded up but with come-hither neon sign still intact). A monthly short-film challenge, "Showdown in Chinatown," was created as a jump-start showcase for local independent filmmakers. With all the new activity, the city's mayor goes so far as to call Honolulu "the only city where the culture and arts are centered in Chinatown." While that stretches the truth for the sake of marketing—homelessness, lack of affordable housing, and other issues of urban blight are everyday concerns for residents, and many areas feel threateningly vacant at night—a revitalized Chinatown has drawn many back to the neighborhood.

Roy Venters, a local artist and another early pioneer in Chinatown, thinks that as long as the neighborhood continues to include working people and isn't too driven by tourism and gentrification, it will thrive. He added that longtime residents like Fong Chan have a unique view when it comes to assessing what the more recent changes in Chinatown will bring. "Fong understands the Chinese side, the Vietnamese side, and the art side—he's a kind of Renaissance man," Venters told me. "He has a mixed perspective, which is what Hawaii is."

VISITORS MAY COME to Fong's gallery looking for someone to tell them about Chinatown, but Chinatown the community also comes calling, to talk about itself. I watched neighbors stop in every morning to say hello, share art-book finds, and examine the latest antiques that Fong brought back from China or Vietnam or the mainland. People came to gossip, to connect. A shy artist named Dennis Yung came with the express purpose of looking at a favorite piece of antique Chinese jade. He visits Chinatown weekly; he and Fong exchanged stories about a famous Chinese brush painter with whom Yung studied at the University of Hawaii. Chinese stick with Chinese, they agreed, even here. Another local, a middle-aged woman named Marianne Mok, stopped in the store with red plastic shopping bag in hand to ask Fong about an exhibit of Buddhist relics he was organizing; she worked a few blocks away in the business district and often picked up produce and pastries in Chinatown. Her mother was Cantonese, she told me when I asked her what coming here meant to her. Now Chinatown is the place where she herself goes to shop and hear the language.

One frequent visitor to Fong's shop told me that his gallery was like a museum to her. But if it's a museum, it's a living one. It reflects a shifting neighborhood that continues to grow and change as the generations come and go. Perhaps most tellingly, it is a gathering place that shows the enduring links between those generations. On several mornings, a tiny, white-haired man peered in the front door and rapped on the glass. Every time, Fong greeted him heartily. "Lum Bok!" he called out—Uncle Lum—using the Cantonese honorific for a respected elder.

At our first meeting, Lum Bok grinned at me and asked, in Cantonese, if I was looking for art. Then he asked me what kind of people I was. "New York has a lot of Toisanese people," he said in response. "Here in Honolulu, we have more Zhongshan people!" He walked around the store in a familiar way, picking up objects and using a little magnifying glass to inspect the glaze on a ceramic vase or the pattern on a piece of jewelry.

Lum Bok, it turned out, was once a major collector and dealer on Hollywood Road, Hong Kong's well-known antique row. Like Fong, he immigrated to Honolulu at the end of the 1970s; worrying about the eventual return of Hong Kong to China, Lum Bok closed his shop and moved his family to Honolulu. Every couple of days, he pays a visit to Fong's shop to look at and talk about Chinese art. Fong says that when Lum Bok visits, the two men become "like children."

"Somehow, Chinese is still looking for Chinese," Fong said, watching his friend examine a miniature carved-wood cricket case. "Even though we aren't in China anymore. You look for your home. Chinatown is like that. So far and so near at the same time. For most people, it's food. But for him, it's the art, a memory, a story." Here, he gestured at me. "Like when he asks you where your people are from. It's a connection between you and him. Maybe later, it will remind him of something else."

The inclusiveness of Honolulu, he says, is what makes it a good place to live. To this end, he shares what he knows with Chinese and non-Chinese alike. Twelve years ago, he began donating his art collection to the Kapiolani Community College for permanent display. It's because he cannot take everything with him when he's gone. Adding other people to what he calls his chain of experience—with links through Vietnam, Indonesia, and Hawaii—is what Fong says keeps a changing culture connected to the past. Having a place to talk about Chinese traditions in Chinatown is a way to keep all of those links alive, "so you can look back and see how it all happened."

James Ho agrees that telling the history is crucial to showing how Chinese have integrated in Honolulu while retaining Chinese customs and traditions, since most people who come to Chinatown have no clue about it. He echoed what I heard in long-standing American Chinatowns from New York to San Francisco to Los Angeles: that insiders have an urge to connect their experiences across generations, and outsiders often have only a vague sense of the meaning the neighborhood holds for the city around it. They don't know that the first Chinese came to Hawaii in 1789, or that Chinatown took shape at the same time that Honolulu's downtown did. "People are astonished that there is so much Chinese history— and so much Hawaiian history—in Chinatown," he said. "And you know, here, you can't separate the two."

To many people here, Chinatown depends on the continuing dynamism of its mix. "I learned so much for my survival," Fong said. "I adapt to myself the positive for the negative. That is what Chinatown is doing. A lot of people say to me, 'So you were born in Vietnam, you are Chinese, you speak Indonesian, now you live in Hawaii. Who are you?'" He pointed to his pale-green Hawaiian shirt. "It's like this shirt. The fabric is manufactured in China, but the label is Hawaiian. This is a lei pattern, this is hibiscus, but the color is more contemporary, more Americanized. The culture here, it's unique. I can learn about things that are American, and I can still be proud of my older culture. As long as you remember where it all came from, there's nothing wrong with that."

Pig delivery at Oahu Market. *Ken Haig*

ELEVEN

NEIGHBORHOOD CROSSINGS

How a local boy became an accidental chef.

block from Honolulu Harbor, a wide pedestrian lane called Kekaulike runs between two rows of old brick buildings, lined with palm trees and cardboard boxes piled high with fragrant papayas, apple bananas, pineapples, and spiky, ruby-colored rambutan. Signs in Chinese advertise the different varieties of tropical produce. Just east of this open-air cornucopia is Maunakea Street, a riot of tiny lei stands in which the flower ladies of Chinatown have woven their delicate, pearly garlands for generations.

Among this Chinatown's distinctive qualities are its characteristic open markets and tropical air. At the end of Kekaulike, in the fish stalls of Oahu Market, Chinatown's oldest, Glenn Chu paced the floors. A fourth-generation, Honolulu-born Chinese American who owns a nationally noted restaurant in Chinatown, Chu is an accidental chef. It all began, he said, with his grandmother, a magnificent, magnanimous presence in his early life, and the trips he took with her and his mother to shop in Chinatown. For him, every space and stall here is a memory.

When Chu talks about Chinatown, his physical, geographical relationship with the neighborhood's streets, shops, and sellers makes itself known. We had in common our repeated tracings of ancestral footsteps, and that shared history, in the context of other people's shared histories, told me that there was something compelling in the act of crisscrossing Chinatown. So we took a walk around the neighborhood together one afternoon, and as we made our way past trays of tuna on ice and trucks stacked with large whole pigs, their flesh still pink, Chu told me it was in this way that he felt connected to his cultural heritage. "It's where my mother and grandmother shopped; it's where I shop," he said, pausing to examine an icy bed of *aku*, what Hawaiians call skipjack tuna. "At the same time it's everyday, it's profound."

The physicality of his relationship to Chinatown is familiar for many Chinese Americans—in Honolulu, and in the rest of America—whose families have been here for generations. It is a different kind of relationship than the one Fong Chan, a first-generation immigrant, has with the neighborhood. It is at once more removed, yet more intimate. Family history anchors them here. Candice Lee Kraughto moved to Honolulu Chinatown as an adult, with her husband. Her girlhood memories are of walks in Chinatown with her grandfather, and of him pointing out the 1916 rooming house where he lived and the bakery where he worked. Her routines today echo those tracks; she walks through Chinatown on weekday mornings to get to work downtown, and buys pastries every weekend from Lee's Bakery, down the street from her own apartment. In these tracings, she says, she keeps little bits of her heritage alive, and in that act, she's not alone.

As Chu and I passed by, one of the fish vendors recognized him and shouted out a greeting, and Chu, a slim man in black jeans and a faded black T-shirt, gave a wave. "I don't speak Chinese, and that hindered my getting to know certain people in Chinatown," he told me. "But I do know some of them very well." Oahu Market is his favorite place to buy sashimi. He buys most of the fish for his restaurant here. When Chu was growing up, his father often came to the market to buy seafood from a friend who owned a fishing boat. "My mom would clean the *aku* outside in the backyard, under a tree," he said. "It was very fragrant, with all these lovely flower blooms. She'd bury the fish guts and use it as fertilizer." People might complain about the smells they encounter in Chinatown's markets, or about how whole fish or animal carcasses are displayed, he said, but that's because American culture sanitizes the experience of buying meat. In Chinese culture, people are taught to use the entire animal, so that nothing goes to waste—the experiences of living and dying are connected. Chu said his grandmother's Taoist teachings showed him that animals make a sacrifice for him, so he should honor their lives by not putting them to waste.

As we stepped around to the rear of the market, Chu pointed out an area where he used to watch live chickens run around. "It has been cleaned up quite a bit—they don't have live chickens here anymore. But I was in Nanjing, China, not too long ago, and my hotel room overlooked a local market. There they had white and black chickens and ducks, and all sorts of fish, everything mixed up together. It was incredible to me—I said to myself, 'That was the market that used to be here!' You reflect back on how things used to be—something might not be there anymore, but you find it somewhere else." In other words, Glenn Chu finds his Chinatown wherever he goes.

CHU GREW UP in Honolulu, in Manoa, a verdant, jungly valley north of downtown that is famous locally for frequent rains and abundant rainbows. To this day, he will call a passing shower "Manoa mist," a local phrase that I love. It was Chu's great-grandfather who first came to Hawaii, in 1864, to work the sugar fields and bring sandalwood trees back to China. On our walk around Chinatown, Chu talked about his relationship to that heritage. "I can imagine him coming off the boat, and the boat would be just down the harbor here," he said, pointing to the water. "The streets in Chinatown go right into the water. It just brings me visions of having him— as well as everyone else who immigrated to Hawaii—coming right to the neighborhood off the harbor. As you can see, Chinatown is not very large, but the whole thing about it is the lure of together-ness. As with most Chinatowns—with the clubs, the associations, the families—the Chinese helped each other out."

Even though the Chinese dispersed from Honolulu's Chinatown early on, Chinatown remained a rendezvous spot almost because of that dispersal, Bill Lum, a trustee of the See Dai Doo Society, one of the most active Chinese associations in Hawaii, told me. Lum helped James Ho start the Hawaiian Chinese Multicultural Museum in 1994. Born in Honolulu in 1926, he calls himself "one of the dinosaurs." His family never lived in Chinatown—his parents were also born in Honolulu, and his father fought with the U.S. Army in World War I—but he grew up two and a half miles away, and his memories of coming to the neighborhood date back to the 1930s.

"Chinese from other areas wanted to meet friends, do their shop-ping, to purchase and cook Chinese stuff. So where do they come to get it? It's Chinatown, it's the gathering place," Lum said.

After the Japanese bombed Pearl Harbor, Glenn Chu's grand-mother moved from the outskirts of Chinatown to a large house on Vancouver Drive in Manoa—a house in which Chu and his par-ents, grandparents, three siblings, aunt, uncle, and two cousins all ended up living together. He remembered being the first Asian fam-ily on the block; their neighbors were the Silversteins. As Chu tells it, the Silverstein family kindly endured what must have been highly unusual goings-on at the house next door: fresh chickens butchered in the backyard, dried rice puffing up in woks atop the outdoor stove, a continuous stream of Chinese visitors.

"What my grandmother brought to this house was her culture

and her heritage," Chu told me. "In the back were her two wood-burning stoves and her two large woks. And she would have us go out and pick up *kiawe* wood, which is like mesquite—it burns very hot and is very fragrant to cook on. She would have these mahjong parties over at the house on Saturdays, with six tables going on at a time, and cook food for something like a hundred people every other week." In this de facto mahjong parlor, Chu grew up with a sense of Chinese community.

The habit was to bring something when you were invited to someone's house, and there was an endless parade of little pink boxes conveyed to the house from Char Hung Sut, a pork-bun shop in Chinatown that is still run by Chu's relatives. From Shung Chong Yuein, a venerable cake shop on Maunakea that recently closed its doors, guests brought moon cakes and other sweets that Chu's grandmother served with tea. These were the kinds of gifts, Chu says, that came from Chinatown to their house.

In Chu's childhood, Chinatown the community was something larger than the neighborhood's geographic boundaries. For Glenn Chu and Bill Lum, who both belong to generations of American-born Chinese for whom Chinatown was never a physical home, a connection to Chinatown as a cultural home was established in the action of going there, and of bringing pieces of it back to outside world. Part of it was practical—Chinatown was the only place to get the traditional things their families wanted—but the act itself became the tradition. "We piled into the station wagon and parked on Kekaulike Street, where the pedestrian mall and low-income housing are now," Chu said. "And we would shop for fresh produce—of course, we're Chinese, so that means bargains. The little shops had everything from sauces to lotus root. Those were the things we went for. And we went because my grandmother was a purist. She would do a dish over and over again until she got it correct."

Chu's grandmother died in 1964, when Chu was thirteen. But

the time he spent with her was formative. "When my family gets together now, my wife, who's Caucasian, says, 'Your family doesn't talk about anything. They don't talk about their feelings. They talk about what they're eating, what they ate, what they're going to eat, and where they're going to eat it,'" Chu said, laughing. "But what she doesn't get is that they *are* talking. They're talking through food."

GLENN CHU calls himself chop suey; by this he means that he is a stew of cultural influences and tastes. Over the course of our conversations, this idea of identity surfaced again and again. "My grandmother wouldn't recognize the food I make now," he said recently, over a prettily presented plate of, among other things, goat-cheese wontons and shiitake mushroom buns paired with an unexpected hoisin-raspberry sauce. But he said she would recognize the principles behind his cooking, principles that she as a devout Taoist instilled in him: balanced elements, wellness in food. In the dimly lit Opium Den lounge of his Eurasian-themed restaurant, Indigo, he explained that as Chinatown has changed over time, so has he. The lounge was created as a tongue-in-cheek reference to a Chinatown past that was a little bit naughty, and Chu feels comfortable claiming it for his own. Similarly, he has taken Chinese traditions to make his own kind of cookery. The dishes he creates reflect his background, but also what he felt he was missing in his growing up. "I don't know how to cook Chinese food," he said. He can't make the beautiful fatty pork his grandmother made, and he doesn't want to. He makes his sauces not with cornstarch, but with French techniques of reduction. His influences include Julia Child and Alice Waters. "It's mine and it's not mine," he told me. "I am Chinese, and I'm deeply influenced by that. But when I came back to Chinatown, it was on my own terms."

Chu's grandmother sent him to Chinese school, but he often played hooky. As a result, he never learned much Chinese. He also attended Iolani School, the same private school Sun Yat-sen graduated from in 1882; unlike that famously fast-learning alumnus, Chu barely managed to graduate. As a teenager, he rejected things that were Chinese. "I loved my *paw-paw*, but I was never really interested in acknowledging my culture back then," he said. Chu went away to college in Michigan, majoring in management. There, he met his first wife, who was apprenticing to be a pastry chef; with the help of Chu's mother's recipe, the couple started a cheesecake business in their basement. In 1979, they moved back to Hawaii, and opened a patisserie and catering company.

Chu continued to travel and try new flavors; at the end of the eighties, he opened a traditional Moroccan restaurant in Honolulu. Then, in the early nineties, someone asked him to come down and look at a space in Chinatown. "Nothing was here then, except for the lounges that attracted the drug dealers and prostitutes," he recalled. But something drew him to the 1903 red brick building and its rear courtyard, which opened out to what was then Chinatown Gateway Park and the old Hawaii Theatre. At the time, the historic vaudeville theater was undergoing a $30 million renovation. Changes were coming. He had an idea of doing something Chinese, but he wanted it to be something new. It was risky to open a restaurant in that part of Chinatown, but memories of his grandmother—of what she did with food—and the location next to the park and theater made him think that maybe, just maybe, he was ready to come back to Chinatown after all.

"Once we opened up those doors to the outdoor terrace space, with the park behind us, I knew people would gravitate to it," Chu said. As we stood in the back garden among the lush greenery and hanging paper lanterns, waitstaff in vivid-blue *cheongsam*—the traditional Chinese long gown—and quilted silk jackets carried dishes from the kitchen. A sun shower burst from the sky. It all had a distinctly tropical feel, with bamboo furniture and elaborately carved screens set up behind the main building and its tall, narrow, blue steel doors. Each of the blue doors led to a tailor's stall; Chu said the doors were originally constructed to resist fires after the bubonic plague and 1900 fire devastated the neighborhood. "You know how I know?" Chu asked me, grinning. "Because one day a little old Chinese lady came into my restaurant and told me she used to live upstairs." His past, it seemed, had come calling.

Two weeks before the restaurant opened, Chu's chef quit. "It was an accident that I became the chef," Chu said. "I knew what I liked, but I wasn't a chef. I never learned to do the back-of-the-house stuff. I'm extremely fortunate that it worked out, because when I was rolling out that first batch of *jin dui*"—glutinous sesame balls that usually have a sweet peanut or coconut filling; Chu's version uses savory roasted duck and apricot—"my grandmother was sitting right there in the kitchen with me as I rolled the dough out with the spider and the wok, saying, 'Glenn, very bad luck if that *jin dui* doesn't turn out.' I could see her right there, standing on the stool, pressing the *jin dui* until they puffed up and got crispy on the outside." Fortunately, they turned out. In 1999, Glenn Chu was proclaimed a rising star of American cuisine by the James Beard Foundation. His restaurant became a destination, and helped to turn the tide on Chinatown's image. The park behind the garden was replanted and revitalized. In 2007, it was renamed Dr. Sun Yatsen Memorial Park, and commemorated with a new bronze statue depicting the revolutionary leader as a thirteen-year-old boy arriving to study in Honolulu.

CHU SAYS THAT Chinatown itself is becoming chop suey. Like Fong Chan, he witnessed a predominantly homogeneous Chinese neigh-

borhood get progressively more mixed as different waves of immigrants came in, adding Filipino lei makers and *pho* shop owners
to longstanding Chinese businesses. He says that that immigration
has enriched the foods available for shoppers in Chinatown. "I've
been to so many Chinatowns and they pretty much have the same
thing, but it's those little jewels that you're looking for—what do we
have that somebody else doesn't have," he said. "What differenti-
ates one Chinatown from the next? In San Francisco, it's street after
street of Chinese stores. Here in Honolulu, it's so combined. And
such a tropical feel. The palm trees and the papaya, the lychee and
mango."

Back on the street, we trolled the markets along Kekaulike
and Maunakea, and Chu pointed out to me the ripe abundance of
Southeast Asian fruits—varietals that have only recently made their
appearance in Chinatown. Now that Hawaii has gotten itself out
of an economy that was concentrated myopically on pineapple and
sugarcane, he said, the opportunity for local farmers to start rais-
ing new things has exploded. In an indoor market on Kekaulike, he
picked up a hard, round green fruit and passed it under my nose.
"This is calamansi, from the Philippines; that's what they use there
instead of limes. We use the zest from it in our pineapple chutney."
He moved to the next aisle. "This bitter eggplant is from Thailand.
As people come and move away from where they have come from,
you'll see their vegetables and their fruit, and I think that's an important gain. You'll see a lot of things that are not Chinese."

The addition of new things to Chinatown doesn't change Chu's
enjoyment of the neighborhood. The tradition of fresh ingredients
still rules, as does the personal element. When Chu needs something, he calls up his regular vendors and they send the produce,
handmade noodles, and meats over to his restaurant. We passed by
Ying Leong Look Funn, a rice-noodle factory, and Nam Fong, the
butcher shop where Chu normally orders his pig. "You can tell a

good butcher shop when you see all the grease splattered in the window," he said, of the handful of small, traditional storefronts that remain. Chu is not the only top chef in Honolulu to do his sourcing in the open markets of Chinatown; other chefs famous for Hawaiian regional cuisine, like Alan Wong, also find inspiration there.

Wong told me that Chinatown is valuable to him because the history of the neighborhood, and of Hawaii, makes it impossible to ignore. "The islands have always been a melting pot of cuisine, a sharing of ideas—that borrowing of techniques happened from a long time ago," he said. "Chinatown to me means a little bit of that. My Chinese grandfather was the kind of man who cooked every meal in the household. I know that, and I know the history, bring me here. Every time I'm in Chinatown, I'm looking for some kind of ingredient to inspire me. You go to Chinatown for that kind of stimulation."

The Chinese have had a big influence on contemporary Hawaiian cuisine. Like Chu, Wong says that he doesn't cook Chinese food at his restaurants—he cooks Chinese-inspired food. But he looks to the culture to know where he's coming from, and where he takes diners with his food: East to West, and West to East. One Chinese fusion restaurant asked Wong for his expertise on a stir-fry dish, and Wong says that in the process of consulting with the staff, he realized that what they needed most was to go into Chinatown. "I said, take a day off, go to Chinatown, go smell it, taste it, go look at the cans and bottles and pickles there," he told me, with rising enthusiasm in his voice. "Throw a few things you see there in your stir-fry. It'll be closer to what you're trying to do than what you are doing now, asking me. When you go to Chinatown, you reinvigorate your senses. It may make you revitalize what you're doing. You remember something."

The mom-and-pop quality of Chinatown also makes it the best place to get things like Hawaiian mango. Every wholesaler might not carry the local fruit at any one time, but Wong told me that he can always find a small store that is selling it. "You can always get it. And when you go there, you're in the moment, you're smelling and seeing and tasting everything, in the Chinese mode of thinking," he said. "That will make your cooking better."

Like Wong, Glenn Chu makes it his business to walk around his neighborhood regularly to stay sharp on inspiration, and to be keenly aware of what's available. On the day of our walk, available items included chicken feet, those ever-lucky phoenix claws. As often happens during Chu's market crossings, the sighting jogged a memory loose. As a college boy in Michigan, he once drove up to Toronto with a girlfriend; the couple ended up in a dim-sum restaurant in Chinatown. "I'm expecting them to come around with the little carts for dim sum," he said. "But they don't. They bring me a menu in Chinese instead. I don't want to claim ignorance, so I just point at a bunch of stuff and order. And when the chicken feet come, I am horribly embarrassed. She goes, 'Oh, what's that for?' And I say, 'Oh—that's to clean your teeth.'" The anecdote was amusing, but it also served as a reminder that the story of Glenn Chu is not a Chinese story—it is a distinctly Chinese-American one.

FRICTION CAUSES HEAT, and change. In a multicultural environment, rituals may be picked up and passed along, but often with changes. Chu took me to Bo Wah, a traditional Chinese emporium, where he pointed out a paper Mercedes designed to be burned as a funeral offering to one's ancestors. His belief in the grounding nature of ritual comes from a childhood spent watching his grandmother perform certain ceremonial movements: burning incense, preparing special tables, honoring the ancestors with shrines. As he shared these stories, they reminded me of my own childhood, when my family visited the Chinese cemetery to honor long-gone relatives—

we burned ghost money and brought food so that they would be happy and well provided for in heaven. Chu's is a life imbued with the ideas behind those actions, if not with the actions themselves. The *jin dui* that he makes, for instance, may have a different filling, but it has the tradition of glutinousness or stickiness in many Chinese delicacies. "It's that notion of stickiness, bindingness, that keeps the family together. So whenever I teach cooking, I tell them that this is how the Chinese feel—this is why we have so many foods that are sticky. It's that thing that binds us together."

Chu's twenty-year-old daughter had her own ways of incorporating Chineseness. Now a student in Cambridge, England, she has always felt much more rooted in England than she was in Hawaii. Chu said that when his daughter was a little girl, she fantasized about growing up English and going to boarding school. Her knowledge of English fashion history is impeccable. "She hasn't reached out to her Chinese ancestral half yet—she acknowledges the other half now," he explained. "But she's starting to, in her own way. We went to a Chinese restaurant in London that she loves, with dumplings and dim sum, and I said, 'I really like what the waitresses are wearing.' And then she told me this is how these are made, and this is how it's done, and then we find that the person who did the uniforms did the costumes for the Chinese film *Crouching Tiger, Hidden Dragon.* That's why they were so gorgeous and perfect. You're going to have that duality of influences, but some of those rituals in our lives continue. Some of them are lost, but the ones that you come around to claim will continue."

We went on with our walk, and I asked him if this was how he saw Chinatown staying Chinatown while moving forward and changing, and he nodded. "Chinatown here is uniquely Hawaiian," he said. His main hope is for visitors to feel motivated to meet the people of Hawaii rather than the tourists of Hawaii, and the marketplace of Chinatown is a place to do that: a gritty, eclectic mix of humanity that is worth firsthand exploration. When you walk around here, he said, life is not the same as what's found at home. And it shouldn't be. The things you see help you understand the rituals that have carried the Chinese through the centuries, and into their diaspora. In the process of that journey, they changed Hawaii, too.

Hula doll at a bubble-tea stand. *Bonnie Tsui*

TWELVE

HISTORY LESSONS

Chinatown's disenchanted generation,
on preserving the past and shaping the future.

The way a Chinatown looks has always been important to how outsiders perceive it. Much the way that the chinoiserie in San Francisco Chinatown has defined it as an exotic enclave, the low-rise merchants' buildings and marketplaces in Honolulu Chinatown have helped establish its character. In the early Chinatown years, shopkeepers lived upstairs from their businesses. In Honolulu, overcrowding and disease in Chinatown led to its burning—not once, but twice. Perhaps because of the dubious history of government-led destruction in Chinatown, city, state, and federal leaders in recent years have been eager to preserve it as a historic center of Old Honolulu. In 2006, Mayor Mufi Hannemann held a Chinatown Summit and implemented various arts programs and grants to bring more business and foot traffic to the area; that summer, the declaration of Chinatown as a "Preserve America" community by a White House preservation council made it eligible for federal funds. Chinatown's architecture, the mayor said, was one of the unique community assets that needed to be preserved. But in an ironic way, delays in actual funding have held dilapidated, run-down properties and crumbling façades in stasis—visual evidence of a place stuck in perpetual transition.

From their vantage point at a bubble-tea and smoothie stand on busy Maunakea Street, Gloria and Grace Tan have seen some changes come to their neighborhood. They moved to Chinatown fourteen years ago from Fujian, when Gloria and her husband sought a better education for their daughter, Grace. There are a few more cops now, a few more streetlights, a little less drug traffic. But what surprises Grace, now a twenty-two-year-old college student in second-language studies at the University of Hawaii in Honolulu, is how much things stay the same.

A ponytailed young woman whose usual uniform is jeans and a purple hoodie, Grace was assertive about what she disliked about the neighborhood. Like Rosa Wong-Chie, the San Francisco Chinatown youth leader, Grace was uncomfortable with the image projected by her Chinatown. "It's a little bit dirty, and there's too much homeless," she told me. She was a straight shooter who spoke bluntly, calling out the problems as she saw them. "It doesn't feel safe after seven o'clock at night."

I spent a couple of warm December days sitting with Gloria and her daughter at the market, watching their world of Chinatown pass by. Gloria is an easygoing, pleasant woman, with lightly curled hair tinted red. In fourteen years, she hasn't picked up too much English, but she has learned plenty of Cantonese in Chinatown to supplement her native Mandarin. She liked where she lived, she told me, and appreciated the lovely weather and laid-back pace of this tropical American Chinatown. Grace, on the other hand, had a lot more to say about her life education in the neighborhood. The authenticity that visitors seek in Chinatown, she says, is in many ways false. "Those old buildings, that is history about Honolulu Chinatown, but you cannot say that it is authentic or that real Chinese *want* to live in this kind of environment," she said, eyeing the physical condition of her neighborhood. What, she asks, does keeping a bunch of century-old buildings the way they are say about the Chinese in Chinatown today, anyway?

■ ■ ■

THE LAST U.S. Census, in 2000, showed the population of Chinatown as overwhelmingly Asian; the median household income was
below $20,000—62 percent less than the median household income
of Honolulu County as a whole. The neighborhood's past may be
rich to people who don't live here, but for residents, the workday
everyday goes on, because Chinatown, after all, remains a working-
class place.

On days when she doesn't have class, Grace comes by to help
her mother serve fresh fruit smoothies and bubble teas at the Hong
Kong Supermarket, which occupies the ground floor of the Wo Fat
Building. Wo Fat is known for housing what was once the oldest
restaurant in Chinatown; the original building was constructed in
1882, but burned down in the 1886 fire. The current building was
one of the first to go up after the 1900 fire, with a host of decorative
additions slapped on it in the years following. The chop suey house
is long gone, but the vintage neon sign remains: Wo Fat Chop Sui.
A green-sheet awning shields the market's customers from the sun,
but it also hides from view the elaborate façade of the community
landmark, with its red tiles and flared-roof corner tower. Locals will
tell you it is the most beautiful building in Chinatown.

The Tan family still lives in an apartment just down Maunakea
Street from Wo Fat. Chinatown's status as a historic district limits
what property owners can do to the characteristic buildings in the
neighborhood; any changes or improvements have to undergo byz-
antine permitting and zoning processes. Above all, it costs money,
and it's money that many owners don't have. Because of this, Grace
thinks that history can only get you so far. The building her mother
works at is one of only a handful of restored historic buildings in
Chinatown. Though the entire district is protected, few blocks have
yet had the work done to fix facades and bring buildings up to current code.

"Here is not a very beautiful place," Grace said. Though she
started attending school in Honolulu when she was eight, she still

speaks English with a slight Chinese accent and, at times, imperfect grammar. On a Thursday afternoon, the sun was beating down through the palm trees, and the pedestrians in Chinatown were hot and thirsty. As we chatted, a crowd of customers had gathered.

"Two watermelon bobas, boss," a man wearing dirty construction boots piped up. Even before the order was made, she had already started scooping and blending the ice and fruit syrup. The hula-girl doll on the counter wobbled and wiggled with the vibration, her grass skirt rustling.

Grace speed-blended the drinks, bright, bubble-gum pink confections that she handed over neatly, with napkins. Her cell phone rang, and she balanced it on her shoulder, chatting with a friend in Mandarin as she made change of $5 bills. Customers smiled, gave their thanks, and ambled on back to work or on to the next tourist attraction. Some asked her where the nearest A.T.M. was; others requested Chinese restaurant recommendations.

She turned back to me after the rush was over, wiping her brow with one pale wrist. Because of Chinatown's excess of crowds and dirt, she doesn't see many reasons to visit. "People come here looking for Chinese food," she explained. "And maybe they are thinking about some gifts that are very representative of Chinatown. Maybe they are traveling here, and they want to bring something back that is very Chinese to them. Just for the memory—'I have been to Honolulu Chinatown.'"

When I suggested that some people come to experience the historic feel of the place—that they think it tells a story about the area's Chinese-American culture—she became passionate. As a Chinese immigrant who grew up here, Grace derided a citywide marketing campaign that touted Chinatown as "Hawaii's most exciting and mysterious neighborhood" (it is described in this startlingly archaic way on the official Web site for Honolulu Chinatown, which is sanctioned by local Chinese groups). She was eager to establish for me her own takes on "Chineseness," and what it means to live in Chinatown today.

"If you go to China, all the buildings are very new and modern," she said. Every summer, the Tans make the trip back there to visit family and friends. "So you cannot say that, oh, Chinatown is China, or Chinese, or that Chinese-American people's lives are very similar to this. You cannot say that, because these hundred-year-old buildings don't say what Chinese people are like *now*." Protecting culture and history for the next generation is important, she acknowledged, so that they know that society was like this a long time ago. But it doesn't represent Chinese America, not by a long shot, and it does nothing for the people who live here in the present day.

Grace says that the city should be able to establish new, contemporary buildings here and still call it Chinatown. "It's okay, isn't it, to be more modern?" she asked me. "You can also keep the older buildings to show the kids this is how it was a hundred years ago. But you can renew a house without changing the structure. You can walk down Hotel Street and see many, many houses, but they are really old and run-down. Nobody lives in them. They're in dangerous condition."

For Grace Tan, it's not the ornate detailing of the buildings that bothers her—it's the emphasis on preserving these buildings while not improving the quality of life for Chinatown's residents. Who has the money to fix up the buildings? she asks. It isn't the residents. The city has received several hundred thousand dollars of state and federal grants on behalf of Chinatown for the purposes of economic stimulation, but the actual funds are slow in coming (and the money, to be honest, won't go very far). Some buildings sit empty, while others are used for storage by their owners. The tension here is that which Phil Choy, the architectural historian, felt in his assessment of the San Francisco Chinatown skyline: there were stories in those buildings, a value to them, but they couldn't be frozen in time at the cost of the living community. Grace's critiques echo past and current generations of Chinatown activists who called for an emphasis on quality of life, affordable housing, and street improvements.

It's true that run-down buildings and loitering persist in giving the area a dangerous feel at night, despite the police officers on foot patrol I saw making their rounds on the streets. The warm weather and nearby parks make it easy for the homeless to settle in. "After ten thirty, the whole Hotel Street has homeless sleeping over there— it's scary," Grace told me. "Even if nobody does anything, you still feel like something will happen."

Karl Rhoads, the representative in the Hawaii state legislature for the district that includes Chinatown, confirmed that the view of Chinatown is still grim to some. "Chinatown has a high crime rate by Hawaii standards and the perception is even worse than the reality," he told me. "Parents who can afford to move to safer neighborhoods often do."

ALAN WONG, the Honolulu chef, said that he sees the revitalization of Chinatown as a parallel to the revitalization of 42nd Street in New York. "Chinatown had that same kind of red-light image," he told me. "But it's becoming a place that you should be able to feel comfortable visiting at night, to go out to a bar or a nightclub or dinner, to see the cultural things there, to be in a historic part of Honolulu. It's something that people should be able to do without worrying about what's going to happen to their car or to them. It's definitely still in that transition zone. You still have some crime and activity down there, but one good change is the police station that opened right in the neighborhood."

I talked to Kelfred Chang of the Chinatown Merchants Association, a recently formed group of younger volunteers whose goal is to serve the Chinese community by perpetuating Chinese heritage through the next generation. Given that Chinatown is already a bustling daytime place, Chang is part of the contingent that wants people to feel that it's okay to go into Chinatown after hours. His big idea: to bring more families in through events like the newly launched Asian-movie night in Aala Park, which got funding from the mayor's office.

"A lot of the kids in Chinatown now are new immigrants—they're not the second-, third-, or fourth-generation Chinese Americans like many of us have been, so there are different concerns," Chang, who is forty years old and grew up frequenting the neighborhood, told me. "Many of us went to Chinese school, or did things like join the lion-dance troupe. That's how we used to interact with each other and the community. A lot of the newer families are just trying to make a living, and the kids don't want to participate in these things." In other words, if you are a first-generation immigrant, you don't have the time or the money to commit your kids to cultural heritage. Though he thinks Chinatown is actually in better shape today than when he grew up, he also thinks neighborhood perception is skewed by the fact that the current youth population is also not as civic-minded. He hears the difference from the kids on the street. "They'll say, 'Mr. Chang, the streets are so dirty, nobody cares about Chinatown.' And when I ask them, 'Okay, so are you willing to do something about it? Are you willing to get up early and come here to help do a clean-up?'" He laughed when he voiced the answer. "'Oh, no, I'm not, Mr. Chang. We don't want to do that.' They ask me what they get in return for coming out to help clean up. There's not that investment in the community."

Even with the recent media attention in Chinatown, Grace tells me that she doesn't think that the government really cares about her neighborhood. "In the election time, I will see those people come around Chinatown and say, 'Hello, oh, can you vote for me?' After that, they get their position, they go away. You never see them. They make the promises, they ask for your support, everybody is very friendly, but then they don't make any change. Also, they come here and take pictures—for what? To show people that there is a Chinatown here?" At the end of the day, the big media show, she said, with a note of indignation creeping into her voice, is just a show.

Despite her strong opinions, Grace insists that she isn't an activist. Unlike Rosa Wong-Chie, who has reacted to problems in her neighborhood by participating in the political process, Grace has disengaged herself from it. She's just an ordinary person, she told me. "I just say what I saw. This is the normal way that everyone acts. Whoever becomes the president or the governor, I don't care—it doesn't interest me. I don't interest them. I'm not the owner of any store; I'm not the boss of any shop. So I don't care to be the friend of the politician. But you ask me, and that's what I think."

Though she lives in the community and helps her mom at the shop when she can, Grace doesn't know many kids in her neighborhood. Her friends are mostly Asian, but they live outside of Chinatown. Grace and her mother habitually work until five thirty P.M. and then walk home from the store. When the daylight hours get longer, they stay open later. But they and other residents in the neighborhood don't exactly partake of the nightlife that has been so publicized as transforming the streets on which they live. "Some of my friends come to Chinatown to shop and go to restaurants, but I don't go to the bars with them," Grace said. A recent story in the *Honolulu Star-Bulletin* reported that "progress has been like molasses" since the 2006 Chinatown Summit, and that many of the local high-rise residents were not persuaded to go out at night in Chinatown. Most neighborhood business owners agreed that more evening foot traffic was needed to keep the new businesses afloat.

When Grace goes to and from school, she drives. She spends a lot of time at school, and when she hangs out with her friends, it's usually close by the university campus, in Manoa. The evening before we first talked, she had attended a friend's graduation party. "It was a very Chinese-style family party—one table, with ten people, and eight or ten dishes. It was fun," she said, grinning. Her classmate was born in Honolulu, but his parents were Cantonese. "Ten Chinese people sitting together, you know, you can eat a lot. Especially over a long time when you are talking, the whole dinner continues for three, four hours. I like that."

Grace said her parents' friends also tend to live and work outside the neighborhood. "So we are living and working here, but our social life is outside," she explained. "A lot of Chinese people live around here but not exactly in Chinatown, because here it's not easy to get an apartment or house. Actually, here is no house. It's really hard to get one. We got one because we got here a long time ago. All those buildings are for business and office use."

She knows how the neighborhood works, and she knows that people perceive Chinatown as a low-income area. "If I say I live in Chinatown, they are imagining a smaller place, a dirty place, a cheaper place. But you know, if you want to buy an apartment in Chinatown, it's very expensive! It's a stereotype. They think that way a long time, and they can't stop."

AN EDUCATION IN Chinatown has taught Grace more than a history lesson on her neighborhood skyline; it has highlighted the language gap between generations. On the plus side, living in the multilingual environment of Chinatown helped Grace to declare her major in second-language studies. She sees her future at the juncture of two generations: the Chinese-speaking immigrants who don't speak English, and the newer generations who don't know Chinese.

"It goes both ways," she told me one afternoon, as we sat in the white plastic chairs under the shade of the shop awning. "Both the new generation and the old need help. I can speak English and

Chinese. America and China are doing more business together, and more people want to learn Chinese. And I think maybe I can help them."

It was surprising to find that even in Honolulu Chinatown, an ethnic enclave that has only become more multicultural over the last century and a half, Chinese immigrants still get by—securing both jobs and housing—without having to learn much English. Grace says that with all of the Chinese living and working in Honolulu, it is easy to find someone who speaks both Chinese and English to help you out. And the language gap between immigrants and their American-born children—a story that is as old as this country—continues. The generational divide is one that Grace sees in her own household. Her younger brother, Kevin, is ten years old; he can still speak Chinese to his family, but doesn't read or write the language. Almost all of his Chinese-American friends speak English, and Grace can see a time in the not-too-distant future when he will forget it all.

When I asked her why her family still lives in Chinatown, she told me that her parents are used to it. Her family enjoys the markets and being able to buy the fresh Chinese produce they want. "They're really comfortable with the environment. Also, it's convenient—we can walk and we don't have to drive to go shopping." And she added the familiar refrain: people speak Chinese.

Though Grace has a critical view of contemporary issues in Chinatown, at the end of the day she wants to continue to live and work in Hawaii. And with her language studies and abilities, she sees a future for herself here in the Chinatown community. "Even though the homeless and cleanliness are an issue, I am still liking it here," she said. "The weather, the water, the people are friendly. The air—there are no factories, like in China, so it's a nice place to live."

But she thinks there's a way to keep the history in Chinatown without it being in such bad shape, and without having outsiders think about it such an old-fashioned way. Even when she goes to the library, she added, all the books about China and Chinatown on the shelves are old. I tell her that stories like hers will shed light on the way life is lived here today. Being a part of a new book about Chinatown, I explain, might show others another way of thinking about things. She mulled it over before quizzing me with a question of her own.

"When will your book come out?" she asked.

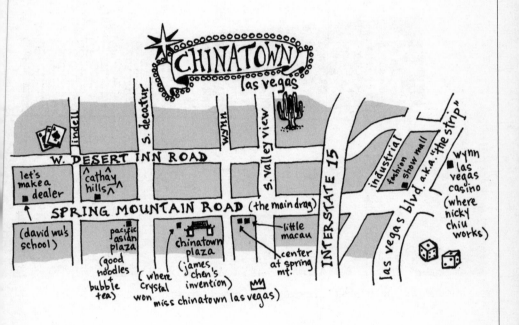

Chinatown interstate sign, Las Vegas. *Courtesy of James Chen*

THIRTEEN

CHINATOWN, NEXT EXIT

*The man who invented a new breed
of Chinatown.*

In many ways, the Chinatown in Las Vegas is just like any other. There is live crab and lobster for sale. There are Chinese herbalists, bubble-tea joints, bakeries, and a Chinese beauty salon. Tucked away behind one storefront is the office of a Chinese-language newspaper, the *Las Vegas Chinese Daily News*. Signs on the interstate direct tourists to "Chinatown Next Right." A slew of Chinese restaurants have typical names evoking the majesty of old China: Mein Dynasty, Harbor Palace, Emperor's Garden. In the afternoons, the restaurants and stores are packed with Chinese shoppers, and cars move slowly, drivers craning their necks, looking around for places to park. There is a community bulletin board posted with Chinese notices advertising rooms for rent, secondhand computer monitors, mopeds. And every year, a Chinese New Year celebration, complete with lion dancing and firecrackers, is held on the premises.

But in Las Vegas, the Chinese New Year celebration is different—it takes place in a parking lot. And in this Chinatown, the live crab is found not in a mom-and-pop seafood shop, but in an Asian supermarket mega-chain named 99 Ranch with branches all over the American West. Most notably, no one lives in Las Vegas Chinatown. That's because Las Vegas Chinatown is a mall, founded in the mid-nineties by a developer named James Chen. It is, as he tells it, America's first master-planned Chinatown.

A MILE WEST of the Vegas Strip, I made my way to Chinatown Plaza to observe its rhythms and to hear the story of its inventor. A trim sixty-year-old with an open, friendly manner, Chen can often be spotted chatting with tenants and customers in his Chinatown. When he spoke, I felt I could see the proverbial wheels turning: he is and always has been very much an idea man. After he arrived in Los Angeles Chinatown from Taiwan in 1971, he brainstormed his first business, a Chinese vegetable farm. He had the idea that new vegetables could be brought to American tastes, introducing more variety to what he deemed a limited palate. "I thought the American food was terrible—all potatoes and burned meat and stuff like that," Chen told me. He brought over a Chinese agriculture expert he knew from Taiwan, and started farming in San Diego County. But after a while he began to realize that nobody in Chinatown was buying his vegetables.

The vegetables, it turned out, were mostly northern varieties. Given that his audience—the Cantonese and Toisanese that populated Los Angeles's Chinatown—hailed mostly from southern China, he had a serious marketing problem. "The Cantonese and Toisanese didn't even recognize what they were," Chen recalled, laughing. "They said, 'Our bok choy is so big, why is this bok choy'—the Shanghai bok choy—'so small?'" Chen was born in Hunan, but his father was an officer in Chiang Kai-shek's Nationalist army, and the family moved to Taiwan when Chen was a year old. Chen was a student, among the first wave of Taiwanese to make their way to the United States.

"I was Chinese and I wasn't Chinese to them, not Chinatown Chinese," Chen says of his experience among the Cantonese during that first decade. In Los Angeles, he faced the same discrimination in Chinatown that Fong Chan did in Honolulu. "They said, *dim gai tong yun m-gong tong wah*—'How come Chinese doesn't speak Chinese?' And me from Taiwan at that time they wouldn't accept me." It was, he explains, a big job for one little businessman to take on: to try to change the habits of a whole community. He eventually learned enough Cantonese to get by, and started other successful businesses in California, one a Chinese food court and another involving Chinese film and television distribution. But what he saw in Los Angeles's Chinatown, his first, got him thinking. As he witnessed the transition in the mixture of Chinese in Chinatown through the seventies, eighties, and early nineties, he began to meditate on the meaning of the phenomenon, and on his own connection to Chinatown. "It was interesting to me," he told me. "Ever since I arrived in the United States, I was always curious about how every major city got to have a Chinatown."

Little by little, he noticed things. He started to make the connections that would culminate in his biggest idea. On his honeymoon trip to Maui in 1977, he opened the phone book in an attempt to find a chop-suey place to take his new bride. They spent three hours driving around. No chop suey. "My wife got mad at me," he said. "We only stay one day in Maui. I thought, why am I so stuck on Chinese food? Why do I have to look for it? One thing about a Chinatown is the food—it's the big draw. You know you will find it there."

In the early 1990s, Chen frequently visited Las Vegas on leisure trips with friends from the Los Angeles area, a mere four-hour drive away. Sin City itself was in transition, starting to shift its strictly gambling image to one with a more tourist-friendly and entertainment-centered focus. More families were vacationing in Vegas. To Chen, Vegas seemed like heaven. Good weather, great shows, plenty of money. It had it all, except for the food he liked. As he did in Maui, Chen tried to find Chinese cuisine. Once again he had no luck. He asked himself why Las Vegas, a city that had everything from volcanoes that erupted on command to a massive casino shaped like an Egyptian pyramid, did not have a Chinatown. Of course Las Vegas was a new city—it didn't have the sizable, isolated Chinese population or the long history that formed Chinatowns in the past. But Chen felt that the warp speed at which Vegas was growing could make something happen. And he couldn't wait.

In the absence of Chinatown, Chen asked himself if it would be feasible to start his own. "Because there were a lot of Asian tourists, from China and from the U.S., they might be looking for those same things I was," he said. "And we know how superior we Chinese think about the food. 'You other guys are great, I can drive your cars, I can live in a nice house, but not the food!'" He chuckled. "But that's the thing I always thought. We can make a Chinatown for the Chinese tourists."

Predictably, most of the advice he received was negative. (His lawyer told him that it would be a "big gamble" to go off the Strip.) But Chen felt that it was not such an outlandish idea, since the Chinese had been coming to Vegas for many years already. As a destination, Las Vegas was popular with out-of-town Chinese. Many casinos ran regular tour buses from Los Angeles's Chinatown, and special programs had been put in place by management to attract the increasingly lucrative Asian and Asian-American gambling markets.

The local Chinese population was growing, too. In fact, Chen pointed out to me, the Chinese were present in significant numbers in the 1870s, during the building of the transcontinental railroad. In 1880, they made up at least 8.5 percent of Nevada's population (and it is likely that many more went uncounted). Though the Chinese had dwindled to less than a quarter of a percent of the state's population by 1950, the post-1965 immigration boom sent the Las Vegas Chinese population skyrocketing, says Sue Fawn Chung, a professor of Chinese-American history at the University of Nevada, Las Vegas (UNLV) who has studied the local Chinese community.

During the 1990s, the Chinese population in the city grew by almost 250 percent, totaling about 15,000 in 2000. Most earned a living as lower-income workers in the casinos or in the food service industry, though by the late nineties many Chinese Americans were employed as dealers.

Chen spent long days researching his Chinatown project, and he realized that to depend on local Chinese residents—as traditional Chinatowns did—would guarantee failure. The rate of population growth was high, but there were still not enough Chinese residents to ensure the survival of a new Chinatown. Though original Chinatowns were seeded by the needs of local Chinese, they would later become destinations for mainstream tourists who were drawn by the culture. This, he says, is the future of Chinatown. "It was a phenomenon I saw, to depend on both—to build a Chinatown for both the tourists and the locals," Chen says. "That's the modern Chinatown."

Several years ago, the *Wall Street Journal* ran a front-page article on Chen and his Chinatown project. It portrayed him as an entrepreneur with a sunny "If you build it, they will come" outlook: "You don't want to be late. You want to be early. That's the game." But Chen says his main point was that the Chinese tourists were there, but no one could see them; businesses did not cater to them, or recognize their importance as a market force. He would make something for the Chinese and Chinese Americans like himself, and the other tourists would follow.

Chen didn't realize it, but he was also following in the footsteps of his forebears in that oldest American Chinatown, San Francisco, and in the rebuilt Chinatown of 1930s Los Angeles. As the San Francisco Chinatown community regrouped after the 1906 earthquake, local leaders knew that the culture and the tourist scenery had to be put in place quickly if Chinatown was to survive. And when Los Angeles's original Chinatown was razed for Union Station, New Chinatown was created by locals as a replacement, with emphasis on maintaining the area as an important visitor attraction. Chen had similar visionary ideas concerning his new Chinatown; even though constructing a Chinese look required more investment, he says that it had to be designed with the architecture to attract the tourists. A regular old American mall would not do. "If it's just a strip mall, it will fade away," he said. "You need to appeal to the Americanized vision of Chinatown." James Chen had decided that Chinatown Plaza couldn't just be a mall. It needed to be a landmark.

When you follow the sign on Interstate 15 and exit west on to Spring Mountain Road for Chinatown, you spot run-down remnants—sky-high piles of wooden freight pallets, abandoned construction sites—that are indications of the area's industrial past. But before long, you see Chinese flourishes along the skyline, in the turned-up eaves and tiled roofs. After passing several Chinese-style shopping centers that have followed Chen's lead (Spring Mountain Square, Center at Spring Mountain), you reach the heart of it, Chinatown Plaza. You know you're there when you see the massive welcome arch; to enter the parking lot, you must drive through it. In its majesty, the arch could be a Chinese version of the Arc de Triomphe. You see the fountain and the towering gold statue of Xuan Zang, a famous Chinese monk who traveled westward in search of Buddhist texts. Chen's commissioned statue of Xuan Zang on a horse is called "Journey to the West" (the statue actually faces east; unfortunately, the Chinese artist forgot to check the actual direction when he made the design). The golden monk gazes out over the span of a parking lot crammed with cars and tour buses.

By the end of the first decade, Chen's Chinatown had achieved that coveted landmark status. The county formally designated Chinatown Plaza the center of Asian-Pacific culture. And nowadays, when Chinese tourists come to Vegas, they come here. My mother's friends, frequent visitors to Vegas, always make a stop in Chinatown Plaza for wonton noodles. A Chinese woman who works as a saleswoman at a jewelry store in Chinatown told me that all her friends in Hong Kong and China are compelled to come here when they visit—it is Vegas's Chinese trademark, one that everyone in China already knows about. Like the Italian tourists I encountered on the Vegas Strip who asked to have their picture taken in front of the Venetian Resort, with all of its faux canals and gondoliers, the Chinese see Las Vegas Chinatown as an American icon. "How do they know this is Chinatown?" I asked the saleswoman. "Because it says so right on the arch, in Chinese characters," she said, matter-of-factly. "*Zhong gwok sing.* Chinatown."

IT MAKES SENSE that the American Chinatown is moving in this direction, and that Las Vegas is the chosen land of this enterprise. The mall was born in America. So was suburban sprawl. And exurban sprawl—the settling of the "suburbs of suburbia," as *New York Times* columnist and cultural commentator David Brooks calls it—is the current pattern of American migration, and it has reached a historic moment. Brooks talks of the booming exurbs in his 2004 book, *On Paradise Drive: How We Live Now (And Always Have) in the Future Tense.* Nevada is one of the fastest-growing states in the country. You can drop a fully formed community, complete with retail outlets and soccer fields, in the middle of the desert. And in Las Vegas, everything is master-planned. It's only logical that ethnoburbs would follow, as different people look for new centers to congregate around.

When I told people I was going to Las Vegas to visit its Chinatown, the response I got was nearly the same each time: "Las Vegas has a Chinatown?" As the common thinking goes, Chinatown is old, crowded, only for Chinese-speaking immigrants—what many Chinese, like Honolulu Chinatown resident Grace Tan, have protested. But newer waves of immigration have brought educated, upwardly mobile Chinese straight to the suburbs, where they can buy their own homes and cars and send their children to better schools. The establishment of suburban, commercial Chinatowns is happening all over America, in places like Quincy, Massachusetts; Albany, New York; Atlanta, Georgia; and Orlando, Florida. Historians like Peter Kwong say that the once-recognizable pattern of urban Chinese settlement is now being "reconstituted" in the suburbs. And even though it's different from how it used to be, it's not necessarily a bad thing. Sue Fawn Chung says that Las Vegas Chinatown, the only Chinatown in Nevada, represents "a new concept," one that combines "both commercial and cultural attractions on ninety thousand square feet of land."

"It's not as independent as San Francisco Chinatown—it's not going to satisfy all your needs," Chung told me. "If you want to go to an Asian church, it's somewhere else in town. If you want to go to Chinese school, you can go to one nearby, but there are also others that you might go to. So it serves some of the cultural needs, though not all."

And unlike traditional Chinatowns, which sprang up because early Chinese had nowhere else to go, you don't have to live here to shop here. The Vegas community remains chiefly commercial, with an Asian resident population that is scattered throughout the city. In fact, there's also an important distinction to be made between Vegas Chinatown and more settlement-driven suburban Chinese areas like Monterey Park or Quincy: sometimes the Chinatown can come before the Chinese do.

In any case, Las Vegas is the site of the most visible and ambitious of these commercially driven Chinatown experiments, and I was eager to walk around what I had begun to think of as "Mr. Chen's Neighborhood." Chen designed his Chinatown to have all the functions of the old neighborhood—to serve Chinese tourists and locals alike—and to contribute an authentic cultural aspect. To this end, he installed educational placards around the mall's covered walkways on topics such as Chinese opera, traditional tea culture, and philosophical thought. To benefit the local Chinese community,

Chinatown Plaza sponsors flu shots and free mammograms, and sets up voting booths during election season. There is the parking-lot Chinese New Year celebration, which attracts in excess of 6,000 people each year, and also a three-day cultural open house for nearly 2,000 local Nevada elementary school students. The kids visit cultural booths to learn how to use an abacus (taught by Chen) and about Chinese calligraphy, Chinese medicine, and Chinese food traditions (how to use chopsticks, family-style dining traditions). Each day culminates in a lion dancing and martial-arts performance by local troupes. These troupes, which Chen helped found, are now frequently employed by Las Vegas casinos to entertain Chinese guests.

The several malls that have sprung up around Chinatown Plaza offer their own arrays of Chinese chiropractors, dentists, restaurants, and real estate agents. They have paid Chen the compliment of copying his mall, but some have the feel of lesser imitations. While it's true that there are Asian businesses under the add-on pagoda roofs of the Center for Spring Mountain—its developers spent $5 million and two years renovating its previous architecture to bring it in line with that of adjacent Chinatown Plaza—there are also plenty of tried-and-true American chains, like Starbucks and Quiznos Sub. But the Chineseness of other malls is indisputable—further west, Pacific Asian Plaza has a variety of grocery stores, restaurants, and other businesses, sporting signs that are almost entirely in Chinese.

On our walk around Chinatown Plaza, Chen and I wandered past the travel agency—where every agent was occupied with multiple customers—and into a shiny, fluorescent-lit video store that had neat white shelves lined with the latest DVDs straight from China. We watched customers mill around the small floor of Diamond Bakery, where many a Chinese wedding cake is ordered ("This is Las Vegas—lots of weddings," Chen said; the mall used to have a Buddhist-style chapel for tourists who wanted to get married and have photos taken of them in traditional Chinese wedding garb, but Chen says that it wasn't as successful as he'd thought it would be) and perused the selection at Great Wall Bookstore, the first and only Chinese bookstore in the state. In Los Angeles, the store would be considered small, but it is unparalleled by Nevada standards. Still other shops sell everything from jade figurines to cell phones and luggage.

We also looked in on the mall's six Chinese restaurants. One serves Hong Kong–style barbecue, another Shanghai cuisine. The others have their own specialties: Cantonese seafood, Mandarin dishes, Szechuan food, and dim sum. There's also a Korean restaurant, a Vietnamese noodle restaurant, a sushi joint, and a Filipino fast-food place. Chen's eldest son, Alan, has run Emperor's Garden, the Szechuan restaurant, for many years, though one of Chen's old friends from Taiwan recently bought the establishment and is moving from Maryland to take it over. When we stopped in for lunch here, there was a healthy mix of customers: casino workers in uniform, tour bus travelers, families. Chen spotted Helen Hsueh, the owner of the *Las Vegas Chinese Daily News*, sitting at a table with her husband, who waved and called over a greeting. Over traditional Szechuan spicy wontons, sweet-and-sour cabbage, and bowls of steaming soybean milk, we talked about the modern reality of what Chinatown is now.

When I observe that the growth of Las Vegas Chinatown has been in the reverse direction of a traditional Chinatown—starting with an appeal to Chinese tourists, with the hope that one day the local Chinese population would come—Chen nods in agreement. "This Chinatown was built to the mix of both," Chen said. "We are aiming for the future: the basic concept is that Chinatown is not only for Chinese. We need all three! We make this ideal with a lot of struggle and adjustment."

During the time I spent with Chen to get the brief history of his Chinatown, perhaps the biggest surprise was finding out that racial prejudice made itself known here just as intensely as it did in every other Chinatown in the history of America. You might think racism wouldn't dog a thoroughly modern Chinatown formed such a short time ago, but Chen has some unexpected tales. When he first started looking at land to purchase for his Chinatown, one owner explicitly told him that he refused to sell to Chinese, "because they bombed Pearl Harbor." In recent years, whenever controversy erupts between the United States and China, racist phone calls inevitably plague Chinatown's management office.

Take the interstate sign, for instance. Chen says that after the county designated Chinatown as a culture center in 1996, the area merchants formed a Chinese Chamber of Commerce. With the Chinese New Year celebrations, voting drives, and other community events behind them, the group went to Nevada senator Harry Reid, now the Senate's Democratic Majority Leader, to request that a sign be put up on the interstate.

"Las Vegas was very Caucasian then, and we got a lot of, 'What are you Chinese guys doing here?'" Chen said. "The feeling was that you can pick up little things, but don't be too crazy. But we went to Senator Reid and said, 'You have to pay attention to us, we're growing.' We had some leverage. Nevada is very unusual—did you know, Nevada at one time had a huge population of Chinese? During the railroad time, when nobody was here. It's an interesting history of our people here. Anyway, Senator Reid was very supportive, and when he got reelected in 1998, I think it was only by a few hundred votes. We gave him three, four hundred votes right here. He even cast his vote in Chinatown."

Reid ordered a sign to be put up on the interstate for Chinatown. But two days after it was mounted, Nevada governor Robert Miller ordered it taken down. "People complained," Chen said. "It was as big as the sign for UNLV"—the University of Nevada, Las Vegas. "They said, 'Who are they? Why do they have a sign that says Chinatown?' Senator Reid said, 'Sorry—I did it, but the governor took it down.' Governor Miller said he didn't think it was appropriate. A year or two later, Kenny Guinn, he wanted to run for governor.

He came to Chinatown to get support from the Asian community—there are a lot of Asian workers in the casino, even though you don't see them on the street. But they are here. So we said, 'When you are elected, will you put the sign back up?' And he said, 'Yeah, I think that's right, it shows the culture.' So after he was elected in 1999, he designated the whole area west on Spring Mountain Road the Chinatown area, and put the sign on the freeway that's there now. We made sure this time he put a sign up of the right size, so it doesn't offend anybody. Something humble. This is the part of the struggle, that we try to get ourselves known."

After the sign was put up, the local news channel came to Chen and asked him how much money he had donated to the government. Chen responded with an indignant negative. "I was targeted by this kind of stereotype. They asked me, 'Are you sure? We can check—we can find out,'" Chen recalls. "And I said, 'Go ahead!' They are always suspecting that Chinese are playing something secret, some tradeoff, some bribe to the politicians. Otherwise, why would they do something nice for us? This is very hard for us. Americans don't like to see Chinese sitting next to their politicians."

To deal with racism, Chen believes that inclusion is important, and that the signs, culture displays, and holiday celebrations at Chinatown Plaza are an important gesture to that end. And the American flag is put up on the Fourth of July and on Veterans' Day, he says, "to show we are American, too, instead of just Chinese Chinese."

But criticism also came within the local Chinese community, who accused Chen and Chinatown Plaza of monopolizing the Chinatown name. "We had to say, no, we are Chinatown *Plaza*, we are the starting point. Right now, it proves that everybody benefits, because we actually brought the tourist money to locals here. If we didn't do it, all of the Asian money would be spent there, on the Strip. The casino is a big vacuum—it takes, it doesn't give. It doesn't give back to the local community. We have been a very rare example in how successful we actually are in bringing the tourist resource to the locals. We hire more people, and all the other services have grown along with us."

Chen gave me a copy of the most recent Las Vegas Chinese business directory, an inch-thick tome that is published by the *Las Vegas Chinese Daily News*. "It used to be very small," he said, flipping through the phone book's pages. Now, there is even a section dedicated to that most traditional Chinese institution: the association. The directory lists more than twenty of them, ranging from the Chinatown Lions Club to the Taiwan Benevolent Association of Las Vegas. Chen marveled at the fact that ASSOCIATIONS had ATTORNEYS beat by a large margin.

Chen's prophecy has turned out to be a self-fulfilling one, though not necessarily in the way he intended. He has created a fully functioning Chinatown, and along with it has come an attendant share of political and social headaches. "When you take the name of Chinatown, you should feel some responsibility to the history and culture of it," he said. "But this was something I never expected—my idea was trying to build some kind of business, and I end up with all these kind of political things, community things, questions about the culture, the future, the image, the government relationship." Here, he gave a wry smile. "I didn't realize I would have to take this on. There is a lot of baggage tied up in the idea of Chinatown."

PHILIP CHOY, THE San Francisco architectural historian, says that the roots of Chinese gambling in America run deep. "Keno came from what Chinese call *bak gup piu*," he told me—"pigeon ticket," a game that used Chinese characters where keno now uses numbers. "It was outlawed in California, and then Vegas and Reno took it over." These days in Vegas, other Chinese influences are obvious. Many casinos have adopted imperial-style décor in their gambling pits. *Pai gow* poker, based on a centuries-old Chinese domino game of the same name, has gained prominence on the gaming floor because it is popular with Asians; so has baccarat.

In a sense, the Chinese have taken over the gambling scene in Vegas. In 2007, the *New York Times* reported that the two-week Chinese New Year holiday is likely the biggest moneymaking period of the year in Sin City's casinos. A traditional emphasis on celebrating good fortune by playing games, especially during holiday periods, has been part of Chinese culture for thousands of years, but the aggressive courting of Chinese clientele has manifested itself only in the last several years. The Chinese potential drives casinos to tailor development specifically to their most prized clientele. Famous Taiwanese pop singers are flown in for concerts, and talented chefs are imported from Hong Kong (and lured away from Las Vegas Chinatown restaurants). V.I.P. lounges are designed with feng shui principles in mind, and tea is served instead of alcohol. One new airline that services Las Vegas, Virgin America, even offers electronic mahjong on its in-flight entertainment system. On a visit I made to Las Vegas during Chinese New Year in 2008, I stayed at The Venetian; the room keycards were gleaming red and gold plastic, and depicted the Chinese character for "rat," to honor the Year of the Rat. The hotel towers were wrapped in red banners that proclaimed the symbols of the zodiac. An executive at the major casino group Harrah's Entertainment told me that the Chinese audience is integral to the city's gaming business.

James Chen says that the casinos' relationship with Chinatown has surprised him. "They bring all of their Chinese big fish here in private limos, because they all want to come for five-dollar noodles," he told me. "They don't want the three-hundred-dollar dinners or the bottles of wine that the casinos want to give them for free. They want to come here. So the casino staff follow, and pay."

The issue of problem gambling, once an unspoken stigma in the Asian community, is also gaining attention; in a recent memoir by writer Bill Lee, who was born and raised in San Francisco's Chinatown, he gives a rare account of a childhood immersed in Chinese gambling culture, his descent into debt as an adult, and his often futile attempts at recovery. There is now a Gamblers Anonymous group that caters exclusively to Chinese gamblers. A handful of other treatment programs in Nevada and California now operate in Mandarin and Cantonese.

When James Chen tried to post information about gambling support groups in Chinatown, he heard from the casinos. "They didn't like it," he said. Chen had briefly considered the idea of opening a Chinese casino in Chinatown, but ultimately decided against it. Gambling, he thought, was better left to the Strip, farther away from the community. In mid-2007, a gaming tavern called Little Macau managed to open its doors in Chinatown, taking up the only spot in the neighborhood zoned for a tavern. As the *Las Vegas Business Press* reported, it became a "gambling giant" in six short months. With the slogan "Drink some, play some, dim sum," Little Macau serves dumplings and other Asian snacks in a lounge-type environment designed to resemble its namesake city (with an annual casino revenue that now eclipses that of Las Vegas, Macau the city is known as the "Monte Carlo of the Orient"). The crowd at Little Macau is heavily Asian—one bartender there told me that Asians make up about half of the customer pool—with many local Chinese casino workers in attendance. Its owner credits the gaming tavern's success to its location in Chinatown.

JAMES CHEN SOUGHT primarily to recreate the comfort of a food culture from the old neighborhood, but ended up inventing something akin to a real community. It is a community to which he feels real responsibility. The local Chinese have been steady in their support over the years, but they are watchful. If Chen is to play the role of the community builder, the community wants to make sure that he is responsible to the name, and image, of Chinatown.

Developers across the United States have called Chen and asked him to build other Chinatowns in new locations. He has declined their invitations, but he is convinced that the future of Chinatown lies along this line of exploration. Years after his community took on a successful life of its own, Chen is still preoccupied with Chinatown's untapped potential. His vision has only been fueled by China's rapid economic growth and global influence.

As much as Chinatown is a tried-and-true attraction in this country, darker elements persist. "In American culture, 'Chinatown' also means negative things," Chen says. "It means filthy, gritty, dirty, produce on the street, people only speak Chinese, isolated, doesn't care about anybody else, or even worse—gangsters, prostitution, that kind of thing. And to be in a new city, Las Vegas, I knew we had to be better. In creating our Chinatown, the Chinese image was at stake. If you have the most modern newest city, Las Vegas, and it has a Chinatown, you want people to see that the Chinese know how to run a business, too, and do it properly. It had to be a modern Chinatown befitting this modern city."

Part of that is expanding the idea of what a Chinatown can be and showing that Chinatown is not just for the Chinese, an idea that is taking root in other new Chinatowns. "Chinatown is a signature," Pomie Lau, president of Florida's Asian Alliance, told *The Orlando Sentinel* when asked about Orlando's recently established Chinatown shopping center. "It doesn't mean Chinese only." Like Chinatown Plaza, the mall bears the name of Chinatown but features other Asian tenants, including a Vietnamese travel agency and an Indian doctor.

Sue Fawn Chung, the historian, says that Las Vegas Chinatown has already gone that direction. It serves as a popular destination for Asians and non-Asians alike, with the grocery store, optometrist, restaurants, and hair salons satisfying daily functions. And she emphasized that the day-long Chinese New Year festivities and street fair, held every year in the Chinatown Plaza parking lot, have done a good job of introducing the general population to Asian cuisine and entertainment—and the inclusiveness of the event has helped make Asian cultures accessible to the community at large.

Pan-Asian establishments have sprung up to the east and west of the neighborhood for several blocks, and Chung notes that Chen's Chinatown success has led to the development of a de facto "Asian Town." On a recent visit, I drove west of the plaza to see how far this Asian Town actually went. Several miles away, a large empty lot had a sign up. "KOREATOWN!" it read. "COMING SOON!"

Crowning Miss Chinatown Las Vegas. *Courtesy of James Chen*

FOURTEEN

MISS CHINATOWN, U.S.A.

Beauty queens and lion dancers in the desert.

Crystal Yuan was twelve years old when Chinatown arrived in Las Vegas in 1995. The daughter of Chinese immigrants who landed on the East Coast and eventually made their way west, Crystal is a rarity for Chinese Americans her age here—she is a born-and-raised Vegas girl. Her parents were among the first of the recent wave of Chinese to settle in the area thirty years ago; as is the case with many locals, they were first employed as casino workers, and then as dealers at the gaming tables. Later, they opened their own insurance business.

Though the Yuans mostly made friends with other Chinese, Crystal found that she was almost always the only Asian in each of her elementary school classes. But she could track the growing Chinese population in the area through the changing makeup of her classmates; by middle school, more immigrants had arrived, and their children had begun to diversify the student pool into something other than just white. And as the wave of immigration grew larger, in high school, she had Asian friends of her own to hang out with in the new Chinatown—they would meet at the boba tea store, or go sing karaoke at the club next door.

She says she never really thought about Chinatown until Chinatown came calling. "When I was growing up, I didn't notice that my heritage wasn't as prevalent in Vegas, because when you're a kid, you don't see in colors," she told me when we met one sunny

217

weekday morning on the upper level of Chinatown Plaza. She is a thoughtful, well-spoken girl with long, eye-skimming bangs over kohl-lined lids and a smattering of freckles. A classically trained violinist, she had recently graduated from UNLV with a degree in music; she was on her way to give a violin lesson to a group of her students. In addition to teaching, she played regularly in an all-girl electric string quartet at various events on the Strip. She pointed to the Chinatown Mall, where the management office for the plaza is housed. "I remember this building being built, but I had no idea what was coming. When Chinatown opened here, I was just starting to become aware of my Chineseness. I wasn't exposed to it when I was young, and I didn't know until later that there was all this Chinatown culture out there."

While the restaurants and shops in Chinatown attracted the older generation, the bubble-tea places and karaoke parlors drew the teenage crowd, and the plaza became a social hub for Crystal and kids her age to eat and congregate. She found she liked eating authentic Chinese food, and she appreciated being able to listen to other people speak her parents' language. Something about the place resonated with her: the feeling that maybe she was not so much in the minority, a burgeoning interest in her cultural heritage. "I grew up with the Chinatown," she told me.

Seven years after Chinatown came to her town, Crystal Yuan would be crowned the first Miss Chinatown Las Vegas.

THE BEAUTY PAGEANT that is Miss Chinatown has roots dating back nearly a century in America, so it shouldn't surprise that a nascent American Chinatown—in a newly built American city like Las Vegas, splashy and shiny as it is—wanted to hold its own marquee event. The first Chinatown Queen on record was one Rose Lew. She was crowned at the Chinatown Carnival, held during the 1915 Panama-Pacific International Exposition in San Francisco. This predated the mainstream Miss America pageant, which was first held in Atlantic City in 1921 as a "promotional gimmick" to keep tourists in town after Labor Day. But in the same way that the Miss America pageant evolved from a local bathing beauty competition to a national event followed by millions for its celebration of the model American woman, Miss Chinatown came to symbolize the Chinese-American female ideal. There was national pride in these pageants—"With her beauty, brains, poise and talent, the American girl has become the most envied and admired girl in the world," one Miss America pageant broadcast gushed in the 1960s—and in the case of Miss Chinatown, there was ethnic pride, too. The San Francisco Chinese Chamber of Commerce further legitimized the concept of Miss Chinatown when it established the pageant as part of its Chinese New Year celebrations in 1954. As avid attendees of Chinese New Year celebrations will know, that set the stage for some form of beauty pageantry to be included in annual cultural festivities in most major American cities ever since. In 1958, the San Francisco pageant began inviting young Chinese American women from all over the country to participate, and the competition officially went national. It was the birth of Miss Chinatown U.S.A.

And in the same way that Chinese Americans of the early twentieth century saw the benefits of having an attractive ambassador of Chinese culture to present to the world, James Chen and others in the Vegas Chinese community saw Miss Chinatown as a positive bridge to local government and larger community relations.

"Probably because of my own limited capability as a Chinese man, I thought it was much nicer for a young Chinese lady to present our image and our voice, to get things done," Chen told me one afternoon in his office. He showed me photos and promotional materials from the inaugural Miss Chinatown Las Vegas, held in 2002. The seventeen contestants beamed winningly from a framed event poster, their pretty faces arranged, somewhat comically, around a giant glittering tiara. "To be an ambassador, a visitor to City Hall—

they were much more welcoming to Miss Chinatown," Chen said. "She spoke the language and got positive attention. It was much easier to build a relationship." Miss Chinatown, he added, was one of the secret weapons of choice for the local Chinese community, a way to achieve wider acceptance and likeability. Chen said it with a laugh, but he meant it with sincerity.

For Crystal Yuan, who was a shy nineteen-year-old college freshman at the time of her win, becoming a secret weapon was not exactly at the front of her mind. Actually, it wasn't on her mind at all. When an organizer for the inaugural Miss Chinatown Las Vegas event first approached her about being a contestant in the fall of 2002, she wasn't interested. Then, as now, classical music was her major occupation; a typical competition involved an audition for a chair as first violin, not a sequined evening gown. "It wasn't really my scene," she told me, cracking a smile. "But then I thought about it more, and it seemed like a good chance for me to play and perform."

This being a beauty pageant, of course, there were also the obligatory, and abundant, measures of cosmetics and coiffed hair. Professional photo and make-up sessions were *de rigueur*. A choreographer was brought in to coach the girls in a traditional Chinese folk dance, which served as the opening number for the final show; they also received lessons from a local modeling school on how to properly walk down a runway. The categories in which the contestants were judged were the expected ones, though with a dash or two of Chineseness: an interview portion that included some trivia questions on Chinese history; a talent portion; an evening gown segment; and a segment featuring the formal Chinese *cheongsam* gown. The winning "queen" would get a $1,000 prize and go on to represent Las Vegas in the mother of all Miss Chinatown pageants, the national event in San Francisco.

On the night of the pageant, Crystal wore a glamorous red and gold *cheongsam* with gold piping along the hem and collar. She had never worn one before, but she told me she liked the way that each contestant had a different look all her own. "Some girls had their *qi pao* custom-made, and some bought them from stores," Crystal said, calling the *cheongsam* by its Mandarin name. Her dress was borrowed from her mom's friend, who had worn it to parties in her younger days, and Crystal liked having that history behind it. "But really, it was about your bearing, and how you carried yourself. I felt like I was kind of able to participate in what my ancestors wore, to join in their traditions."

As we talked inside the Chinatown Mall, outside in Chinatown Plaza the golden monk Xuan Zang was perpetually heading off on a westward pilgrimage. So were the legions of Chinese tourists who made the trip every year to Las Vegas Chinatown. But for a Chinese daughter born in America, the new Chinatown was a place to travel in the opposite direction—to turn eastward and learn about her cultural heritage. For her Miss Chinatown talent, Crystal prepared a traditional Chinese song called, appropriately enough, "Journey to China." She played the piece on a traditional Western violin, but used different bowing techniques from those to which she was accustomed. "It was hard," she recalled. "Sometimes it sounded like a *pipa*"—a four-string Chinese lute—"and sometimes it sounded like a *guqin*," a seven-string zither that is considered the most classical Chinese instrument. "Or the *erhu*, you know, the Chinese violin. I thought it would represent who I am, in a way. I've been playing the violin since I was five, and I thought it would showcase my talent and also show that I appreciate my Chinese heritage in music, too. Like, I grew up classically trained, I was learning Western music, but I'm Chinese, and I'm American, at the same time." It was the old familiar story, she told me—East meeting West all over again.

CHINATOWN HAS ALWAYS been a site of negotiation between the Chinese and Western worlds, and the Miss Chinatown pageant is no different. In a 1997 essay on the history of the Miss Chinatown

U.S.A. beauty pageant, social historian Judy Tzu-Chun Wu pointed out that organizers from the outset "had an ideal image of Miss Chinatown contestants as the perfect blend of Chinese and American cultures." The best contestant was a modern, educated Chinese-American woman. She spoke English and Chinese, exhibited artistic talent, and still had a figure that could fill out a *cheongsam* modified with a lower neckline and higher cut to emphasize cleavage and legs (after all, this was modernity by 1950s pinup standards). The pageant was considered a Western appeal to younger, American-born generations of Chinese as they were becoming assimilated into mainstream culture. Part of this approach was due to the popularization of the beauty pageant in general. In 1954, the same year that San Francisco first put on a Miss Chinatown competition as part of its Chinese New Year festivities, the Miss America beauty pageant was televised for the first time.

The postwar popularity of the beauty pageant lasted for many decades, but the Miss Chinatown U.S.A. pageant had a certain added cachet in the American Chinatown community. Tickets always sold out well in advance, and the event itself was simulcast over local Chinatown radio and to Chinese radio stations across the country. Marisa Louie, the curator of the Chinese Historical Society of America's recent "Miss Chinatown U.S.A." exhibit, told *Asian Week* magazine in March 2007 that the pageant was once "the social event in Chinatown." The executive director of the Chinese Historical Society of America, Sue Lee, said that she remembered watching her grandparents read the *Chinese Times* newspaper and squabble about which girl was going to win the pageant. "It was a big thing for them," she told *AsianWeek*. "They would wait for the Miss Chinatown and they would watch the Miss America pageant. For us, we could see somebody who would look like us and be a beauty queen, who wasn't white, blonde and long-legged. We were just legitimate like Miss America. So that really strikes a chord with Chinese Americans."

The inaugural Miss Chinatown Las Vegas pageant wasn't televised, but it got a lot of local attention. Hundreds of people crowded into the 12,000-square-foot auditorium at the Chinatown Mall, and the contestants' supporters came to cheer them on. Flashbulbs strobed; local elementary school kids performed; the city's Chinese- and English-language newspapers flocked to cover the event.

Crystal wasn't just the first Miss Chinatown Las Vegas—she was the only Miss Chinatown Las Vegas. After the pageant, the Chinese Chamber of Commerce and Chinatown Plaza were criticized by a local Chinese paper, the *Southern Nevada Chinese Weekly*, for judging the competition unfairly. "It's a small community," James Chen told me. "The parents got crazy and upset. The children, they liked being in the event, but it was too much competition and politics for their parents and everyone else. Even in the Chinese New Year banquet we had after the pageant, it was all about who got to sit next to who. After that, I thought we should just concentrate on the health, flu, and scholarship stuff, the culture fair, the Chinese New Year festival—all this kind of stuff is not so controversial. It's not about winning and losing."

CRYSTAL WAS INVITED to appear at a number of Las Vegas events— she and her court of four princesses visited the mayor and also presided over the Chinese New Year celebrations in Chinatown that year, where she performed onstage with several of her young music pupils, and though she missed the deadline for the 2003 national pageant, she went on to compete for Miss Chinatown U.S.A. in San Francisco the following year. During the event, she spent two weeks in downtown San Francisco, and she loved every minute. The national pageant was similar in format to the Vegas event, but the depth of history there was immediately palpable to a girl who was used to a city and Chinatown that were brand-new by comparison.

"The San Francisco pageant had of course been happening for

many, many years—decades—and you could tell there was a lot more tradition settled in it," she said. "We did a lot of association visiting, and that was very interesting to me because it's something we don't really have here." Though associations are listed in Vegas's Chinese phone book, most people don't have much to do with them. In San Francisco, the associations have played important, longtime leadership roles in the community; in a nod to that, each of the pageant contestants went to visit her surname association if she had one, making modern-day connections to Chinatown history.

When I asked her if it was interesting to meet Chinese-American girls her own age from all over the country, Crystal nodded. The most inspiring part about it, she said, was getting to know other ambitious Asian women with similar interests in school. Though Crystal was the only contestant who was artistically inclined—most had professional interests in banking, business, or marketing— the young women with whom she spent the most time presented a refreshing change from the population in Vegas, where, she says, "a lot of people are stuck in the entertainment industry."

"It was fun to meet girls my age who were aspiring to do something," Crystal told me. National Miss Chinatown contestants are required to be between the ages of seventeen and twenty-six, and to never have been married. In Vegas, she says, there isn't as much of a priority on education. She still keeps in touch with many of the girls she met during the national pageant, and recently stopped to see her San Francisco-based friends during a trip to visit relatives in the Bay Area.

What she also got out of her pageant experience was a new viewpoint on Chinatown. Even as an adolescent, Crystal had the feeling that her Chinatown was different from the other ones she had visited in New York and Los Angeles. When she went to San Francisco, the time she spent there helped put them collectively into perspective. "When you really look into it deeper, and if you've lived with one, you'll definitely see different things about each Chinatown," she told me. In New York, the Chinatown seemed busier and more like a big city—what she herself called a "city within a city." It represented New York itself, she said, as a very bustling place with a lot of people. In San Francisco, Chinatown was old and traditional, with a vibe that was integrated into the mainstream downtown.

She saw similarities, too. "Like maybe they all started out in a certain way," she said. "Of course, with Vegas, it's probably very different from the other ones—it's much newer, just like Vegas is the newer place. It's the first of its kind here. It's definitely added to the different cultures of Las Vegas. It's added another attraction, something else besides the Strip."

In comparison with San Francisco Chinatown, she calls Las Vegas Chinatown "more of a mash-up." Her social hangout is a place that is frequented by a lot of different Asian groups, including those who are more Westernized. Like Honolulu Chinatown has been, this Chinatown is now a place that facilitates a melting-pot culture. Crystal says that the combination of Koreans, Filipinos, Vietnamese, and Chinese reflects Las Vegas today, with an Asian community that is not as segregated as it might be in other places. Given the lack of ethnic diversity in her early life, it is a mix that she appreciates.

When Crystal travels to other cities for music gigs, she tries to visit their Chinatowns. She has always thought of her hometown Chinatown as being another shade to an already colorful city, and she says this holds true for the other neighborhoods she goes to explore. "Every city has its own thing going on, and then each Chinatown has its own thing going on, too," she said, thoughtfully. "It also reflects the rest of the city. Even though it's Chinese or Asian or whatever, it reflects the rest of the city no matter where it is."

She told me that she thought it was nice that I came down to Vegas to check it out. Most people, she says, don't even know that Chinatown is here.

■ ■ ■

I CHECKED IN with Crystal shortly after the arrival of Chinese New Year 4706—the Year of the Rat, in February 2008. We met at one of her favorite tapas restaurants, a café at the Fashion Show Mall that overlooked the Vegas Strip where it crossed Spring Mountain Road. Afternoon crowds milled about, and loud music blared from outdoor speakers. She asked me if I'd been to the Chinese New Year celebrations in Chinatown earlier that week; she had gone with friends to sample the street food and check out the scene for a few hours.

I, along with almost 7,000 other people, had indeed shown up at Chinatown Plaza that Sunday, and by all accounts it was the most diverse crowd yet. Lines snaked around the parking lot, composed variously of families, groups of punky local teenagers, and Chinese tourists. I spotted one African American boy running around in blue Chinese silk pajamas, and a young Latino girl toting a small Chinese drum. When I saw the event lineup of Chinese lion dancers, Japanese taiko drummers, Shaolin kung fu performers, and Polynesian dancers, I was reminded of what Crystal had said about Chinatown being a "mash-up."

Among Crystal's crowd, the feeling is that the Chinese New Year celebration is starting to become more a part of the local community. "Word is starting to get out that there is this celebration, and people are looking for that kind of thing to go to," she said. "That Chinese celebrate the new year at a different time and in a different way. For some people it's becoming more of a tradition for them— they're learning about this culture. When I was growing up, I never saw the banners and lanterns and decorations that they now have on the Strip. They didn't used to make such a big deal about Chinese New Year."

The fact that nobody walks in Vegas, other than on the Strip, probably adds to the appeal of the event. It's a rare opportunity to experience something akin to the street life and market culture of other Chinatowns in other major cities, an experience that is conspicuously missing here. Crystal says the community feel is an attraction, replicating the pedestrian experience in other places. It's the kind of close-quartered event in which a local might run into someone she knows, as Crystal did when she encountered one of the girls who competed with her in the Las Vegas pageant. The girl—whom Crystal described as "really nice and really cute"—was one of the only other contestants with whom she stayed friendly. I asked her if she knew what the other pageant contestants were doing now; it turns out that the "really cute" young woman now works at the Playboy Club in the Palms Casino. Every once in a while, Crystal sees other ex-contestants elsewhere around Las Vegas. One is a DJ at a local hip-hop radio station. About a year ago, Crystal did a modeling job with another former pageant girl at The Venetian, during an event for which the casino had requested Asian women to pose as geishas.

As we watched passersby stroll by, their faces upturned, burnished by the sun and competing flashing marquee displays, Crystal said her reign as Miss Chinatown still surprises her. As the beauty pageant has historically done for participants, Miss Chinatown Las Vegas opened up professional opportunities. But she found its focus on competition and appearance problematic. It's the same kind of focus she sees on the Strip, day after day. She told me she had decided to apply to graduate school and get her master's degree in classical music performance. "I can get a whole bunch of gigs right now, but in ten years, they'll probably start to dry up for me," she explained. "I want to have more success as a musician, and not just because I look good."

In Kathy Huang's poignant documentary, *Miss Chinatown, U.S.A.*, which premiered at the 2007 Tribeca Film Festival in New York, contestant Katie Au was similarly conflicted about participating in the pageant. "I didn't want to do it," she told Huang in the film. Her mother had enrolled her in the Seattle competition without telling her. She eventually came around, because she saw that it would mean a lot to her parents, especially her father. Other girls had told her that winning the pageant or even placing would open up different opportunities, "whether it be dancing in Vegas or working in a bank with the community." But she worried about how she would be perceived.

"I would want the judges to see me as me," she said. "Maybe on that night, with all that makeup, they won't." Katie Au ended up winning fourth princess in the 2006 Miss Chinatown U.S.A. pageant, but at the end of the night, she found that there weren't any clear answers waiting at the winners' podium to enlighten her with regard to identity, career, or family.

Crystal Yuan's MySpace page hinted at the identity conflicts in her own life—her photos showed her at a gig on the Strip, wielding a purple electric violin and wearing a miniskirt over fishnet stockings. Her home page quote read, "If you're sexy and you know it, add me!" The visuals would seem to play up the image of a hip, young, Vegas-showgirl-style performer. Yet the three musical recordings she had posted were of her playing the Intro and Rondo Capriccioso by Saint-Saëns, the Bartok string quartet No. 5, and the Brahms string quartet No. 2—well-performed, professional pieces suggesting that the violinist in question would like to be taken seriously.

At the Miss Chinatown Las Vegas pageant in 2002, a local troupe of little girls entertained the crowd with a traditional Chinese dance; many of them became Crystal's violin students. They are now in middle school. "Their parents saw me in the pageant, and then put them in lessons with me. The pageant was mainly why they wanted lessons—all the little girls wanted to be beauty queens." At home, Crystal has a photo of one of her students presenting her with flowers on the day she won.

Her MySpace page also links to her students' pages. On their profiles, she has noticed, even the half-Chinese, half-white kids identify themselves as Asian. "They have a great deal of Asian pride," she says, admiringly. In much the same way she was trying to parse out her identity and her cultural self in middle school, when Chinatown arrived in her city, she recognizes that the kids are working out their own ways of fitting in. They don't have a Miss Chinatown anymore, but they do have Chinatown.

A few years ago, the Chinese government announced its plans to build a museum in Beijing to document the global Chinese diaspora. By 2006, it had already collected 10,000 relics from around the world, including significant items from Chinese American communities in San Francisco and New York. By the Chinese government's estimate, 30 million people born in China now live in other countries. In an interview with the *San Jose Mercury News* San Francisco's Chinese cultural consul, Shixun Yan, said, "It's important for your mother country to recognize what you've done in another land and for Chinese to know this history of overseas Chinese."

One of the locally donated items was a red silk *cheongsam* worn by Betty Ng in 1957, when she won the title of San Francisco's Miss Chinatown. One day, in a Beijing museum that has yet to be completed, young, middle-school Chinese girls may see it, and wonder just what it's like to be a Chinese-American beauty queen.

Craps practice at dealer school. *Bonnie Tsui*

FIFTEEN

THE NEW TENANTS

The new immigrant generation on the Strip.

A couple of traffic lights west of Chinatown Plaza, the new American Dream is being dealt out at the felt-covered craps tables and *pai gow* poker stations at Let's Make A Dealer, a private dealer school run by David Wu. There are about seven dealer schools in Vegas proper, and two are Chinese-owned. Wu is a former V.I.P. host for the Mirage. In late 2007, he took over an existing dealer school, revamping and modernizing its image and moving into a new building on the corner of Spring Mountain Road and Red Rock Street. During a blazing-hot week in late June, I spent a day in the school's spacious, air-conditioned facility getting acquainted with a variety of popular casino games—craps, poker, roulette, blackjack, *pai gow* poker—and the people who aspire to deal them for a living.

For working-class Chinese immigrants, the historic jackpot may have been gold mountain, but today it's a dealer job on the casino floor. For those without much education, dealing means good money—not the salary itself, but the lucrative tips that can come from customers flush with winnings. It also means benefits, and significantly less labor than that which is required for a traditional restaurant or cleaning job. The newcomers come from all over China—including big-city Guangzhou, Shanghai, and Beijing, and their outskirts—and, like twenty-one-year-old Steven Chan does, they see dealing as a way to get a foot in the door of America. It may not be what they aspire to do for the rest of their lives—"if I could do anything, I would be a doctor," Steven told me—but with a little bit of training, dealing is an option that is available to them now.

The speed at which newcomers get involved in the gaming world can be startling. The morning I visited the school, a young Chinese woman was standing at a *pai gow* poker table near the front door, clumsily throwing down cards from a deck in her left hand. She looked at me shyly and said hello, but in the hesitant way of a foreigner unused to the word. I asked her, in English, how long she'd been in Vegas, and she answered with a shake of her head: "Ah, no English." I repeated the question in Cantonese, and she smiled.

"When tonight comes, it will be three days," she replied proudly. Her sister-in-law, a Vegas dealer for nearly twenty years, had already brought her and her two friends—fresh arrivals all, from Toisan—to the school to begin their training.

The mother hen for all these new arrivals is Pamela Wine-Gaulding, the educational director of Let's Make A Dealer, an outgoing blonde with a warm, patient manner and a slow-drawl way of speaking. She herself deals part-time at the Ritz-Carlton, Lake Las Vegas, and sees dealing as a flexible trade, much the way bartending or carpentry might allow someone to find work almost anywhere in the world. Most students at the school are trying to move out of housekeeping and restaurant jobs, though there is also the occasional Silicon Valley refugee or business type looking for a change. "It's the closest thing to that income level," Wine-Gaulding explained as she showed me around, noting that a full-time dealer could make anywhere from $20,000 to $120,000 a year, including tips.

The classes are generally taught in English, but since many of the instructors also speak Cantonese and Mandarin and most of the students are immigrants, the soundscape of the school's large, open rooms is a polyglot one. Separate conversations in Filipino, Chinese, and Ethiopian dialects were punctuated by cries of "Press!" and "Seven, seven, seven—push!" at the craps tables, amid the clatter of stacking chips and shooting dice. Later, I saw Bosco Yeung, the school's *pai gow* consultant, lead a cluster of students in a demonstration of the game. The lesson was conducted entirely in Cantonese.

WINE-GAULDING HAS her favorite students, and her comfort with the Chinese students—"I have a Chinese connection, too, because my ex-husband is Chinese," she explained—was palpable, despite the language barrier. (She doesn't speak Chinese, but she has picked up a few words here and there.) She checks in the students when they arrive during practice hours, and she gets to know their stories. It was Wine-Gaulding who introduced me to Steven Chan, a thin young man with glasses who moved from Guangzhou to Las Vegas with his family in 2005.

The Chans live near Chinatown. When Steven arrived, he didn't know any English. He attended ESL classes at the College of Southern Nevada for two years, and enrolled at the dealer school for lessons in craps and blackjack. Three months ago, he started working full-time as a craps dealer at El Cortez, a somewhat worn downtown hotel and casino that serves as a "break-in" house for newbie dealers. As we sat at the roulette table—he is learning the game to add to his dealing repertoire and better his chances of getting a position in a higher-paying casino—another student spun the wheel and collected mock bets from the two of us. We watched as the ball bounced and rolled around, seeking a landing spot to settle in, and I asked how his job was going so far.

"It's not bad," he said. Then he paused, trying to figure out what to say next. Thinking I would be helpful, I asked him to describe the break-in house for me, and he and Wine-Gaulding started to laugh.

"It's like . . . the exact opposite of the Bellagio," Wine-Gaulding said, naming the swank hotel and casino that starred alongside George Clooney and Brad Pitt in the movie *Ocean's Eleven*. "The clientele, you know . . . he's getting quite an education right now.

But he's learning to be a stronger dealer." We both looked at Steven's face, which was fixed in an expression that was equal parts amusement and pain.

A casino day is divided into three eight-hour shifts: the day shift (generally eleven A.M. to seven P.M.), the swing shift (seven P.M. to three A.M.), and the graveyard shift (three A.M. to eleven A.M.). The exact hours may vary slightly from casino to casino, but the shift pattern is the same. Steven works the swing shift at El Cortez. He had not yet slept that day, and he would practice at the school for about two hours before going home to bed. "If you find a good casino, it's a good job—it's a better job than working at a small casino, which is kind of terrible," he told me, fiddling with his chips. "To get to another casino, you learn more games, and practice and practice and practice." A pause. "And be very good."

Craps was his favorite game. "It's the most exciting, and busy, and fast-moving," he said, gesturing over to the three craps tables on the other side of the room, where other students were practicing. "People can win and lose very quickly." He has friends who are happy at their casino jobs, but he is not sure where he ultimately wants to end up.

"Well, listen, it's like this," he said, switching to Cantonese. "A lot of people come here and they don't know what to do, so they do dealing. This kind of job, it's more for those people. For me, it's just for now to be a dealer." Here, he switched back to English. "I dream of being a lawyer or a doctor. But"—heavy sigh—"my English is very bad."

In Guangzhou, Steven's father was a skilled mechanic. Here in Vegas, he works in a restaurant. "He doesn't know any English, so that's where he works," Steven told me. He says he knows well the importance of language in America, where a lot of people who don't know English work in restaurants or housekeeping. And as exhausted as he is, hopping from his casino shift to school and back again, he knows the going could be a lot tougher. He doesn't complain.

■ ■ ■

UNLIKE THE ENFORCED artificial lighting and absence of clocks in most casinos, Let's Make A Dealer has floor-to-ceiling windows that let in plenty of daylight and a clock that reads "Lady Luck Casino." But David Wu has otherwise tried to approximate a real-life work atmosphere with casino carpeting, music, and flat-screen televisions. The gaming tables bear the logos of the houses they came from: Paris, Nevada Palace. In a couple of months, the school will expand into the finished space just next door.

If anyone is familiar with the highs and lows of the contemporary Chinese immigrant experience in Las Vegas, it's Wu. In the early 1980s, he and his parents moved from Hong Kong to Los Angeles's Chinatown, where Wu's grandmother had been living for more than fifteen years. Wu describes the experience as "culture shock." A teenager who had never worked a day in his life, he was immediately pressed into service as a busboy at a relative's restaurant in Chinatown. Six months later, he was uprooted again when his father got a job in Las Vegas. "My dad met a guy named Jimmy at the supermarket in Chinatown," Wu told me. "Every week, he drove his truck to Los Angeles to pick up stuff for his little grocery store in Vegas." Back then, the population of Chinese was miniscule. "Jimmy basically supplied all of Las Vegas's Chinese with Chinese groceries. My dad got a job with this guy, and that's how we got to Vegas." The family moved into a house next door to Valley High School, a couple of miles east of the Strip, and Wu would later graduate from there.

You could say that Wu's path to the casino industry was lined with Chinese restaurants. He began working at local Chinese food establishments, which eventually led to work inside the casinos themselves. He spent five years at the Chinese restaurant in Caesar's Palace, and another five years managing the one at the MGM Grand. By the end of his tenure at MGM, he got to know all of the Chinese high rollers who came regularly through the restaurant. One day, he got a call from the casino's vice-president of Asian marketing, who was moving on to the Mirage.

"She said, 'David, you're always taking care of my Chinese customers in the restaurants, and you know pretty much everybody. Are you interested in coming with me to do international marketing?' And what I found out is that marketing is pretty much the same as restaurant service—you make sure that when the customer shows up everything is taken care of." In this way, Wu not only became intimately familiar with the local Chinese community but with the tourist Chinese community that traveled to and from the city. At times, as shown by James Chen's story, those communities blurred, as tourists made the transition into locals.

The growth of the Asian gambling market for Las Vegas followed the Asian economic boom. It began in Hong Kong, moving through South Asia, Taiwan, and Japan, and finally to China. As a country's economy flourished, so did its gaming traffic to Vegas, and the casinos paid attention.

Wu is a hip-looking man in his forties, with long shaggy hair and red-framed glasses. On any given day at the dealer school, he is normally attired in flip-flops, a T-shirt, and jeans. Pam Wine-Gaulding, who has known Wu and his wife for many years, said that his casual appearance is a way of rebelling against his buttoned-up years in suits and ties serving all the Chinese "whales"—casino-speak for extremely high rollers. When I asked Wu what his former job required him to do on a daily basis, he laughed.

"You go to a restaurant, you sit down, and you order, right? As a server, you make sure the order comes in a timely manner, that it's correct, that service is good. For the casino clients, it's the same thing. You go to the airport to pick them up, you go with the private jet, you take them to the golf course. I hate golf, but I played it when I was asked. Sometimes it's very particular stuff: this guy doesn't like this food, he is diabetic, he cannot take sugar, and you have to arrange the room service. Tedious things. Sometimes, because of the language barrier, you have to go shopping with them." For Wu, the most ridiculous experience came on a trip to the mall, when a Chinese client wanted him to barter with the boutique owner: $3,000 for $6,000 worth of high-end shirts and slacks. "One thing I really hate is when the guy says he only wants to pay five dollars for the ten-dollar stuff. But it's the job. And it works. You keep the games going, you have them spend money, and they come back."

Wu doesn't have to interact directly with casino clientele anymore, but he's now in the business of teaching others how to do the right thing at the gaming tables. He speaks Cantonese and Mandarin, which makes it easier for him to communicate with the large percentage of his students who are Chinese. Of the Chinese student body, some come from China by way of Los Angeles, as he did, but increasingly they come directly from China. Many find the school through the Chinese newspaper, or through word-of-mouth recommendations from friends.

There are roughly 300 students enrolled at the dealer school, but they don't all come to class at once. Throughout a single day, forty or fifty students will drift in and out according to their own schedules. They take advantage of the free practice time in the two hours before and after classes, which are held between noon and six P.M. The instructors, like fifty-one-year-old Chaco Yang, who presides over the craps tables, are experienced working dealers.

Yang is a feisty veteran who arrived in Vegas from Taiwan in 1972; he graduated from the Las Vegas School of Dealing in 1978. As I perched next to him at the edge of a craps table, he explained the four positions on a dealing team: the stickman, who announces the roll and collects the dice with a long stick; the second base and the third base, who both collect and pay out bets from either side of the table; and the relief, who is on break (each dealer on the team works for one hour at a time, rotating through each position in twenty-minute increments). There is also a boxman, who supervises the game. Acting as the boxman, Yang watched as a young woman named Elaine retrieved the dice and paid out money to a player seated at the table. "Ah, ah, ah—that's a bad habit," he called out good-naturedly, shaking his head. "You know what, the stickman never hands out the money to the player. It's the dealer. So tomorrow, when you go to audition, don't touch the money!" Chastised, Elaine laughed and covered her mouth. Yang told me that Elaine would be going on her first audition the following day, at the casino where he worked as a supervisor. Given the extreme heat in summer, there were fewer tourists, so it was a slow hiring period for the casinos. But with any luck, she would have a good experience at the tryout and make some contacts.

Yang began teaching at the school at Wu's behest; the two are longtime friends. "Since I began, I've seen that about seventy or eighty percent of the students are Chinese," he told me, eyeing the students practicing at the table. "It's easier here for new arrivals, because we are able to speak to them in their own language if they have trouble understanding. But we tell them that they have to take some English class—you have to be able to communicate with the customer." The casinos themselves, he added, have lately become stricter in their language requirements for hiring.

Yang told me that when he first moved to Las Vegas, his English was poor. He speaks English quickly now, still with a heavy accent, but fluently. "A lot of people are afraid to talk because they'll say something wrong and people will laugh," he said. "But I say, hey, it's like me, when I first started talking, I said a lot of words wrong. But people helped me, and corrected me, and that's how you learn. You just can't be scared. You say something wrong—so what?" He shrugged. "You have to realize you are here now—you're not in Taiwan or Hong Kong anymore."

■ ■ ■

IN THE STATE of Nevada, where the Asian-American population is growing the fastest, the Chinese population is booming even bigger in the twenty-first century. The rash of new hotel and casino development on the Strip has created plenty of work for newcomers. Along Las Vegas's Chinatown strip, parking lots filled with beat-up minivans and Ford pickups parked next to gas-guzzling H2 Hummers and shiny silver Lexus convertibles reflect the modern reality of the Chinese in America. In this Chinatown, the new immigrant generation hits both ends of the economic spectrum: rich and poor, tourist and local, high roller and blue collar.

In other words, the educated class also finds its way to the casino, seeking employment through hospitality programs and business internships. A former colleague of David Wu's at the Mirage, Nicky Chiu is a V.I.P. host for the Far East market at the Wynn, a sleek, high-end casino owned by Vegas impresario Steve Wynn. She first arrived in Las Vegas in the early nineties, as a graduate student at the UNLV hospitality program. "When I was little, my parents took me to travel a lot around Taiwan on summer vacations," Chiu, an animated forty-something woman with streaks of red blazing through her hair, told me. The experiences she had gave her the feeling that travel should make "a happy mood" all the time, and it was a vision that she brought with her to Las Vegas. "Of course it's not happy all the time in reality," she said with a laugh, "but that was my inspiration." These days, it's her job to make a happy mood for her clients.

I sat down one morning with Chiu in the Wynn's baccarat lounge, a cushy, chandelier-lit room with an impressive Chinese morning buffet of dumplings, hot soy milk, traditional rice porridge, long sticks of fried dough, and thousand-year-old eggs. Sheer curtains separated it from the gaming floor. "This room is mostly for high rollers," she said as we passed by a series of smiling attendants and a sign marked INVITED GUESTS ONLY.

Chiu left Vegas in 2001 but came back in 2005 for the opening of the Wynn. Upon her return, she was floored by the huge jump in the Chinese population. "The whole Spring Mountain Road is now called a Chinatown Street for us," she told me. For locals, the word "Chinatown" has expanded beyond Chinatown Plaza to include the several miles west of it. These days, Chiu is more drawn to big franchises from Taiwan, like Diho Supermarket, than she is to the original Chinatown Plaza. For noodles, she and her family will go to Champion, a Taiwanese snack shop; for pastries, she will go to Leslie Bakery. "They are more like the places where I grew up," Chiu told me. "The owners and the managers are from Taiwan. And they have the kinds of things I know and like to eat."

The chains that have popped up are an indication of the change in the people coming here: better-educated and wealthier immigrants from all over China, Hong Kong, and Taiwan. They come with their families, and enroll their kids in Chinese schools located on Spring Mountain Road. According to Chiu, education is the chief difference between frequenters of Las Vegas's new-breed Chinatown and the population in a more traditional Chinatown.

"It's not like a hundred years ago, when the Chinese came here to work on the railroad or gold mountain to mine gold," Chiu told me. "Nowadays the Chinese come here for school, like myself. I came for a degree, and I ended up staying here. And once your language is good and you are capable of getting around, then you don't have to stay around the Chinatown. You can go wherever you want, live wherever you want. That's the biggest difference I see."

Most of Chiu's casino clients are businessmen, involved in manufacturing and property investment. They hail from Taiwan, Hong Kong, and mainland China (the mainlanders typically jet in from Beijing, Guangzhou, and Shanghai, since people in certain provinces and occupations have an easier time getting visas to travel to the United States). "People are so rich now," Chiu said, describing the Chinese economic boom. In the last ten years, a prosperous urban middle class—roughly 150 million people strong—has taken shape in China. The number of millionaires, 236,000 in 2004, continues to soar. "Living standards are so high—much better than before."

With reference to the Chinese clientele, Chiu told me that sometimes it's not really the number of people, but how much they spend in the casino that makes them significant to the rest of the population. And that makes the clientele valuable and worthy of attention.

"They feel comfortable with us, they don't need to worry when they come here. They know what to expect," Chiu said of her clients. "The Chinese, they just don't want to have a surprise. We make it perfect for them."

AS THE DIFFERENT classes of Chinese find their fortune in Las Vegas, the Chinatown community is steadily growing, and changing, around them. In a town where an entire shopping center can go up in three months and a condominium complex can appear to have sprung fully formed, overnight, from the desert itself, Chinatown has rapidly become much more than a series of Asian-themed commercial businesses chiefly serving tourists. And though it seemed improbable from the start, the residential component has finally taken shape: people have begun to live in Chinatown.

As in a traditional Chinatown, homes and apartments around this Chinatown strip attract new immigrants with limited English ability. At Pacific Asian Plaza, I inspected a bulletin board filled with housing listings advertising proximity to Chinatown as a selling point. "Townhouse for rent in Chinatown behind 99 Ranch," one flyer read. For $850 a month, you could have a 1,200-square-foot two-bedroom house with private parking and a swimming pool, not to mention a multilingual landlord: "Renter speaks Cantonese, Mandarin, and English." Many ads were in Chinese, and some listings specified Chinese-only tenants.

The establishment of a Chinatown in Las Vegas has obviated the need to speak English for many newcomers. It is the same safety net as that found in the old Chinatown. Geoffrey Hsueh, a student at Let's Make A Dealer who rents a house five minutes from Chinatown, says that he knows many immigrants for whom the most important thing about Chinatown is the language. "Because if you live there, you don't hear any English," he told me. "They just speak Chinese. Everybody knows that."

A former health-foods entrepreneur who moved to Las Vegas six months before from Taiwan, Hsueh attends dealer school while working part-time driving foodstuffs between Los Angeles and a restaurant in Las Vegas's Chinatown. He was introduced to dealing by his sister's friend, a longtime dealer at the MGM Grand. A games and math aficionado, Hsueh thought he could excel at the job. His hope is to secure a full-time dealer position by the time his daughter arrives in California for graduate school in the coming year. The school has become his social hub, and he has lots of friends here. "Many of them are Chinese, but some are American, too," he told me. He and his fellow dealers-in-training head out together to eat after class and visit the casinos—not to gamble, but to watch and to learn.

Even younger, English-speaking Chinese Americans rent apartments in Chinatown, for their older, non-English-speaking parents. Hidden behind Chinatown Plaza, Cathay Hills, and the other business complexes lining Spring Mountain Road, there are red-tiled condominium developments and two-floor stucco apartment buildings with courtyards and garages. "Some elderly people will just live there and walk to Chinatown, since they don't have a license and can't drive, even though their children speak perfect English," Nicky Chiu told me. "So you still have the old generation and new generation here. Even though it's kind of mixed up, it's still similar to the traditional Chinatown in this way. The kids are busy working, and on weekends or on days off they will come and drive their parents around to eat, shop, or visit the Strip. But during the weekdays, the parents are able to be more self-sufficient."

■ ■ ■

LOOK AT Las Vegas's new breed of neighborhood alongside the iconic, long-standing Chinatowns of San Francisco, New York, Los Angeles, and Honolulu, and you will find the dovetailing of the traditional and new Chinatowns. As traditional Chinatowns are places where life's primary experiences take place, this "concept" Chinatown has also taken on that weight. And the traditional Chinatowns themselves have moved in the opposite direction, coming closer to commercial products. Merchants and residents of those Chinatowns increasingly weigh their own value as an ethnic commodity, and see this as important to their continuing survival. They form neighborhood and business associations to discuss issues of gentrification and how to improve sales figures and foot traffic; they hold fairs, festivals, night markets, and other events to capitalize on the Chinatown name.

From the beginning, appealing to an American notion of Chineseness has been a crucial part of what makes up a Chinatown in this country. Las Vegas's Chinatown is undoubtedly a commercial product—Las Vegas being in many ways the ultimate representation of how culture is sold—but it has come to resemble traditional American Chinatowns in more substantive ways. It figures significantly in the lives of various classes of Chinese immigrants living in Las Vegas. All of the Chinatowns discussed here cater both to American sensibilities and to the practical demands of Chinese immigrants. Chinatown's physical space is itself an artifact of cross-cultural negotiation, as well as the field on which that negotiation continues to happen. That cultural hybridity lets outsiders—who can gaze at the clannish people, faux-pagoda rooflines, and Eastern wares—get what they need, and it satisfies insiders, too, by providing a place for cultural comfort, cheap lodgings, and the transaction of business. The vibrancy and relevance of these American Chinatowns depend upon both their integrity and their integral relationship with the community at large. The idea of Chinatown persists because it is something America *needs*, and it encompasses much that is negative and positive in the Chinese American experience.

Chinatown in Vegas is new, observes Nicky Chiu, but it doesn't make it less significant. "We do have quite a big number of Chinese now—looking at the Chinatown shows how Chinese people are developing here," she told me. The speed of that development has amazed her. "The majority work in casinos, and now there is even a dealer school that is owned by Chinese."

It was three o'clock in the afternoon in the poker room at Let's Make A Dealer, when two instructors and four dealers-in-training entangled me in a game of no-limit Texas Hold 'em. I protested that I didn't play poker, but Annie Lim, an instructor and veteran dealer at The Venetian, cheerfully convinced me that it was for the good of the students that I practice at the table with them. As I attempted to bluff my way through several hands, my pile of chips quickly clicked down to nothing. But my seat at the table afforded a bird's-eye view into this community. As Lim patiently dealt out the game, a Chinese student three seats over translated the rules for her friend. There was hot gossip: one of the school's graduates had won a coveted job as a dealer for the World Series of Poker. Chinatown restaurant recommendations floated around the room. There was talk of meeting up after class. Everybody here taught each other, learned from each other, helped each other out. It occurred to me that Chinatown might be the realest community in Las Vegas, in part because it transcends the geography in which it is set. A community has shared values, institutions, and interests; it is responsible to itself. In a way, Las Vegas's Chinatown carries the weight of all the Chinatowns that came before it, and its center of gravity attracts new immigrants, non-Chinese, and Chinese tourists alike. If that isn't a community, what is?

CONCLUSION

Moving Pictures

In his 1897 short story "The Third Circle," writer Frank Norris famously characterized his view of San Francisco's Chinatown with these opening lines: "In reality there are three parts of Chinatown—the part the guides show you, the part the guides don't show you, and the part that no one ever hears of." Even so early in the neighborhood's history in this country, an American fascination with a "hidden" Chinatown was plain. And though I don't believe in the idea of self-conscious secrets in any Chinatown, I hope the stories collected in this volume serve to open up a newly expanded view into these neighborhoods as revealed by multiple generations of residents.

The stories we tell about a place give it power. The word "Chinatown" has long been shorthand for a whole other world. What world that is, however, depends on what we choose to see, and how deeply we want to look. As they unfolded their lives to me, the people I met reclaimed Chinatown from those who exoticize it as an unknowable place with mysterious denizens, a violent gangland setting appropriate for a video game entitled "Grand Theft Auto: Chinatown Wars." Rather than be characterized simply as dangerous, foreign, dirty, crowded, or persistently the "other," Chinatown residents changed the signposts for the neighborhood to read more complicated, and more constructive, phrases: working class *and* gentrifying, insular *and* interconnected, progressing *and* contracting, touristy *and* local, Chinese *and* American.

The truth is that Chinatown is a space of self-invention. The oldest Chinese immigrants—including but not limited to those who landed in the port cities of New York, San Francisco, Los Angeles, Honolulu—had to create a community setting that was palatable to the white society at large. These days, new immigrants continue to come for a new life, and a search for cultural identity brings Chinese Americans of many generations back to walk alongside them.

The myth of America lies in its patchwork heritage. Though the United States hasn't always tolerated difference, it continues to this day to be built by immigrants. This contradiction in founding myths led to an ethnic awakening—the birth of a cultural pride that is still evolving. Visitors to Chinatown today have a role, just as residents do, in the bartering of cultural currency. If there is authenticity to be experienced, it's that of an immigrant enclave that continues to be vital. It's a reminder of what makes America special.

For me, Chinatown has been a kind of compass by which to find where I belong in this country. I haven't always felt at ease in my Chinese skin, and as a young adult it was comforting to know that there was a place I could go in my city where everyone else looked like me. Like the teenagers in L.A., like the beauty queen in Vegas, I could identify with what young Chinatown residents like John Tan told me. I felt proud of the fact that, when approached in a Chinatown subway station, I could give directions in Cantonese as needed. It was fun to be on the inside for a change—to listen to waiters gossip about customers in a restaurant, to know which hole-in-the-wall shop had the best noodles.

When I went to other Chinatowns, in Boston, Sydney, Buenos Aires, they felt familiar, of course, but curiously different. In these places, I as a visitor could toe the line between insider and outsider. When I went to China to visit my father—who had moved back to Hong Kong, and then on to Beijing, and Guangzhou—I had a revelation. China was where my family came from, but it wasn't where I was from. So, when I returned to Manhattan to live, I got to know the Chinatown there as my own. The everyday things I did there—food shopping, meeting friends for lunch, taking Chinese lessons—were on my own terms.

Perhaps the most meaningful challenge to my identity as a Chinese American came when I moved to San Francisco and met its Chinatown. Somehow, this one confounded me most. I found myself an outsider in a city in which I now lived; like any outsider, I had to dig deeper. It led to this book.

Being in Chinatown in a new city opens up another dimension of place for me. What I take away from a Chinatown when I leave, even from Las Vegas—perhaps the most manufactured place one can think of—is a sharpened sense of why Chinatown still matters. It is, as Norman Fong told me, heartland Asian America. After a century and a half of Chinese immigration, Chinatown is still the first step for new immigrants into America, and for American-born Chinese into their Chinese heritage. Their personal stories are narrative epics; by reading them, we find out what Chinatown means to its people at present. And by looking behind, we also get a sense of what may lie ahead, beyond its borders.

SOURCE NOTES

INTRODUCTION

10   *the Chinese even outnumbered Caucasians in the islands:* In 1884, there were 18,254 Chinese in Hawaii, 9,967 Portuguese, and 6,612 "Other Caucasian." For a table of Hawaii's population by ancestry between 1853 and 1940, see William C. Smith, "Minority Groups in Hawaii," *Annals of the American Academy of Political and Social Science*, 223, Minority Peoples in a Nation at War (September 1942), p. 38.

ONE: AMERICAN PAGODAS

13   *The Oldest:* By 1852, the dramatic rise in immigration following the Gold Rush had resulted in a population of about 25,000 Chinese in California; the city of San Francisco experienced explosive growth in this period, including the formation of the oldest Chinatown around Portsmouth Square. See Library of Congress, *The Chinese in California, 1850–1925*, American Memory Collection (http://memory.loc.gov); and Peter Kwong and Dusanka Miscevic, *Chinese America: The Untold Story of America's Oldest New Community* (New York: The New Press, 2005), p. 45. By 1854, the first Chinese-language newspaper was published by William Howard to serve the Chinese community; see "The Founding of *Golden Hills' News* (1854)," *Chinese American Voices: From the Gold Rush to the Present*, ed. Judy Yung, Gordon H. Chang, and Him Mark Lai (Berkeley: University of California Press, 2006), p. 13.

15   *a gift from Taiwan—but in 1969:* According to Anna Naruta and Judy Hu, Chinese Historical Society of America.

16   *"veritable fairy palaces":* Look Tin Eli, a rich San Francisco merchant and founder of the Bank of Canton, is credited with creating an Oriental city of "veritable fairy palaces." See Philip P. Choy, "The Architecture of San Francisco Chinatown," *Chinese America:*

248

History and Perspectives 1990, vol. 4, p. 49; Look Tin Eli, "Our Oriental City," *San Francisco: The Metropolis of the West* (San Francisco: Western Press Association, 1910); and Mae M. Ngai, "How Chinatown rose from the ashes," *International Herald Tribune*, April 18, 2006.

17   *"Keep Grant Ave Narrow, Dirty, and Quaint"*: For documentary photos of Chinatown's first demonstrations in 1968, see Judy Yung, *San Francisco's Chinatown* (San Francisco: Arcadia Publishing, 2006), p. 98.

20   *"eight hundred sons"*: See Christopher Rand, "A Reporter at Large: Aspects of a Meeting Place-I," *New Yorker*, November 16, 1957, p. 125.

21   *since 1848*: See *The Gold Rush*, a PBS documentary presented by American Experience, 2006 (www.pbs.org/wgbh/amex/goldrush).

21   *63,000 Chinese in America*: See Library of Congress, "California as I Saw It": First-Person Narratives of California's Early Years, 1849–1900, American Memory Collection (http://memory.loc.gov); and Ronald Takaki, *Strangers from a Different Shore: A History of Asian Americans* (Boston: Little, Brown, 1989), p. 79.

21   *"unassimilated foreign community"*: See Choy, "The Architecture of San Francisco Chinatown."

22   *By 1854, California laws had been put in place*: "In the (1854) case People v. Hall, the California Supreme Court reversed the convictions of George Hall and two other white men who had murdered a Chinese man. Hall and his companions had been convicted based on testimony of some Chinese witnesses. In its reversal the court extended the California law that African Americans and Native Americans could not testify in court in order to include the Chinese. The reversal made it impossible to prosecute violence against Chinese immigrants." From "People & Events: Chinese Immigrants and the Gold Rush," supplementary material to *The Gold Rush* (www.pbs.org/wgbh/amex/goldrush).

22   *In 1882, the Chinese Exclusion Act was passed*: See Wei Li, "Chinese Americans: Community Formation in Time and Space," in *Contemporary Ethnic Geographies in America*, ed. Ines M. Miyares and Christopher A. Airriess (Lanham: Rowman & Littlefield, 2006), pp. 216–17; and the 2003 PBS documentary *Becoming American: The Chinese Experience* (www.pbs.org/becomingamerican).

24 *On May 26, 1910:* San Francisco campaigned for (and won) the right to hold the 1915 Panama-Pacific International Exposition with this ad, "Further Reasons Why the Panama-Pacific International Exposition, 1915, Should Be Held in the City by the Golden Gate," *The Washington Post*, May 26, 1910, p. 16.

24 *Marlon Hom, has called the stylizing of Chinatown:* See Vanessa Hua, "The Great Quake: 1906–2006, Out of chaos came new Chinese America," *San Francisco Chronicle*, April 13, 2006.

24 *Felicia Lowe dramatized the human fact of the ghetto:* Felicia Lowe, from the 1997 documentary film, *Chinatown* (www.pbs.org/kqed/chinatown).

TWO: ALLEYWAY KIDS

32 *the newly rebuilt I-Hotel:* For a discussion of the importance of the I-Hotel to the city's Chinese and Filipino community, see Kantele Franko, "I-Hotel, 30 years later," *The San Francisco Chronicle*, August 4, 2007; and Estella Habal, *San Francisco's International Hotel: Mobilizing the Filipino American Community in the Anti-Eviction Movement* (Philadelphia: Temple University Press, 2008).

41 *The average SRO costs $350 to $600 per month:* From interviews with Rosa Wong-Chie and Norman Fong; facts and figures from the Chinatown Community Development Center (www.chinatowncdc.org) and the Marguerite Casey Foundation (www.caseygrants.org).

THREE: CHAIN MIGRATION

49 *Of the working-age Chinese residents in San Francisco . . . thousand dollars a year:* Cited in Susie Smith, Tim Lohrentz, and Tse Ming Tam, "Building Bridges to Help Chinese Families Reach Economic Self-Sufficiency," an economic report prepared by the National Economic Development and Law Center for the Chinatown Families Self-Sufficiency Coalition, San Francisco, November 21, 2005.

51 *the 1965 Immigration Act:* See Li, "Chinese Americans: Community Formation in Time and Space," pp. 217–18.

51 *The year 1965 was a benchmark:* See Helen Zia, "The New Immigration Wave," *Asian American Dreams: The Emergence of an American People* (New York: Farrar, Straus, and Giroux, 2000), pp. 50–52.

55 *That gap is only beginning to be examined:* Sabina Chen has since left her post at the Chinese Culture Center.

FOUR: CITY WITHIN A CITY

59 *The Biggest:* The New York metropolitan area is now home to over half a million Chinese—the largest Chinese population in the United States. The densest concentration is still in Manhattan's Chinatown: four census tracts within the neighborhood have the highest density of Asians in New York City. Despite population shifts, Chinatown is bigger today than it ever was, home to 80,000 residents—55 percent of all Lower Manhattan residents. See Chinatown Census Information, fall 2004, and America's Chinatown: A Community Plan, April 2004 (www.rebuildchinatown.org): also Census Profile: New York City's Chinese American Population, and Neighborhood Profile: Manhattan's Chinatown, two reports issued by the Asian American Federation of New York Census Information Center, 2004 (www.aafny.org). By contrast, San Francisco's Chinatown has an estimated 15,000 residents, though the numbers are likely much higher. See San Francisco Planning Department's "Chinatown Area Plan" (www.sfgov.org/site/plannning); and Steven Knipp, "U.S. Top Six Chinatowns," *South China Morning Post*, September 13, 2004.

61 *By 1920, 40 percent of all the Chinese in America:* See Takaki, *Strangers From a Different Shore*, p. 245.

62 *For generations, New York made more clothes:* See Daniel Soyer, ed., *A Coat of Many Colors: Immigration, Globalization, and Reform in New York City's Garment Industry* (New York: Fordham University Press, 2005), p. 3.

62 *Manhattan persists as America's fashion capital:* See New York State Department of Labor, 2006, Q2. In the *New York Industrial Retention Network 2007 Manufacturer's Almanac*, p. 13.

63 *no jobs for the mostly rural population of Chinese refugees:* See "Out of Luck," *Time*, January 4, 1960.

66 *Between the end of the sixties:* See Kwong, *Chinese America*, p. 319; also Xiaolan Bao, "The Geographical Movement of Chinese Garment Shops: A Late-Twentieth-Century Tale of the New York Garment Industry," *A Coat of Many Colors: Immigration, Glo-*

balization, and Reform in New York City's Garment Industry, ed. Daniel Soyer (New York: Fordham University Press, 2005), p. 70.

67 *contributing significantly to the city's economy:* See Bao, "The Geographical Movement of Chinese Garment Shops," 70.

67 *the garment and restaurant trades:* From interviews with Wing Lam; also Bao, "The Geographical Movement of Chinese Garment Shops," 71.

68 *where tip-stealing by restaurant owners:* From interviews with Wing Lam and Jei Fong; also Mary Reinholz, "Chinatown restaurant is served with $700,000 fine for biting tab," *Downtown Express*, February 9–15, 2007.

68 *20,000 Chinatown garment workers:* From interviews with Wing Lam; also Bao, "The Geographical Movement of Chinese Garment Shops," p. 21.

69 *In 1994, a tramp steamer named* Golden Venture: See Nina Bernstein, "Making It Ashore, but Still Chasing U.S. Dream," *New York Times*, April 9, 2008.

72 *Jiang was among five workers:* See Zeng Liu v. Jen Chu Fashion Corp., 2004 U.S. Dist. Lexis 35 (S.D.N.Y. January 7, 2004).

73 *Donna Karan International settled:* See Suzanne Kapner, "Karan Pays $500K+ in Sweatshop Settlement," *New York Post*, September 9, 2003.

73 *Jiang's employer:* From interviews with Feng Ying Jiang; also Zeng Liu v. Jen Chu Fashion Corp., 2004.

74 *In the four years after September 11:* "Before the attacks, there were 246 garment factories in the neighborhood, employing 14,000 workers. Last summer, the [Asian American F]ederation counted only 102 garment factories . . ." From Brian Kates, "Chinatown Gets Left in the Dust," *New York Daily News*, January 8, 2006.

74 *The New York metropolitan area is now home:* See Census Profile: New York City's Chinese American Population; and Neighborhood Profile: Manhattan's Chinatown. Reports issued by the Asian American Federation of New York Census Information Center, 2004 (www.aafny.org).

74 *"the hardest-working neighborhood":* See introduction to the Chinatown Film Project (www.wjtalk.com/moca).

75 *the vast majority of Chinese residents are still poor:* "Census data for Community Board 3, which covers the bulk of Chinatown and the increasingly affluent Lower East Side, shows that the percentage of Chinese residents defined by the federal government as poor or near poor rose to 69 from 64 between 2000 and 2006 . . . ," From Saki Knafo, "Dreams and Desperation on Forsyth Street," *New York Times*, June 8, 2008.

FIVE: THE NEW CHINESE SCHOOL

78 *Chinese schools in various U.S. cities:* See "To Open Chinese Schools: China Would Prevent Her Children from Forgetting Parent Language," *New York Times*, October 24, 1908.

78 *generations of Chinese American kids:* For a superb discussion of Chinese schools in the United States in the twentieth century, see Him Mark Lai, "Chinese Schools in America before World War II," and "Chinese Schools in America after World War II," *Becoming Chinese American: A History of Communities and Institutions* (Walnut Creek: AltaMira Press, 2004).

79 *within a decade, China is expected to surpass:* See National Geographic Geopedia: China, "China by the Numbers" (ngm.nationalgeographic.com/geopedia/China).

80 *a tumultuous period in Shuang Wen's history:* From interviews with John Tan; Yori Yanover, "Three Schools in Two Buildings," *Grand Street News*, October 2006; and Susan Saulny, "Elementary School Parents Feel Squeezed and Ignored," *New York Times*, November 4, 2005.

SIX: FORTUNE COOKIES

96 *In 2008, the fortune cookie turned ninety:* See Reyhan Harmanci, "'Killing of a Chinese Cookie': Finding Fortune," *San Francisco Chronicle*, March 20, 2008; and Vincent Cheng, "A Four-Legged Duck?" Chinese Restaurant Culture in the U.S. from a Cross-Cultural/Inter-Cultural Communication Perspective," *China Media Research*, April 2007, vol. 3, no. 2, p. 99.

96 *the fortune cookie in Japan:* See Jennifer 8. Lee, "Solving a Riddle Wrapped in a Mystery Inside a Cookie," *New York Times*, March 18, 2008.

98 *In 1983, Wonton Food bought a small mom-and-pop:* From interviews with Derrick Wong and Eric Ng.

99 *Approximately forty other fortune cookie factories:* See Jeremy Olshan, "Cookie Master," *New Yorker,* June 6, 2005, p. 34.

106 *Chinatown is still larger now:* See "America's Chinatown: A Community Plan," a report issued by Asian Americans for Equality, April 2004, p. 8 (www.rebuildchinatown.org).

SEVEN: CHINATOWNLAND

115 *Charlie Chaplin filmed here, as did Buster Keaton:* Charlie Chaplin filmed scenes for *The Kid* and *Caught in a Cabaret* in Chinatown, while Buster Keaton used the neighborhood in his famous short film, *Cops;* see John Bengtson's *Silent Traces: Discovering Early Hollywood Through the Films of Charlie Chaplin* (Santa Monica: Santa Monica Press, 2006) and *Silent Echoes: Discovering Early Hollywood Through the Films of Buster Keaton* (Santa Monica: Santa Monica Press, 2000).

115 *Hollywood crowd:* Actress Dorothy Tree was a guest of Tom Gubbins "at one of those famous Chinese dinners in the Chinatown quarter . . ." See Read Kendall, "Around and About in Hollywood," *Los Angeles Times,* January 21, 1935.

115 CHINATOWNLAND *. . . its own Los Angeles landmark:* See Andre Yi and Annie Shaw's official Chinatownland site (www.chinatownland.net).

116 *"Una Merkel took a group of friends to Chinatown":* See Read Kendall, "Odd and Interesting Hollywood Gossip," *Los Angeles Times,* October 14, 1935.

116 *a displaced population:* Exact numbers are unknown, but the Chinese Historical Society of Southern California estimates the displaced community at about 3,000.

117 *force behind New Chinatown:* From the Chinese American Museum's permanent exhibit on New Chinatown, Los Angeles.

117 *Its developers were careful to address locals' concerns:* From interviews with Pauline Wong; also Lisa See, *On Gold Mountain: The One-Hundred-Year Odyssey of My Chinese-American Family* (New York: Vintage Books, 1995), p. 214.

117   *a full-page ad in the* Los Angeles Examiner*:* From the Chinese American Museum archives.

117   *China City:* Christine Sterling was also responsible for the creation of Olvera Street, an "Old Mexico"–themed tourist attraction that was intended to save the historic Plaza district, the city's birthplace. A discussion of image and historic communities can be found in William D. Estrada's "Los Angeles' Old Plaza and Olvera Street: Imagined and Contested Space," in *Western Folklore*, vol. 58, no. 2, *Built L.A.: Folklore and Place in Los Angeles* (Winter, 1999), pp. 107–29. See also the Chinese American Museum's excellent permanent exhibit on Old Chinatown, China City, and New Chinatown.

118   *people like Tom Gubbins:* See filmography for Tom Gubbins, courtesy of Turner Classic Movies (www.tcm.com).

118   *Born in China to an English family:* See Kevin Brownlow, *Behind the Mask of Innocence* (New York: Knopf, 1990), p. 332; and Bruce Henstell, *Sunshine and Wealth: Los Angeles in the Twenties and Thirties* (San Francisco: Chronicle Books 1984), p. 91.

119   *War pictures featuring Asian faces:* See Barbara Miller, "Oriental Film Actors In Demand," *Los Angeles Times*, September 26, 1937; also interviews with Esther Lee Johnson.

120   *The distinction between the original Chinese American settlements:* Wei Li, an Asian Pacific American studies professor at Arizona State University, coined the phrase "ethnoburb." For more discussion of ethnoburbs vs. Chinatowns, see Li's "Ethnoburb versus Chinatown: Two Types of Urban Ethnic Communities in Los Angeles," *Cybergeo*, Colloque "les problèmes culturels des grandes villes," December 8–11, 1997, article 70, modified May 15, 2007 (www.cybergeo.eu/index1018.html).

120   *Anna May Wong:* See Leslie Camhi, "A Dragon Lady and a Quiet Cultural Warrior," *New York Times*, January 11, 2004.

121   *Her parents' friends:* See Harry Carr's interview with Anna May Wong, "I am Growing More Chinese—Each Passing Year!" *Los Angeles Times*, September 9, 1934.

121   *Anna May was allowed one kiss:* See Camhi, "A Dragon Lady and a Quiet Cultural Warrior."

121   *Her tribulations served as the inspiration:* See "No One Ever Tried to Kiss Anna May Wong," by John Yau, in *Radiant Silhouette:*

New & Selected Work, 1974–1988 (Santa Rosa: Black Sparrow Press, 1989).

121   *embodying an "'authentic' Chineseness"*: See Shirley Jennifer Lim, *A Feeling of Belonging: Asian American Women's Public Culture, 1930–1960* (New York: New York University Press, 2007), p. 72.

122   *by 1940, more Chinese in the United States were American-born*: See Kwong, *Chinese America*, p. 171.

122   *Anna May's obituary*: See Richard Corliss, "Anna May Wong Did It Right," January 29, 2005.

123   *"Roaring Through China Today"*: See a version of the *Peking Express* movie poster (http://themave.com/Cotton/posters/peking.htm).

126   *Steven Spielberg's 1987 film*: See Andrew L. Yarrow, "Boy in 'Empire' Calls Acting 'Really Good Fun,'" *New York Times*, December 16, 1987.

EIGHT: HOMETOWN CHINATOWN

131   *Old Chinatown's Garnier Building . . . City Hall*: See the Chinese American Museum's discussion of the historic building's significance (www.camla.org).

133   *knowing the past led to useful realizations*: For an excellent historical briefing of the Chinese in Los Angeles, see the Chinese American Museum's timeline (www.camla.org).

NINE: PREACHER MAN, TEACHER MAN

144   *"new Chinese immigrants still favor the three main cities"*: See Kwong, *Chinese America*, p. 341.

149   *Out of the 760 kids*: Statistics from Cheuk Choi and Castelar Elementary School.

TEN: KAPAKAHI CHINATOWN

155   *first visited by the Chinese in 1789*: See Arlene Lum, ed., *Sailing for the Sun: The Chinese in Hawaii, 1789–1989* (Honolulu: University of Hawaii Press, 1990), p. 10–11; also James Ho, *Untold Fragments of Hawaii's History, Volume I* (Honolulu: Hawaiian Chinese Multicultural Museum & Archives, 2003).

155 *More than half of Honolulu's population is Asian:* From the U.S. Census Bureau: State and County QuickFacts. Data derived from Population Estimates, 2000 Census of Population and Housing, 1990 Census of Population and Housing, Small Area Income and Poverty Estimates, County Business Patterns, 1997 Economic Census, Minority- and Women-Owned Business, Building Permits, Consolidated Federal Funds Report, Census of Governments.

155 Li hing mui, *the preserved, salted plums:* See Rachel Laudan, *The Food of Paradise: Exploring Hawaii's Culinary Heritage* (Honolulu: University of Hawaii Press, 1996), p. 81.

156 *more Changs than Smiths, more Lums than Joneses:* See Honolulu Phone Book, White Pages, 2007–2008 (11 columns of Changs vs. 8 columns of Smiths, 8.5 columns of Lums vs. 3 columns of Joneses).

157 *sugarcane industry in Hawaii:* See Hawaii's Labor History Timeline, Center for Labor Education and Research, University of Hawaii, West Oahu, (http://clear.uhwo.hawaii.edu/Timeline.html#1870).

161 *birthplace of Sun Yat-sen:* See "About Iolani" and "Dr. Sun Yat-sen" on the Iolani School site (www.iolani.org).

161 *Since 1997, Zhongshan has been designated:* See Resolution 97–179, Re: Sister City Relationship, Zhongshan City, Guangdong Province (www.honolulu.gov/refs/bill/status/1997/r179.htm).

164 *acted as a Chinese ghetto:* See Sen-dou Chang, "Community As Catalyst: The Chinese in Honolulu," *The Chinese Diaspora: Space, Place, Mobility, and Identity*, ed. Laurence J. C. Ma and Carolyn L. Cartier (Lanham, MD: Rowman & Littlefield, 2003), p. 302.

164 *presented by "a higher power":* See Helen Geracimos Chapin, *Shaping History: The Role of Newspapers in Hawai'i* (Honolulu: University of Hawaii Press, 1996), pp. 107–8.

164 *the 1900 fire* James C. Mohr, *Plague and Fire: Battling Black Death and the 1900 Burning of Honolulu's Chinatown* (New York: Oxford University Press, 2005).

165 *In 1973, the federal government listed Chinatown:* See Chinatown Historic District, #73000658 (www.nationalregisterofhistoricplaces.com/hi/Honolulu/districts.html).

166 *city's mayor goes so far as to call:* See City of Honolulu Public Communications, "The City and County's Month in Chinatown Will

Celebrate Chinese New Year," January 11, 2008 (www.co.honolulu.
hi.us/csd/publiccom/honnews08/chinatownnewyear.htm).

ELEVEN: NEIGHBORHOOD CROSSINGS

177 *Iolani School:* See "Dr. Sun Yat-sen" (www.iolani.org).

178 *Dr. Sun Yat-sen Memorial Park:* See "City to Dedicate Statue and
Rename Park to Honor Dr. Sun Yat-sen," Release No. M-122-07,
November 7, 2007, City and County of Honolulu Public Commu-
nications Division.

TWELVE: HISTORY LESSONS

185 *Chinatown's architecture:* See Chinatown Summit remarks (www.
co.honolulu.hi.us/mayor/chinatownsummit_mr.htm).

187 *The last U.S. Census:* According to Census 2000, American Fact-
Finder, Median Household Income in 1999 for Honolulu County,
Hawaii was $51,914; Median Household Income in 1999 for Cen-
sus Tract 52 (Chinatown), Honolulu County, Hawaii, was $19,606.
Also in the Census Tract 52 that encompasses Chinatown, the 2000
Census had the total population as just over three thousand (3,056).
The neighborhood is overwhelming Asian (about 70 percent of the
residents are Asian [69 percent Asian alone]).

189 *The city has received several hundred thousand dollars:* See Nina
Wu, "Chinatown: Getting beyond First Friday," *Honolulu Star-
Bulletin*, October 21, 2007.

192 *"progress has been like molasses":* See Wu, "Chinatown: Getting
beyond First Friday."

THIRTEEN: CHINATOWN, NEXT EXIT

202 *In 1880, they made up at least:* See Sue Fawn Chung, "The Chi-
nese," *The Peoples of Las Vegas: One City, Many Faces,* ed. Jerry
L. Simich and Thomas C. Wright (Reno/Las Vegas: University of
Nevada Press, 2005), p. 99.

203 *"You don't want to be late":* See Barry Newman, "For Asians in
U.S., Mini-Chinatowns Sprout in Suburbia," *Wall Street Journal*,
April 28, 2004.

207   *add-on pagoda roofs:* See Hubble Smith, "Shopping center renovation nearly done," *Las Vegas Review-Journal,* April 4, 2003.

212   *the two-week Chinese New Year holiday:* Steve Freiss, "Las Vegas Adapts to Reap Chinese New Year Bounty," *New York Times,* February 21, 2007.

213   *a gaming tavern called Little Macau:* See Howard Stutz, "Up in smoke: Local tavern business suffers under weight of smoking ban, weak economy," *Las Vegas Business Press,* November 29, 2007.

214   *"Chinatown is a signature":* See Babita Persaud, "Chinatown on the rise: It may not look traditional, but a 50-store plaza in Pine Hills aims to be the community's core," *Orlando Sentinel,* July 13, 2007.

Fourteen: Miss Chinatown, U.S.A.

218   *The first Chinatown Queen on record:* See Judy Yung, *Unbound Feet: A Social History of Chinese Women in San Francisco* (Berkeley: University of California Press, 1995), p. 148.

219   *Miss America pageant:* "1921, September 7: The first Miss America Pageant, called the 'Inter-City Beauty Pageant,' takes place in Atlantic City as a part of a Fall Frolic to attract tourists. There are seven contestants. Sixteen-year-old Margaret Gorman from Washington, D.C., wins the title, Miss America." From "Timeline: Miss America," part of the 2002 PBS documentary film *Miss America* (www.pbs.org/wgbh/amex/missamerica/timeline/timeline2.html).

219   *"With her beauty, brains, poise and talent":* From the transcript of *Miss America* (www.pbs.org/wgbh/amex/missamerica/filmmore/pt.html).

219   *The San Francisco Chinese Chamber of Commerce:* See J. K. Hom, "50 Years With Miss Chinatown USA," *AsianWeek,* March 2, 2007.

219   *In 1958, the San Francisco pageant:* From "Miss Chinatown USA: An exhibit on the history and culture of the pageant," press release from the Chinese Historical Society of America, February 21, 2007.

222   *"had an ideal image of Miss Chinatown":* See Judy Tzu-Chun Wu, "'Loveliest daughter of our ancient Cathay!': representations of ethnic and gender identity in the Miss Chinatown U.S.A. beauty pageant," *Journal of Social History,* Fall 1997.

222 *a certain added cachet:* See Hom, "50 Years With Miss Chinatown USA."

227 *In Kathy Huang's poignant documentary:* See *Miss Chinatown, U.S.A.,* 2006 (www.kathyhuangfilms.com).

229 *A few years ago, the Chinese government:* See K. Oanh Ha, "China collects the relics of diaspora's lives; Museum to Highlight Roles in U.S.," *San Jose Mercury News,* July 15, 2006.

FIFTEEN: THE NEW TENANTS

231 *There are about seven dealer schools:* From interviews with David Wu and Chaco Yang; also the Las Vegas Yellow Pages, 2008.

239 *In the state of Nevada:* See Chung, "The Chinese;" also Haya El Nasser, "In a twist, USA's Asians are heading to the Mountain West," *USA Today,* July 6, 2008.

240 *In the last ten years:* See *National Geographic Geopedia:* China, "China's Middle Class" (ngm.nationalgeographic.com/geopedia/China).

241 *the number of millionaires:* See Country Profile: China, August 2006, Library of Congress, Federal Research Division.

CONCLUSION

245 *1897 short story "The Third Circle":* See Frank Norris, *The Third Circle* (New York: John Lane Company, 1909).

ACKNOWLEDGMENTS

THIS BOOK WOULD not have been possible without those who so generously and openly shared their Chinatown stories with me. Many of the people I met were surprised that I wanted to know about their lives. You saw your daily challenges as pedestrian, the rich, dynamic melee of your community as "nothing special." But you also saw the value in having a place to belong and in identifying a future that expanded beyond the boundaries of Chinatown. I hope this book reflects that clear-eyed honesty—and I hope it succeeds in bringing your narrative epics to the world by revealing the realities and vibrant complexities of modern life in each distinctive neighborhood. I wasn't able to include every story, but I am changed by the collective history of strength, patience, and sacrifice I found in Chinatowns across America.

Certain individuals were especially helpful and generous in sharing their research, archives, and expertise. My deepest gratitude to Anna Naruta at the Chinese Historical Society of America, Alyson Lee Suzuki and Karen Ho at the Joy Lok Family Resource Center, Eric Ng at New York's Chinese Consolidated Benevolent Association, Wing Lam at the Chinese Staff and Workers' Association, Derrick Wong at Wonton Food, Patrick Kwan, Pastor Ken Yee at the First Chinese Baptist Church of Los Angeles, Cheuk Choi at Castelar Elementary, Eugene Moy at the Chinese Historical Society of Southern California, Danee Prasert and Jennifer Tang at the Los Angeles Chinatown Service Center, James Ho at the Hawaiian Chinese Multicultural Museum, and Sue Fawn Chung at the University of Nevada, Las Vegas.

I would like to thank William Clark, my agent, for championing this idea from the beginning, and Elizabeth Stein for believing in this "telling of contemporary history." Thanks to Amber Qureshi, my hardworking editor at Free Press.

A special thanks to my dear readers: Esther Chak, Frances Duncan, Adam Felchner, Sara Houghteling, Peter Pihos, and Adam Baer. Your smart and thoughtful feedback means more than you will ever know. I also want to thank my friend Tom Davidson for all those marathon days of work and moral support. Thank you as well to Tim Sinnott for so cheerfully sharing your mapmaking finesse.

A big thank-you to my family, as always, for your love and encouragement. My mother in particular deserves my deepest appreciation, not least for being on call at all hours with cultural and linguistic support. And many thanks to my husband, Matt, who is the bedrock on which I rest.

About the Author

Bonnie Tsui is a frequent contributor to the *New York Times*. A former editor at *Travel + Leisure*, she has written for *National Geographic Adventure, Salon*, and *Condé Nast Traveller*. She is the editor of *A Leaky Tent Is a Piece of Paradise*, a collection of essays on the outdoors, and is a recipient of the Radcliffe Traveling Fellowship, the Lowell Thomas Travel Journalism Award, and the Jane Rainie Opel Award. She lives in San Francisco and can be reached at www.bonnietsui.com.